POCKET GUIDE TO THE
REPTILES
AMPHI
of Eas

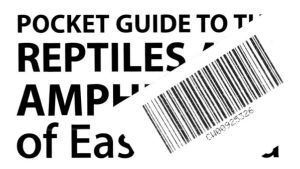

**STEPHEN SPAWLS, ᴵ ᴼWELL
AND ROBERT C. ᴿEWES**

B L O O M S B U R Y

LONDON • NEW DELHI • NEW YORK • SYDNEY

First published in 2006 by Bloomsbury Publishing Plc

Bloomsbury Publishing Plc
50 Bedford Square
London
WC1B 3DP

www.bloomsbury.com

BLOOMSBURY and the Diana logo are trademarks of Bloomsbury Publishing Plc

A CIP catalogue record for this book is available from the British Library

ISBN (print) 978-0-7136-7425-5

10 9 8 7 6 5 4 3

Printed and bound in China by RRD South China

Contents

Acknowledgements

To our great pleasure, the publication of our original field guide in 2002 has acted as a stimulus to naturalists in many places in Africa, particularly in East Africa. During the last three years we have received a constant flow of interesting information concerning East African reptiles, most hearteningly from the people who are actually working in the field with the animals. Much of that information is incorporated herein. We would like to thank those people who have taken the trouble to contact us. They include Sanda Ashe, Teddy Berhanu, Gordon Boy, Don Broadley, Gary Campbell, Graham Dangerfield, Marc De Bont, Squack Evans, Brian Finch, Emily Fitzherbert and Toby Gardner, Paula Kahumbu, Chege Kariuki, Chris Kelly, Patrick Malonza, Dino Martins, Glenn and Karen Mathews, Tomas Mazuch, Michele Menegon, David Moyer, Petr Necas, Ian Parker, Damaris Rotich, Norbert Rottcher, Howard Saunders, Itai Shanni, Sisay Taye and Victor Wasonga. Our particular thanks are also due to Alan Channing, who generously allowed us access to his unpublished amphibian data. Steve Spawls would also like to thank Glenn and Karen Mathews, Andrew Botta, Gordon Boy, Joy and Ian MacKay for kindly putting up with him on recent trips to Nairobi, and Martin Mulwa for his faultless logistics. Steve also thanks his sons Timothy and Jonathan Spawls for producing the line drawings in this book, Joe Beraducci, who once again has kept us updated on herpetofaunal discoveries in Tanzania, and two friends overlooked in the acknowledgements from our last book: Carol Hancox, whose computer expertise enabled us to produce the maps, and Dr Maurizio Dioli, who collected and allowed us to photograph some beautiful lizards from inaccessible areas of north-eastern Africa. Angelo Lambiris kindly allowed us to base our frog drawings on the pictures in his *Frogs of Zimbabwe*.

Once again, we would like to thank our friends and colleagues who have lent us animals and photographs, shared information and spent time with us in the field. They include Sabine Baer, Joe Beraducci, Wolfgang Boehme, Don Broadley, Alan Channing, Michael Cheptumo, Lynn and Barry Bell, Dave Brownlee, Haile Demissie, Dietmar Emmrich, Paul Freed, Wulf Haacke, Barry Hughes, Alex Kupfer, Dong Lin, Simon Loader, Stefan Lotters, Jill Lovett, Ian MacKay, Andrea Maggi, Glenn Mathews, Mike McLaren, Dave Morgan, Charles Msuya, Deone Naude, Wilirk Ngalason, Martin Pickersgill, Gerald Rilling, Mark-Oliver Roedel, Mills Tandy, John Tashjian, Royjan Taylor, Colin Tilbury, Lorenzo Vinciguerra, Jens Vindum, James Vonesh, Philipp Wagner, Chris Wild, Danny and Nana Woodley and George Zug. We thank also Harald Hinkel, whose excellent photographs and expertise on the reptiles and amphibians of the Albertine Rift have proved invaluable. We have benefited from specimens and data collected by Frontier-Tanzania, a cooperative research programme between the Society for the Exploration of the Environment (SEE) in London and the University of Dar es Salaam. Simon Loader and David Gower at the Natural History Museum, London are thanked for their critical reading of our section on caecilians.

As before, our thanks go to the museums and administrators of those museums with significant East African collections, in particular the California Academy of Sciences, the National Museum, Kenya, the University of Dar es Salaam and the Natural History Museum, London. Without museum collections, no taxonomic work can be done or distributional data plotted. Likewise, we recall with gratitude the early explorers, collectors, museum administrators and herpetologists who added to the total of our knowledge of the East African herpetofauna; details of these stalwart individuals are given in our original field guide. We thank Nigel Redman and his team at A&C Black; Nigel's cheerful enthusiasm has brought this book to fruition. Our particular thanks are due to Julie Bailey, for her meticulous and patient shepherding through production, and Tina Tong for the design. The authors are also grateful to their spouses and families, who patiently tolerated the time we committed to preparing this book.

Since the East African field guide was written, sadly, two members of our original team, Alex MacKay and James Ashe, have died. Alex and Jim, we hope this book is a decent memorial to your lifelong work in East Africa. Safari Njema, marafiki zetu. Mwanzo kokochi, mwisho nazi!

Stephen Spawls
Kim M. Howell
Robert C. Drewes

Introduction

In 2002, we published a field guide to the reptiles of East Africa. As a consequence of it being the first work of its kind, it is a heavy book, of over 500 pages, weighing nearly 1.5kg and not very portable. Consequently, we decided to produce this smaller and more compact, illustrated guide, which we hope will be useful and more accessible for field workers in East Africa. In it, we have described about 190 prominent East African reptiles (just under half the total) and we have also added around 85 amphibians. We have chosen the animals we feel the public are most likely to encounter. However, there are over 420 species of reptile and over 200 amphibian species known from East Africa. Readers should be aware that not all species are covered in detail here. We have provided brief notes on some of the species we have not illustrated and described, including maximum size, general appearance and broad distribution (within East Africa only). Those looking for more background information on the reptile species illustrated here, for information on reptiles we have not illustrated, for a comprehensive key for identification or for a species that does not seem to be here should consult our field guide (*A Field Guide to the Reptiles of East Africa* by Stephen Spawls, Kim Howell, Robert Drewes and James Ashe, A&C Black 2004, ISBN 0 7136 6817 2). For more information on the amphibians, especially those we have not illustrated, consult Alan Channing and Kim Howell's *Amphibians of East Africa* (2006, Cornell University Press). In general, expanded versions of all the introductory sections here can be found in our field guide.

How to use this book

This book is meant for use in the field - put it in your field bag or your car. When you see a reptile or amphibian, leaf through the book and try to match it with the picture. If it matches, then check the distribution map; is it in the right area? Then look at the notes; we have tried to emphasise key points of identification. Check the maximum size; this is particularly useful for snakes. If you don't have this book, or the animal doesn't appear to be shown, take a photograph or make some notes. This is particularly useful identification pointers are the colours and patterns of the animal, its location, its size and any behaviour it displays. With turtles and tortoises, the shape of the shell is useful, with lizards the head shape and any head ornamentation (spikes, horns, ear holes visible). With snakes, the shape of the head, the type of pupil and the behaviour may give clues to its identity. For amphibians, the head shape, the appearance of the eye (size, iris colour, pupil shape), the colour, and the appearance of the back (smooth, ridged) are useful aids, as is the call, although this is only likely to be heard at night.

Please note: no East African frog, turtle, tortoise or lizard is venomous (although some of the larger lizards can bite and scratch, and amphibians may have toxic skin secretions). Thus they may be safely approached. However, you should not go too close to an unidentified snake, as it may be dangerous. A distance of twice the snake's length is as close as you should get, unless you suspect the snake is a spitting cobra, in which case do not go closer than three metres. Beware also of approaching any snake, particularly a large one, that appears to be agitated (spread hood, raised head or neck, hissing loudly, opening its mouth) as it may strike or rush forward if cornered. Unless you are an expert, you should never handle snakes. This includes apparently dead ones; they might not be dead. Beware also of crocodiles, which in parts of East Africa will attack humans.

East African reptiles and amphibians and their zoogeography

The five countries of East Africa (Tanzania, Kenya, Uganda, Rwanda and Burundi) have an area of over 1.8 million square kilometres. The altitude varies from sea level to snow-capped mountains over 5,800m; the vegetation includes true desert, semi-desert, savanna, woodland, alpine moorlands and a wide range of forests, from hot coastal forest through true rain forest to cold montane forest. East Africa is also riven by two gigantic, north–south Rift Valleys, which have created a landscape of block-faulted mountains, valley floors, escarpments, lakes and volcanic mountains. On the eastern side of our region there is a chain of ancient crystalline mountains, the Eastern Arc. The two maps below show variation in altitude and vegetation.

Altitude   **Vegetation**

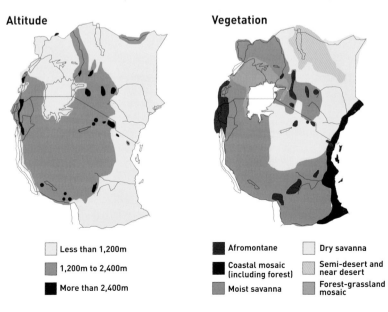

☐ Less than 1,200m	
▨ 1,200m to 2,400m	
■ More than 2,400m	

■ Afromontane	☐ Dry savanna
■ Coastal mosaic (including forest)	▨ Semi-desert and near desert
▨ Moist savanna	▨ Forest-grassland mosaic

Reptiles and amphibians are present throughout the East African landscape, being absent only from areas above the snowline. About 200 species of snake, 200 species of lizard and 200 species of amphibian occur in East Africa; there are also 22 species of turtle and tortoise, three crocodiles and ten worm lizards - a diverse tropical fauna.

Most of our East African reptiles and many of our amphibians are savanna animals, and fall into three main groups: animals of the relatively moist savannas of south-eastern Africa (Zambezian Savanna), animals of the drier savannas of West and Central Africa (Sudan Savanna) and species from the dry country of north-east Africa, the Somali-Masai fauna. There are also a few Palaearctic species, originating in the northern half of Africa, that reach East Africa. Our coastline is inhabited by some reptiles and amphibians typical of the East African Coastal Mosaic fauna, dwellers in the moist thicket and woodland that may once have extended almost continuously from the shores of north-eastern South Africa and Mozambique to southern Somalia. The animals of the great Guinea-Congolian forests of West and Central Africa are represented by a number of forest species on the western side of East Africa, in particular amphibians, many of which reach their easternmost limits in the Albertine Rift forests of Uganda, Rwanda and Burundi. There are also a number of endemic reptile and amphibian species, found only within East Africa. Most of these endemic animals are associated with hills, mountains and forests, in particular the forests of the ancient East Arc Mountains, that extend from southern Kenya through Tanzania to Mlanje Mountain in Malawi. This is why it is important that these regions should be protected.

The present structure of the East African reptile and amphibian fauna has been largely shaped by three main factors: firstly, the geological events (formation of rift valleys, volcanic activity, watershed movement, river capture, flooding and erosion); secondly, various climatic changes over the last 30,000 years (variation in rainfall, changes in lake levels, shrinkage and expansion of forests and deserts); and thirdly, human activity.

Observing and collecting reptiles and amphibians

In general, amphibians and reptiles are best left in the wild; that is where they live and they are an important part of the ecosystem. In addition, many areas in East Africa are protected, and animals there are not permitted to be collected. It is our hope that the users of this book enjoy watching amphibians and reptiles in wild places, and their successful identification adds to the enjoyment. However, we are also aware that in certain circumstances, collecting amphibians and reptiles is justified. Consequently, we give here some advice on observing, finding and collecting amphibians and reptiles. The notes on collecting are aimed at those with appropriate permission from local authorities.

Weather is significant. In East Africa, the broad climatic picture is of dry and wet seasons. The wet season may be a poor time for seeing big game in wild areas, but it is the best time for observing reptile and amphibian activity. Amphibians in East Africa lead a curious life; most species are dependent upon seasonal pools for breeding. So when the rainy season begins there is a frenetic cycle of activity among amphibians: emergence, mating, egg-laying, feeding, growth of tadpoles and young, burial; the cycle must be finished before the pools dry up. There is almost no amphibian activity in the dry season, and consequently, as a result of the importance of frogs in the snake food chain, greatly reduced snake activity.

Amphibians and reptiles are secretive: they spend much of their time hidden. Those in the open, if approached, tend to freeze or move away unobtrusively. The casual observer in the wild may see a few, but a little expert hunting will increase your chances of seeing these creatures. There are various techniques you can use. Turning over ground cover such as rocks, logs and vegetation heaps will expose hiding animals, but take care where you put your fingers, and replace the cover afterwards. Lifting up rock flakes, breaking up fallen logs, and removing dead bark from trees may reveal animals, but bear in mind that this destroys habitats. Areas around rural housing or abandoned buildings are often prime reptile habitat. In forest areas, raking through leaf litter will often expose frogs, lizards and snakes. When walking in the bush, keep your eyes open. Move slowly, look around. You can also look for tracks in sandy areas and follow them back to where the animal is hiding: it may be buried, or in a hole. If you sit and watch a termite mound on a warm day animals may emerge to bask. In open areas, lizards are often active. Rocky hills, especially those with sloping sheet rock areas and cracks, are usually excellent places to see lizards. In open country, isolated big trees are important refuges. Around buildings, amphibians will hide near water sources, in such places as behind sinks, between pipes, in tanks and cisterns and just inside drains.

Water sources are good places to see reptiles and amphibians. During the day, frogs will hide under waterside vegetation, between reed stems, or between the leaf stem and the trunk of fleshy plants, especially bananas. Frog-eating snakes may be in waterside vegetation. Except for puddle frogs (*Phrynobatrachus*) and a few others, frogs are rarely found in the water during the day. Birds and some mammals, especially squirrels, may give away the presence of a snake. If you hear birds or animals mobbing something, then investigate.

Because of the unique nature of their skin, most of our amphibian species are nocturnal. Looking for amphibians (and reptiles) at night can thus be very rewarding. You will need a good lamp or torch. At the beginning of the rainy season, frogs can be located by their calls. A group of frogs around a pool can make a noise audible hundreds of metres away. The male frogs are the callers, producing advertisement calls that attract females of their species and at the same time warning other males of their presence. Each of our numerous frog species has its own unique call, and these calls are a very familiar part of the African night scene. Where we are familiar with them, we have described these calls onomatopoeically. For example, the Senegal Kassina has a frequency-modulated call that sounds like a drop of water in a bucket. We have rendered it as 'boink'. A frog expert can sit by a waterhole at night and tell you 'who's home' without ever seeing a frog. In some of our really diverse localities, like the Arabuko-Sokoke Forest on the Kenya coast, or the Zaraninge Forest in Tanzania, there may be over 20 frog species calling at once, and in great numbers.

Many types of snakes are also active at night, as are geckos. Some reptiles, especially chameleons and green snakes show up clearly at night; they look pale against dark vegetation. However, apart from crocodiles, reptile eyes do not reflect light well, and it is no good looking for reptilian eyeshine. In urban areas, walls and drains act as traps and snakes or frogs may be found crawling along them. Storm drains often trap animals. Geckos may be hunting around lamps at night. Frogs will sit under a lamp, catching falling insects. Diurnal lizards may be sleeping on vertical rock faces. Reptiles and amphibians moving at night often make a surprising amount of noise, especially in well-vegetated areas; once in a while turn off your lamp and listen. Bear in mind that if you want to look for amphibians and reptiles at night you should check if there is a watchman present, and not walk at night in areas you haven't surveyed during the day; you might get lost, or wander into danger (a cliff, a swamp, or into the presence of big game). Wear stout footwear at night and take care not to tread on snakes.

Driving slowly at night (20 to 30 kilometres per hour) can also be rewarding, especially on tarred roads, with your headlights dipped; you may encounter frogs, geckos and snakes either lying on the surface to absorb heat or just crossing the road, especially if the road is wet. Bear in mind that there are hazards involved in night-driving in East Africa; they include unlit vehicles, roadblocks, and livestock on the road.

Useful equipment for the amphibian and reptile collector may include a tape of frog calls with a player, plastic bag for amphibians, a long-handled net, cloth bags with sewn-in drawstrings and screw-topped plastic jars for little animals. Remember to keep containers with live animals in them away from sunlight or excessive heat, and take care not to squash them. A hooked stick is useful for turning ground cover, removing tree bark, poking about in holes and pressing down snakes. For dangerous snakes, a grab stick, pair of tongs and a pair of goggles (for spitting cobras) will be needed. A pair of industrial leather gloves are also useful, for protecting the hands when digging. Other useful equipment might include a small shovel or trowel for digging out holes, and some plastic tubing, for sticking down holes so you don't lose your way when digging them out. Lizards may permit close approach and can be noosed using fishing line on a light rod (e.g. an old radio aerial or a long thin stick). Animals can sometimes be flushed out of holes with chloroform, petrol, mothballs or smoke, but such techniques may permanently damage the refuge, kill the animal in the hole or start a bush fire; thus their use should be carefully considered. A tortoise in a hole, if poked with a pool cue makes a most distinctive thwock. A small pair of binoculars is useful. You don't always have to walk in East Africa to observe the smaller wildlife; the quiet watcher with binoculars in an elevated spot can often see a surprising amount.

Local help is often available in East Africa. People will come and offer their services; they often have a lot of local knowledge, and a little money goes a long way. If you have a book with you and speak the local language, you can show pictures of what you want. But never ask or allow people to catch snakes for you; if someone gets bitten there will be major problems.

Serious scientific collectors will need preservative and containers. Valuable specimens are often found dead. A 10% formalin solution or a 50–60% alcohol solution can be used to preserve specimens. All specimens should be labelled; mark the label with soft pencil. Locality is the most important piece of data; a specimen without a location is virtually useless. Larger animals should be cut open along the abdomen, and/or injected with preservative into the soft body parts. In an emergency, you can preserve specimens with methylated spirit, petrol or concentrated salt solution. Specimens should be deposited in a public-access collection, such as a museum.

Anyone intending to collect dangerous snakes should be thoroughly experienced, and be part of a team with adequate medical insurance. Snakebite treatment may involve blood transfusions. The field worker should also have suitable protective clothing, food, drink and medical supplies.

Conservation

Reptiles and amphibians suffer from an image problem. A lot of people dislike them, and snakes and certain lizards are actively feared and killed if encountered. Environmental education may help with this problem, but even in highly developed countries, many people do not like reptiles and amphibians. It is for this reason that places such as reptile parks serve such an important function in bringing the public face to face with reptiles and amphibians, thus giving them a chance to appreciate their beauty and usefulness. For the same reason, any enthusiast who keeps local amphibians or reptiles and shows them to their friends is benefiting conservation. In addition, reptiles and amphibians are an important part of ecosystems. They eat pests, and they possess both known and untapped potential in culinary, economic and medical terms.

In many ways, the future is bright for East Africa's reptiles. Kenya, Tanzania and Uganda all have active tourist industries that employ many people and bring in outside money; thus their governments have a financial interest in protecting wild places and their inhabitants. There is a large, well-developed and protected national park and reserve system, helped to some extent by the forest reserves. In addition, amphibians and reptiles are relatively small and secretive; they are not as vulnerable to habitat loss and exploitation as larger wild animals and can survive on farmland and in suburban areas.

East Africa's vulnerable amphibians and reptiles are the endemic species, especially those with limited ranges that live in areas suitable for agriculture or exploitation. Many live in tiny habitats, which are often forested. With population increases, these forests are vulnerable, for their timber and potential use for farming. At present, our conservation priorities should be to identify such habitats, especially those with no protection, document their fauna and flora and implement protective strategies.

We would like to draw attention to the importance of museums in conservation activities. The ranges of almost all species documented in this book are based upon museum specimens. Without those specimens, ranges would be unknown, and taxonomic status impossible to clarify; thus no conservation strategy would be possible. There is a modern school of thought that decries collecting, and states that rare creatures should always be left alive and that range mapping should be done using field observations. This may be possible with larger mammal and bird species; it is not possible with amphibians and reptiles. There are few observers and few specimens, reptiles and amphibians are hard to see and find, the difference between many similar species is not obvious in the field and field identification is difficult. Museum specimens are necessary, and it is most important that specimens are deposited in local collections to assist indigenous researchers. A list of institutions involved with East African herpetology is given at the back of this book (see pages 233–234).

Safety and reptiles

In other publications (our field guide, and *The Dangerous Snakes of Africa* by Stephen Spawls and Bill Branch) we have dealt at length with avoidance of snakebite, and how to treat it, and we included details of how to deal with venom in the eye after an encounter with a spitting cobra. We refer interested persons to those publications. A few rules for safety are given here.

The Nile Crocodile is a dangerous reptile; it may attack humans in order to eat them. You should never wade or swim in water bodies where Nile Crocodiles live. It is advisable to stay at least 8–10m from the water's edge.

A number of East African snakes are dangerously venomous. To avoid being bitten, always treat snakes with respect. Don't try to catch or kill them. Snakes never make unprovoked attacks. If confronted with a snake, move backwards slowly. The most important rule is always look where you are going. Wear adequate shoes, and don't put your hands or feet in places you cannot see. Use a lamp or torch at night. Don't sleep on the ground, or gather firewood after dark. If someone gets venom in their eyes after an encounter with a spitting cobra, the eyes should be gently washed out with large quantities of water (or other bland fluids such as milk), and the victim taken for a medical check-up. If someone has been bitten by a snake, treat it as a medical emergency, abandon other plans and organise rapid safe transport to hospital. Do not try to catch or kill the snake. Leave the wound alone; don't start cutting it, giving shocks, using ice, etc. Immobilisation therapy may be useful in some cases, as detailed in our other publications. But don't let fears about snakebite put you off going into wild places; the risks are very small.

Identifying reptiles

Some species are easy to identify, others are not; this is true for most tropical areas. It is worth having a good look at the pictures in this book before you go into the field, to get an idea of what you might encounter. However, many reptiles are easily identifiable in the field. We give below a number of general rules, to help with field identification of our reptiles. They are applicable to East African animals only, and you should use them with caution, particularly where snakes are concerned.

First, there are no venomous lizards in Africa, despite local legend that indicates that some lizard species (especially agamas and chameleons) are. In addition, no species has poisonous excreta. However, reptiles (especially captive ones) may have bacteria on their skin. These are unlikely to cause any problems, however, provided handlers thoroughly wash their hands after holding animals, and avoid touching their eyes and mouth while handling.

Most chameleons can be readily identified by their swivelling eyes set in turrets, their grasping feet and prehensile tail. Monitor lizards are large; most are over 70cm long, and no other East African lizard is that big. Worm lizards look like worms. Large male agamas have broad, bright heads, usually green, blue, red or pink. The smaller agamas often have blue on the throat. Agamas can also be identified by their broad heads and very thin necks.

Geckos are the only lizards active at night. Most have vertical eye pupils and soft skin. Skinks have shiny bodies, are often striped and/or brightly coloured, with little limbs and no distinct narrowing of the neck. Lacertid lizards are

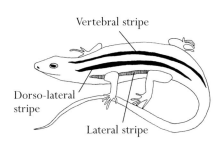

Lizard stripes

Vertebral stripe

Dorso-lateral stripe

Lateral stripe

small, fast-moving, often striped and most common in arid country. Plated lizards have an obvious skin fold along the flanks, and are relatively large.

There is no single way to tell a harmless snake from a dangerous one. Any fat snake over 4m long must be a python. Any snake with more than one conspicuous stripe running along the body is probably back-fanged and not dangerous. Any snake over 2m long is probably dangerous. Any grey, green or greenish tree snake over 1.3m long is almost certainly dangerous; it will probably be a mamba, boomslang or vine snake. If it is over 1.3m long and

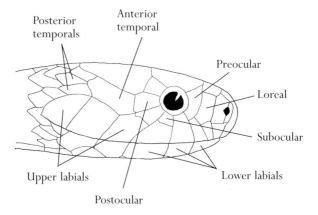

Head scales of a colubrid snake, side view

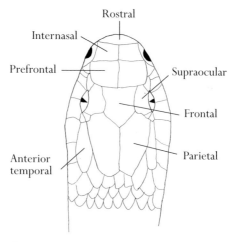

Head scales of a colubrid snake, from above

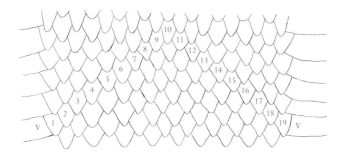

How to count the dorsal scale rows of a snake, count obliquely
V= ventral scale

inflates the front half of its body in anger, it will be a dangerous back-fanged tree snake (boomslang or vine snake).

Any snake that spreads a hood, flattens its neck or raises the forepart of the body off the ground when threatened is almost certainly dangerous, and will probably be an elapid (other possibilities include night adders and the Rufous Beaked Snake). Any snake with conspicuous bars, cross-bands, rings or V-shapes, especially on the neck or front half of its body, on the back or on the belly is probably dangerous. Most cobras have dark bars or blotches on the underside of their necks. A fat-bodied snake, with a sub-triangular head, that lies quietly when approached, is probably a viper or adder. Small black, dark grey or brown snakes with tiny eyes, no obvious necks and a short fat tail that ends in a spike will almost certainly be burrowing asps.

Most bush vipers are a mixture of greens, blacks and yellows, with broad heads and thin necks, and are usually in a bush or low tree. A little snake with conspicuous pale bands on a dark body is probably a garter snake. Any snake with rectangular, sub-rectangular or triangular markings on its back or sides, or rows of semi-circular markings along the flanks, is probably a viper. A snake that forms C-shaped coils and rub them together, making a noise like water falling on a hot plate, will be either a carpet viper (dangerous) or an egg-eater (harmless). Any small snake with a blunt rounded head <u>and</u> a blunt rounded tail, with eyes either invisible or visible as little dark dots under the skin, and with tiny scales that are the same size all the way around the body will be either a blind snake or a worm-snake, and harmless.

Identifying amphibians

Amphibians in East Africa belong to two orders. The order Gymnophiona contains the caecilians. These have no legs, moist shiny skins and are worm-like in appearance. Most of their lives is spent buried in damp soil, usually in forests. The order Anura consists of the more familiar frogs and toads.

Adult frogs and toads may be identified using a combination of features. Identification of larval anurans, the tadpoles, is not attempted in this guide. Many adult frogs can be identified using colour pattern but, often, a more careful examination is required. Below we have tried to briefly describe the more easily observed features useful in identifying frogs. Specialists use a more detailed number of structures and measurements to help determine the various species. In some genera, species are extremely difficult to tell apart using only physical characters. For those, studies of male vocalisations (the call) and even molecular and genetic studies, are required. We point out cases in which our knowledge of the identification of species is wanting.

Initially, have a look at our illustrations and see if you can observe trends among the groups. What groups of frogs show the most startling range of colours? What does a typical toad look like? What sort of pupils do the different genera have? What is distinctive about puddle frogs (*Phrynobatrachus*)? If you can answer these questions, you are well on the way to field identification of East African amphibians to genus level.

A number of amphibian groups can be quickly identified. Most toads of the genus *Bufo* are warty, and various shades of brown and grey, with paired markings on the back. The ridged frogs, *Ptychadena*, have long pointed noses and longitudinal glandular ridges and stripes. The reed frogs (*Hyperolius*) are tiny, never more than 3 or 4cm long without legs outstretched, often green or other vivid colours, their big eyes have horizontal pupils and their digit tips are big and rounded for climbing. The leaf-folding frogs (*Afrixalus*) look like reed frogs but have diamond-shaped or rhomboidal pupils. The Kassinas (*Kassina*) are smooth-bodied frogs with high-contrast blotches and stripes and vertical pupils. The tree frogs (*Leptopelis*) have squat, dumpy bodies, huge eyes with a vertical pupil and big rounded tips to their digits.

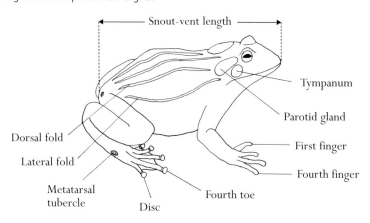

Amphibian features

If you encounter a frog in the field, the actual location will often provide useful clues. Almost all the hyperoliids (spiny reed frogs, reed frogs, and tree frogs) can climb and are likely to be found on plants; the only exception in this family are the Kassinas, which live on the ground. The rhacophorids (foam-nest tree frogs) are also usually found on vegetation (or buildings). These frogs rarely descend to the ground. Finger and toe shape help identify climbers. Do the digits have enlarged, rounded discs, indicating good climbing ability, or not? Many treefrogs have expanded discs allowing them to obtain purchase on grass stems and trees. Are the digits bundled into opposing pairs, as in the foam-nest frogs, *Chiromantis*?

The pipids (clawed frogs) are nearly always in water, and very rarely emerge. They have a very distinctive shape. Rocket frogs (*Ptychadena*) do not climb, but are often found sitting on the banks and edges of water bodies. The *Bufo*, or typical, toads are often a long way from water. If the night seems quite dry and a frog is moving about on the ground, it will often be a toad or a sand frog (*Tomopterna*).

Behaviour will also give useful clues. The best jumpers, that can make long direct powerful leaps of a metre or more, with limbs tucked in, are the rocket frogs (*Ptychadena*). When the hyperoliids (tree frog, reed and spiny reed frogs) and the foam-nest tree frogs jump, they tend to have their limbs outstretched to assist with landing, in an ungainly manner. If you watch them jumping you will see how distinctive this is. Toads can only hop; they rarely make big jumps. The Kassinas walk. The leg shape may give clues, before the frog moves; ridged frogs have long legs, burrowing frogs like the rain frogs have short muscular legs. The feet will also give clues to identity. Are the digits of the legs webbed at all, or with little webbing, as is the case for many terrestrial species which do not spend much time in water? Are they connected by extensive webbing (as is found in forms which are good swimmers)?

Examine frogs closely. None are dangerous, and almost all can be safely picked up, (except bullfrogs, which can bite), but you must wash your hands thoroughly afterwards, as some frogs have sticky, toxic skin secretions (for this reason, don't let them touch any open wound). Look closely at the colour. Examine the eye. Look at the underside. How big is your frog? When you put it down, how does it behave?

Size is a useful feature when identifying species. A species may be classed as small, medium or large. In most frogs, the females reach a larger size than the males. Unless stated otherwise, all our lengths are snout-vent lengths, that is the overall length of the frog when sitting with the legs folded. Traditionally, the snout to vent length is taken in millimetres. However, amphibians have been sampled at relatively few points in East Africa, and we make no claims that the sizes we present are authoritative and, in some cases, we have had to use extralimital data. Two similar genera that are fairly readily distinguished by size are the tree frogs (*Leptopelis*), rarely smaller than 4cm snout-vent length, and the reed frogs

(*Hyperolius*), rarely larger than 3cm. The biggest frogs of all are the bullfrogs (*Pyxicephalus*), some of the toads, and the Groove-crowned Bullfrog (*Hoplobatrachus occipitalis*).

The shape of a frog may provide much information: is its body relatively sleek and streamlined (ridged frog) or is it more muscular and stronger (bullfrog)? Is the snout pointed (ridged frog) or rounded (bullfrog)? Is the snout small and hard, as in the snout-burrowers (*Hemisus*)? Is the body evenly proportioned (large toads), or is it stout and plump (rain frogs, snout-burrowers, long-fingered frogs and others)? The shape of the pupil may be horizontal or vertical and is a useful character. The eardrum or tympanum may be large and conspicuous, small and less so, or it may not be visible at all.

The head may bear features which make a species easy to identify, for example, a groove running across the back of the head (Groove-crowned Bullfrog), or a fold of skin as is found in the snout-burrowers. Many frogs have a dark band of colour running from about the nostril through the tympanum; this gives the impression of a dark 'mask'.

The skin of the back (dorsal surface) of a frog may be relatively smooth or be very rough and warty (most toads). The back may have little in the way of distinct patterning, or may have a complex combination of marks that render the species difficult to see, or the colour on the back and sides may be very bright and conspicuous. Often there is a mid-dorsal line extending the length of the back; it may be very narrow or relatively wide.

Some of the large toads have distinctive, well-developed glands on the skin just behind the eye (parotid glands), and various enlarged areas of glandular skin may extend down the side of the body (Red Toad, *Schismaderma*), or occur as large swellings on the legs (forest toads, *Nectophrynoides*). The upper surface of the legs is often banded with darker colour than the basic colour of the back. To separate some species, it may be useful to examine the pattern of pale lines found on the upper surface of the thighs (particularly ridged frogs).

Many frogs are capable of altering their colour and an animal seen at night may look very different from the same animal in daylight. The underside of the animal (ventral surface) is often paler than the dorsal side and may be more or less uniformly coloured, or have varying patterns. Colour is a very useful means of identification. Any frog that is really bright green, yellow or with a complex, vivid colour pattern is likely to be a reed frog. Kassinas have high-contrast dark blotches on a lighter background.

Many frogs have hardened structures of the skin, the tubercles, in the metatarsal and other areas of the foot; the size and shape of these may be diagnostic. Some species have large, spade-like tubercles that are used as digging implements. One genus, the African clawed frogs, *Xenopus*, has dark, claw-like structures on some of its toes.

Most male frogs give an advertisement call, produced by expelling air from the lungs into a vocal sac, which swells like a balloon when they are calling.

This vocal sac may be single or double, and may have a gular gland (often of a particular colour) on it. It is relatively easy to learn to identify these calls and thus to identify the species. Bullfrogs and the big toads have very loud, harsh calls, and often live near habitation. The Red-banded Rubber Frog has a trill like an electronic alarm clock. The reed frogs have short, high-pitched calls; the Kassina call sounds like water falling into a bucket. If you hear frogs calling at a pond, go and have a look with a torch. They will often go quiet when you get near, but if you switch your torch off and wait, they will recommence calling and you can switch on and spot them.

About the authors

Stephen Spawls was born in London but moved to Kenya when he was four. He lived in Kenya for 17 years, and subsequently worked in Ghana, Egypt, Botswana and Ethiopia, spending nearly 40 years in Africa. Herpetology is his major interest; he has published several books and papers on African reptiles. At present he lectures in science and mathematics at City College, Norwich.

Dr Robert C. Drewes is Curator of Herpetology at the California Academy of Sciences, San Francisco and Research Professor of Biology at San Francisco State University. His three and a half decades of African field work and research have spanned the continent. His wife and four children have accompanied him to Africa on a number of occasions, and his research programme is described at www.calacademy.org/research/herpetology

Kim M. Howell has lived and worked in East Africa for the past 38 years. A Professor in the Department of Zoology and Wildlife Conservation, University of Dar es Salaam since 1989, he is extremely fortunate to have had family, friends and colleagues who over the years have encouraged him in his fascination with reptiles and amphibians.

Tortoises, Turtles and Terrapins
Order Testudines

There are nearly 300 species of turtle, tortoise and terrapin worldwide. Twenty-two species occur in East Africa: five sea turtles, five land tortoises, two soft-shelled turtles and ten terrapins. They are all easily identifiable owing to their protective shell. Most species can totally or partially withdraw the head, limbs and tail inside the shell. They are long-lived, and may take several years to reach maturity. All lay eggs, which they bury in soil or sand. Land tortoises mostly eat plants, although some may eat invertebrates; water-dwelling species are largely carnivorous. Due to their relative size, they take a long time to gain heat, and thus are rarely found above 1,500m altitude in East Africa. Some species are at risk from fires, and from collecting for the pet trade; sea turtles are exploited for their shells, meat and eggs.

Identification of the East African land tortoises is straightforward. Leopard Tortoises are large, with a domed shell that slopes uniformly at both ends. The two hinged tortoises are smaller; the shell slopes steeply at the back, gently at the front. The Pancake Tortoise has a flat, flexible shell. The only problem is distinguishing between the two species of hinged tortoise; the differences are not clear cut. Some authorities, however, believe the split is artificial and that there is only a single, quite variable species.

Speke's Hinged Tortoise
Kinixys spekii

Identification: Up to 22cm. The slightly domed shell is yellow or tan, with darker markings, and rounded at the back, with a hinge at the back of the carapace.

Habitat and Distribution: Dry to moist savanna and coastal thicket,

from sea level to nearly 1,600m altitude, often in rocky areas. From the Kenya coast westwards across Ukambani and northern Tanzania to southern Burundi, isolated records from Rwanda and Kerio Valley.

Natural History: Diurnal, most active during rainy season. Spends the night (and aestivates) in holes, in rock cracks or under boulders. Males fight in the breeding season. Lays two to four eggs, roughly 3cm diameter. Omnivorous, eating plants, invertebrates and carrion.

Bell's Hinged Tortoise
Kinixys belliana

Identification: Up to 22cm. A brown, yellow and brown or yellow and black tortoise, the shell is rounded at the back and slopes gently forwards. There is a hinge at the back of the carapace.

Habitat and Distribution: Dry to

moist savanna and coastal thicket, from sea level to nearly 2,000m altitude. Eastern Tanzania, coastal Kenya, extreme northern Kenya, western Kenya, central and north-west Uganda.

Natural History: Diurnal, most active during rainy season. Spends the night (and aestivates) in holes, in rock cracks or under boulders. Males fight in the breeding season. Lays two to seven eggs, roughly 3cm diameter. Omnivorous, eating plants, invertebrates and carrion.

Leopard Tortoise
Geochelone pardalis

Identification: Up to 70cm. A large tortoise with a black and yellow domed shell, and no hinge.

Habitat and Distribution: Semi-desert, dry and moist savanna, from sea level to about 1,500m. Northern half of Tanzania, eastern Kenya, sporadic in northern Kenya, extreme eastern Uganda.

Natural History: Diurnal, shelters during midday, active in rainy season. Males fight in the breeding season, and are equally rough with females. Up to 30 eggs, about 5cm diameter, are laid, possibly several clutches in a season. They eat plants.

Pancake Tortoise
Malacochersus tornieri

Identification: Up to 22cm. A small, broad, flat tortoise with a uniquely flexible shell.

Habitat and Distribution: At low altitude, in and around rocky hills in savanna. Endemic to Kenya and Tanzania. In Kenya, south from Mt Nyiro to Samburu, Ukambani and Tsavo. In Tanzania, from Mkomazi across the central plateau, south to Ruaha National Park, west to Serengeti and south of Lake Victoria.

Natural History: Diurnal, maybe crepuscular. Expert climbers on rocks. Hide in rock cracks and under boulders (sometimes in holes) when inactive, often in groups. While mating, the male bites the female's legs and neck and tries to turn her over. A single egg (5 x 3cm) is laid. They eat plants and invertebrates.

Other land tortoises found in East Africa

Forest Hinged Tortoise *Kinixys erosa* A vivid yellow, brown and black, hinged tortoise, in forest in Uganda.

Aldabran Tortoise *Dipsochelys dussumieri* A huge grey tortoise, introduced, on Zanzibar.

Hawksbill Turtle
Eretmochelys imbricata

Identification: Up to 90cm. A small sea turtle with a noticeable beak and elongate carapace, the overlapping carapace scales marked with radiating streaks.

Habitat and Distribution: Circumtropical, in tropical and

even temperate seas. Found along the length of the East African coast.

Natural History: East Africa's most common turtle. May forage close to the reef, sometimes enters the lagoons inside the reef, but usually nervous. Mating occurs in shallow water. Lays between 50 and 200 eggs, roughly 4cm diameter, on the beach. Juveniles eat mostly vegetation but adults eat marine invertebrates, sometimes fish and plant material.

Green Turtle
Chelonia mydas

Identification: Up to 1.4m. A big, hard-shelled, deep-bodied sea turtle with a small blunt head, the carapace olive or brown, the shields streaked with tan or yellow.

Habitat and Distribution: Tropical and warm temperate seas, found

along the length of the East African coast.

Natural History: May forage in shallow water, often enters the lagoons inside the reef, found on seagrass beds. Quite tolerant of humans if not persecuted. Mates close to shore. Nests at night, all along the East African coast on secluded beaches, lays usually 100 to 150 eggs, about 4.5cm diameter. Up to six clutches per season recorded. Juveniles eat invertebrates, adults are herbivorous.

Helmeted Terrapin
Pelomedusa subrufa

Identification: Up to 30cm. A small, flat, smelly terrapin with a broad head. Shell mottled grey or brown, often stained green.

Habitat and Distribution: Dry and moist savanna and semi-desert, from sea level to about 1,600m altitude. Found in water bodies; dams, pools, swamps, streams and small rivers but rarely in large rivers. Probably occurs throughout lowland East Africa, but few records from northern Kenya and southern Tanzania.

Natural History: Aquatic, may bask in the water or on land. Will walk across country looking for pools. Quite quick moving. Swims quickly; if disturbed in pools it will dive into the mud and bury itself. Buries itself in mud at the start of the dry season. Mating occurs in water. Usually 10–30 eggs laid, roughly 3cm diameter. Eats anything living it can catch, including insects, amphibians, fish, even carrion and plant matter.

Yellow-bellied Hinged Terrapin
Pelusios castanoides

Identification: Up to 23cm. An olive-brown hinged terrapin with a long neck. Shell olive-brown.

Habitat and Distribution: In water bodies along the Tanzanian and southern Kenyan coastal plain, inland up the Rufiji River, usually in backwaters.

Natural History: Aquatic, active by day, buries itself in the mud in the dry season. Lays up to 25 eggs. Eats insects, water snails and floating vegetation.

Serrated Hinged Terrapin
Pelusios sinuatus

Identification: Up to 55cm. A huge, grey or black hinged terrapin with a serrated rear carapace.

Natural History: Aquatic, active by day, often basks on shorelines, logs and exposed rocks. In the dry season may bury itself in mud,

or walk across country to find water. Lays up to 30 eggs. Eats molluscs, snails, fish, amphibians and arthropods.

Habitat and Distribution: In rivers and lakes almost throughout Kenya and Tanzania, below 1,600m altitude, absent from Lake Victoria.

Nile Soft-shelled Turtle
Trionyx triunguis

Identification: Up to 90cm. A big, flat, soft-shelled water turtle, without scales, with a long tubular nose.

Natural History: Aquatic, apparently active by day, basks on shorelines. Sometimes partially

buries itself in mud. Lays 25 to 100 eggs. Eats fish, frogs and aquatic invertebrates. Will bite if incautiously handled. Can respire partially through its skin.

Habitat and Distribution: Rivers and lakes, known from Lake Turkana, Lake Albert and the White Nile downstream from Murchison Falls. Probably in the Daua River.

Other turtles, sea turtles and terrapins found in East Africa

Olive Ridley Turtle *Lepidochelys olivacea* Medium-sized dark turtle, with smooth shell with very regular scales, sporadically recorded all along the coast.

Loggerhead Turtle *Caretta caretta* A big, reddish sea turtle with a huge head. Only recorded from southern Tanzania

Leatherback Turtle *Dermochelys coriacea* A very big (up to 1.8m) black turtle, with a leathery skin, not scales. Sporadic records along the coastline, but mostly offshore.

Adanson's Hinged Terrapin *Pelusios adansoni* A small (19cm) hinged terrapin with a yellow-brown or brown shell, might occur on the Albert Nile in Uganda.

Lake Turkana Hinged Terrapin *Pelusios broadleyi* A small (18cm) hinged terrapin, with a finely speckled grey-brown shell. So far only recorded from Lake Turkana.

Congo Hinged Terrapin *Pelusios chapini* A large (30cm) hinged terrapin with a brown shell, yellow plastron. Recorded from Lake Albert and its feeder rivers.

Forest Hinged Terrapin *Pelusios gabonensis* A large (30cm) hinged terrapin with a yellow-brown or grey shell, the shell has a black central stripe, broadening to a V at front, carapace scales black outlined with yellow. Known only from the Bwamba forest, extreme western Uganda.

Zambian Hinged Terrapin *Pelusios rhodesianus* A small (25cm) hinged terrapin with a black or dark grey shell, plastron dark with central yellow blotches, sometimes uniform yellow. Known from lagoons and weedy estuaries bordering Lakes Victoria, Tanganyika and Malawi.

Pan Hinged Terrapin *Pelusios subniger* A small (20cm) hinged terrapin, shell brown or grey brown, lower edges yellow with black edging. Plastron scales yellow with black edging. Found in isolated water bodies in Burundi and central and south-western Tanzania.

Williams's Hinged Terrapin *Pelusios williamsi* A medium-sized (25 cm) hinged terrapin, shell black or dark brown, plastron black with a yellow rim and mid-seam. Known from Lake Victoria, and feeder rivers, the Uganda Nile system (including lakes) and Lake Edward.

Zambezi Flap-shelled Turtle *Cycloderma frenatum* A large (55cm) soft-shelled turtle, shell brown mottled with black, pale below, neck long and striped, eyes small and bright. River systems of south-eastern Tanzania and Lake Malawi.

Lizards and Worm Lizards

Order Squamata
Suborders Sauria and Amphisbaenia

The order Squamata, or squamate reptiles, contains three suborders. They are: the lizards, suborder Sauria, the worm lizards, suborder Amphisbaenia, and the snakes, suborder Serpentes (see pages 86–155). Worldwide there are about 4,450 lizard species, 155 species of worm lizard and 2,900 snake species.

Around 200 species of lizard occur in East Africa. None are venomous, despite legends to the contrary. All lizards have scales and most have four limbs; there are a few legless forms. Most lizards have external ears, and most can close their eyes. Most can shed their tails, and the regenerated tail often has a different shape to the original. They usually lay eggs; a few species retain the eggs internally until they are about to hatch. Lizards largely eat invertebrates, although a few take larger animals and some eat plant food.

Lizard identification There are 20 families of lizard, of which eight occur in East Africa. Lizards can usually be identified to their family quite quickly. The **geckos** are small, mostly nocturnal, with a soft granular skin, often with enlarged scales, called tubercles. The nocturnal geckos have curious vertical slit-like pupils; no other East African lizard has vertical pupils. The dwarf geckos, active by day, are small, with round pupils and enlarged toe-tips. The **agamas** are diurnal, relatively large lizards, with scaly, spiky bodies, big rounded heads, and thin necks; the head often has spiky scales. They often sit in prominent places, and the males of several species have brightly coloured heads. **Chameleons** are slow-moving, with rotating eyes set in little turrets, and with grasping feet. Most are green, live in trees or bushes and have long prehensile tails; the pygmy chameleons are brown with stumpy tails. The **monitor lizards** are huge, with forked tongues, muscular limbs and tails that are flattened sideways. The **skinks** all have shiny bodies and fairly long tails; most have little limbs and there are a few limbless species. Many are striped. Any lizard found buried underground or pushing through leaf litter will be a skink. The **lacertids** or 'typical' lizards have rough scales; they usually have long tails, and most of the dry country species are striped or barred. Many are very quick-moving. A small, very fast-moving ground lizard in dry country will be a lacertid. The **plated lizards** are relatively large; two species are striped, one is big and brown, but all have a curious and distinctive skin fold along their sides. This family also contains a plated snake lizard, with a very long tail and no front limbs. The family of **girdled lizards** and their relatives contains three genera. A single species of flat lizard (*Platysaurus*) is found only in southern Tanzania. Two species of slim, limbless, striped brown grass lizard or snake lizard occur in highland areas. The girdled lizards are brown, rough-scaled lizards with spiny heads and tails.

Geckos: Family Gekkonidae

Over 750 species of gecko are known; 55 are so far recorded from East Africa. Geckos are small, plump, mostly nocturnal lizards. They have a soft, granular skin. Most shed their tails very easily. Unlike most nocturnal animals, they hunt by sight, so they have large eyes and no eyelids (with the exception of the Somali-Masai Clawed Gecko). Some can squeak. They have a limited ability to change colour, from dark to light. Most geckos have feet adapted for climbing, with enlarged toe pads, which have claws and minute hair-like structures that grip the surface. Most eat insects, and a number will forage around lamps at night. Nearly all geckos lay two eggs in a cavity; the eggs harden after laying. Some species lay eggs communally.

Somali-Masai Clawed Gecko
Holodactylus africanus

Identification: up to 11 cm. A slow-moving banded terrestrial gecko with claws and eyelids.

Habitat and Distribution: Semi-desert and savanna at low altitude. Known from Kajiado southwards into dry central Tanzania, eastwards to Mkomazi, sporadic records from southern Lake Turkana, dry central Kenya and the Mandera area, probably more widespread.

Natural History: Nocturnal, emerging from deep burrows and beneath rocks at darkness, feeds on invertebrates, especially termites and beetles. Two eggs are laid in a burrow.

Other unusual gecko species found in East Africa

Madagascan Clawless Gecko *Ebenavia inunguis* A small (8cm) brown gecko with no claws and a pointed snout. A distinct pale stripe through eye. A Madagascan species, recoded from Pemba.

Elegant Gecko *Stenodactylus sthenodactylus* A small (10cm) spotted gecko, with claws but no toe pads. Sporadically recorded from desert and semi-desert at low altitude in north and north-west Kenya.

Usambara Forest Gecko
Cnemaspis africana

Identification: Up to 10cm. A quick-moving gecko, with a round pupils, feet with claws, not pads, on long thin toes. Colour greenish-brown with a vertebral stripe, yellow below.

Habitat and Distribution: Woodland and hill forest, from sea level to 2,000m altitude. Endemic to south-east Kenya and north-east Tanzania, on most hills and mountains south and east of Mt Meru and Kilimanjaro, also the Shimba and Taita Hills.

Natural History: Diurnal and crepuscular, lives on trees, rocks and earth banks, may shelter in leaf litter. Lays eggs, eats insects.

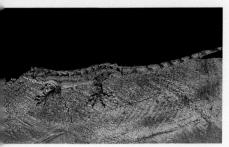

Four-lined Forest Gecko
Cnemaspis quattuorseriatus

Identification: Up to 9cm. A quick-moving gecko, with a round pupils, feet with claws, not pads, on long thin toes. Colour brown or grey with a vertebral stripe, bordered with grey chevrons. Tail barred.

Habitat and Distribution: Woodland and hill forest, of the Albertine Rift, from Kibale south through western Rwanda.

Natural History: Diurnal and crepuscular, lives on trees. may shelter in leaf litter. Lays eggs, eats insects.

Other forest geckos found in East Africa

Uluguru Forest Gecko *Cnemaspis barbouri* A small (6cm) olive or grey gecko, with chevron markings. On trees in hills (Usambara, Uluguru) or coastal forests in eastern Tanzania.

Dickerson's Forest Gecko *Cnemaspis dickersonae* A medium-sized (9cm) slender, olive-grey gecko, with chevrons down the back, sporadically recorded from forests of central East Africa, including Mt Elgon, Mt Kadam, the Nyambeni Hills, Mt Hanang and Lake Manyara.

Elgon Forest Gecko *Cnemaspis elgonensis* A large (up to 10cm) grey or olive gecko, with chevrons on the back, known from forest and hills in western Kenya (Kakamega area, Mt Elgon), eastern Uganda (Mt Kadam) and the Ruwenzori Mountains.

Udzungwa Forest Gecko *Cnemaspis uzungwae* A small grey to brownish grey forest gecko, with chevrons along the back. Known only from the Udzungwa Mountains, Tong'omba and Kiwengoma forest in eastern Tanzania.

Brook's Gecko
Hemidactylus brooki

Identification: Up to 15cm. A chunky gecko, body and tail covered with small prominent tubercles, grey or brown, with sub-rectangular markings down the back and a banded tail.

Habitat and Distribution: In forest, woodland, savanna and semi-desert, from sea level to over 2,400m. Widespread almost throughout the northern half of Tanzania, south-eastern and north-western Kenya and most of Uganda.

Natural History: Nocturnal, will hunt on the ground, climb trees and rocks, will forage around lamps at night. Shelters under rocks, in holes or under bark. Lays two eggs. Eats invertebrates.

Uniform-scaled Gecko
Hemidactylus isolepis

Identification: Up to 8cm. A slender, grey, brown or pinkish gecko, often with white or yellow spots.

Habitat and Distribution: Dry savanna and semi-desert. Sporadically recorded from much of northern Kenya, at low altitude.

Natural History: Terrestrial. Shelters in holes and under ground cover by day, active by night. Lays two eggs, sometimes communally. Eats insects and other arthropods.

Tropical House Gecko
Hemidactylus mabouia

Identification: Up to 15cm. A robust gecko, very variable in colour, may be grey, pink, white or yellow, with irregular darker markings on the back, can change colour. Usually dark crossbars on tail.

Habitat and Distribution: Semi-desert, savanna, forest and woodland, from sea level to over 2,100m, although rare above 1,700m. Occurs virtually throughout Tanzania. Rwanda, Uganda and the southern half of Kenya, records from northern Kenya sporadic.

Natural History: Nocturnal, active on the ground and on trees and rocks. Probably the most common gecko in East Africa, and often seen on building walls, especially at low altitude, eating insects and other arthropods that come to lamps. They lay two eggs. They have a curious clicking call, sometimes described as a 'tiny laugh'.

Tree Gecko
Hemidactylus platycephalus

Identification: Up to 19cm. A robust gecko, very variable in colour, may be grey, grey-brown or yellow-brown, with irregular darker markings on the back, can change colour. Usually dark crossbars on tail.

Habitat and Distribution: Semi-desert, savanna, and woodland, from sea level to 1,500m. Widespread in south-eastern Tanzania and eastern Kenya, sporadic from northern Kenya.

Natural History: Nocturnal, active on the ground and on trees and rocks. Fairly common, and like the Tropical House Gecko (which it closely resembles - some authorities think these two are the same species) often found around human habitation. They lay two eggs.

Prince Ruspoli's Gecko
Hemidactylus ruspolii

Identification: Up to 10m. A dark, robust gecko, with many obvious tubercles, the regenerated tail is usually distinctively carrot-shaped. Usually grey, brown or black, with darker sub-rectangular markings, the tubercles are often bright yellow. Like other geckos can change colour. Usually dark irregular markings on the tail.

Habitat and Distribution: Semi-desert, and dry savanna at low altitude. Widespread in central northern and north-eastern Kenya; sporadic records from Tsavo and Kitui areas.

Natural History: Nocturnal, active on the ground, by day shelters under rocks, logs and in holes. Occasionally found under tree bark. They lay two eggs.

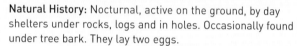

Nyika Gecko
Hemidactylus squamulatus

Identification: Up to 9cm. A small grey or brown gecko, with irregular darker crossbars or wavy back markings, and a dark line through the eye.

Habitat and Distribution: Semi-desert and savanna, from low altitude up to 2,200m but usually below 1,500m. Widespread in north-central Tanzania, in eastern and southern Kenya, west to Masai Mara.

Natural History: Nocturnal and terrestrial. Shelters under rocks, in holes, in old logs etc. Lays two eggs; laying sites include termite mounds and rock cracks.

Other species of *Hemidactylus* geckos found in East Africa

Barbour's Gecko *Hemidactylus barbouri* Up to 9cm, a slim dark-brown or grey gecko, finely spotted. Occurs on the coast, from Malindi south to Bagamoyo.

Somali Banded Gecko *Hemidactylus bavazzanoi* Up to 8cm long, a vividly banded orange and black gecko. Known only from Mandera, north-east Kenya.

Pacific Gecko *Hemidactylus frenatus* Up to 13cm long, a pinkish, brown or grey gecko, without tubercles on the body. Recorded only from Lamu Island, probably a waif.

Archer's Post Gecko *Hemidactylus funaiolii* A little gecko, less than 8cm, with overlapping body scales, hazel-grey with brown spots. Recorded from Laisamis and Archer's Post in northern Kenya.

Boulenger's Gecko *Hemidactylus macropholis* A large (14cm), gecko, with many tubercles, resembles Brook's Gecko, light pink or brown with darker crossbars. Sporadically recorded from north-eastern Kenya and near Arusha in Tanzania.

Tana River Gecko *Hemidactylus modestus* Up to 8cm long, a brown gecko, sometimes with darker dorsal markings. Known only from a few localities in south-eastern Kenya.

Richardson's Forest Gecko *Hemidactylus richardsoni* A large, (up to 16cm), silvery-grey gecko, with a distinctive dark flank stripe and dark back markings. Recoded from the Bwamba Forest in western Uganda.

Somali Plain Gecko *Hemidactylus robustus* A brown or rufous gecko, with irregular darker crossbars. Known only from Mandera, Kenya. There are doubts about this species' status, it might just be a variety of the Turkish Gecko *Hemidactylus turcicus*.

Dutumi Gecko *Hemidactylus tanganicus* A big gecko, up to 16cm, buff-coloured with a pink tinge, and six dark blotches on the back. Known from Dutumi and Mkomazi Game Reserve in Tanzania.

Ogaden Gecko *Hemidactylus tropidolepis* Up to 7cm long, a little gecko, various shades of brown, with a semi-circular darker marking around the back of the head, darker wavy markings or crossbars on the head. Sporadically recorded from eastern Kenya (Voi, Tana Delta, Wajir).

Dwarf Geckos, *Lygodactylus* species, are a difficult taxonomic group. These little colonial, diurnal geckos are prone to translocation, especially of communal nest sites. Their behaviour has not been well studied, and the distribution of several species, at present, does not make zoogeographic sense. Bear this in mind if you encounter an unusual looking species. See the notes in our field guide.

Cape Dwarf Gecko
Lygodactylus capensis

Identification: Up to 8cm. A brown or grey dwarf gecko, with a paler irregular dorso-lateral stripe.

Habitat and Distribution: Woodland and savanna, from sea level to 1,800m altitude. Sporadic records from south-western Kenya, widespread in central to south-east Tanzania and south-west Tanzania.

Natural History: Diurnal, active on tree, bushes and fences. Live in structured colonies with a dominant male. Lay one to two eggs under bark or in rock cracks, communal nests are known. They eat small arthropods. May feign death if picked up.

Forest Dwarf Gecko
Lygodactylus gutturalis

Identification: Up to 8cm. A brown or dark grey dwarf gecko, can look almost black in shade.

Habitat and Distribution: Forest, woodland and well-wooded moist savanna, from 700 to 1,800m altitude. Sporadic records from Mt Elgon, and the Sesse Islands, widespread in western Uganda, Rwanda, Burundi and north-east Tanzania.

Natural History: Diurnal, active on forest trees and saplings, may descend to the ground. Lay one to two eggs under bark or in rock cracks, communal nests are known. They eat small arthropods.

Kenya Dwarf Gecko
Lygodactylus keniensis

Identification: Up to about 8cm. A grey dwarf gecko, with a distinctive pale yellow and black head.

Habitat and Distribution: Widespread in dry savanna and semi-desert in northern Kenya,

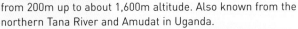

from 200m up to about 1,600m altitude. Also known from the northern Tana River and Amudat in Uganda.

Natural History: Diurnal, active on trees and bushes. Lay one to two eggs under bark or in rock cracks; communal nests are known. They eat small arthropods. Colonial but territories seem to be fairly small; on one tree 21 males, 15 females and 10 juveniles were found.

Yellow-headed Dwarf Gecko
Lygodactylus luteopicturatus

Identification: Up to about 9cm. A grey dwarf gecko, with a distinctive bright yellow and black head. Females are more subdued in colour. The male has a black throat; the female's throat is white.

Habitat and Distribution: Coastal

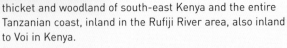

thicket and woodland of south-east Kenya and the entire Tanzanian coast, inland in the Rufiji River area, also inland to Voi in Kenya.

Natural History: Diurnal and arboreal, active on trees and bushes, often on buildings. Very agile, and uses scansors on its tail to balance. Colonial, like other dwarf geckos. Lay one to two eggs in glued pairs under bark. They eat small arthropods, but will also take vegetable material and honey from stingless bee nests.

Mann's Dwarf Gecko
Lygodactylus manni

Identification: Up to about 9cm. A grey dwarf gecko, with a dull yellow-brown and black head.

Habitat and Distribution: Medium altitude moist and dry savanna, from about 1,000 to 1,800m altitude. Occurs from the south-east shores of Lake Victoria north and east to Lake Baringo in Kenya.

Natural History: Diurnal, active on trees and bushes. Live in small structured colonies with a dominant male. Lay one to two eggs under bark or in rock cracks. They eat small arthropods.

White-headed Dwarf Gecko
Lygodactylus picturatus

Identification: Up to about 9cm. A grey, black-speckled dwarf gecko, with a distinctive yellow and black head. Colour quite variable, as is the extent of the black markings on the back. The male has a black throat; the female's throat is white.

Habitat and Distribution: Coastal thicket, dry and moist savanna and riverine forest of south-eastern Kenya, from the headwaters of the Tana River south and east to the coast.

Natural History: Diurnal and arboreal, active on trees and bushes, often on buildings, common on Kenya's north coast. Colonial, like other dwarf geckos. Lay one to two eggs in cracks, under bark or in tree holes. They eat small arthropods, but will also scavenge things like sugar and bread in homes.

Other species of dwarf gecko found in East Africa

Angolan Dwarf Gecko *Lygodactylus angolensis* Up to 7cm, olive-brown, with pale spots on the upper flanks. Sporadically recorded from south-central Kenya and widely scattered localities in Tanzania.

Angulated Dwarf Gecko *Lygodactylus angularis* Up to 10cm, brown, with chevrons under the chin. Found between the top end of Lake Malawi and the Udzungwa Mountains.

Grzimek's Dwarf Gecko *Lygodactylus grzimeki* Average size 6cm. Grey in colour, with fine parallel dark throat stripes. Found around Lake Manyara.

Broadley's Dwarf Gecko *Lygodactylus broadleyi* About 6cm long. Colour unknown, presumably grey. Coastal forests of eastern Tanzania. Red median stripe under male's tail.

Conradt's Dwarf Gecko *Lygodactylus conradti* A small grey dwarf gecko with distinctive pale dorso-lateral stripes, yellow or orange belly. Found only in the Usambara Mountains and associated forests.

Bunty's Dwarf Gecko *Lygodactylus grandisonae* About 5cm long, light brown or grey, three brown chin lines join on throat. Known only from Malka Murri, north-east Kenya.

Usambara Dwarf Gecko *Lygodactylus gravis* Large (9cm) dwarf gecko, yellowish to blackish grey above, belly yellow. Found in forests in extreme north-east Tanzania.

Dar es Salaam Dwarf Gecko *Lygodactylus inexpectatus* Nothing known about it, only one was ever found, in Dar es Salaam. The description makes no mention of colour.

Kim Howell's Dwarf Gecko *Lygodactylus kimhowelli* Looks like the White-headed Dwarf Gecko but body striped in black and grey (females) or black and blue (males), bold black and yellow head. Known only from the north-east Tanzanian coast, but recently reported from coastal forest on the Kenyan side of the border.

Side-spotted Dwarf Gecko *Lygodactylus laterimaculatus* Up to 7cm long, grey, with big black spots on the sides. Voi, Taita Hills, vicinity of Mt Kilimanjaro.

Scheffler's Dwarf Gecko *Lygodactylus scheffleri* Length 5 to 6cm, olive-brown with darker and lighter mottling. Known from Kibwezi, the Chyulu Hills and Mt Hanang. Kibwezi/Chyulu specimens have a red-brown to black neck blotch; Hanang form have a big brown neck blotch.

Scortecci's Dwarf Gecko *Lygodactylus scorteccii* Length 8cm, grey, bright yellow and black head. Recorded only from the north bank of the northernmost sector of the Tana River.

Somali Dwarf Gecko *Lygodactylus somalicus* Up to 6cm long, light brown with darker head and neck stripes. Widespread in extreme north and northeast Kenya.

Uluguru Dwarf Gecko *Lygodactylus uluguruensis* Maximum size 6cm, grey all over, with dark grey back blotches. Occurs only in the Uluguru mountains.

Copal Dwarf Gecko *Lygodactylus viscatus* Pale to dark brown or grey. No throat markings at all. Forests of eastern Tanzania.

Turquoise Dwarf Gecko *Lygodactylus williamsi* A small (6cm) gecko, absolutely unmistakeable as bright blue (males) or greenish blue (females) in life. Found only in the Kimboza Forest, Tanzania.

Turner's Thick-toed Gecko
Pachydactylus turneri

Identification: Up to about 20cm. A big, stocky gecko, with distinctive enlarged toe tips and no claws, grey or brown, spotted with white.

Habitat and Distribution: Moist and dry savanna with big trees and rock outcrops, from sea level to about 1,800m altitude. From Olorgesaille southwards into north-central Tanzania, also found in southeast Tanzania and one record from north-west Rwanda.

Natural History: Nocturnal, sheltering in tree or rock cracks during the day. Occasionally found on buildings and will forage around lamps. Squeaks if picked up, and bites hard. Two eggs laid in rock fissures or under bark. Eats arthropods.

Tuberculate Thick-toed Gecko
Pachydactylus tuberculosus

Identification: Up to about 17cm. A big, stocky gecko, with distinctive enlarged toe tips and no claws, usually grey or brown, with faint darker crossbars.

Habitat and Distribution: Open and wooded savanna from sea level to

1,700m altitude. Widespread across most of central Tanzania.

Natural History: Nocturnal, sheltering in trees and buildings and will forage around lamps. Squeaks if picked up. Breeding details unknown. Eats arthropods.

Other gecko species found in East Africa

Tete Thick-toed Gecko *Pachydactylus tetensis* A stocky pale grey gecko, up to 18cm length, with big toe tips, recorded from extreme south-east Tanzania.

Banded Velvet Gecko *Homopholis fasciata* A stocky gecko, up to 16cm length, brown and brownish-grey chevrons on the back, tail banded brown and grey. Sporadically recorded from savanna in central and north-west Tanzania and eastern and northern Kenya.

Cross-marked Sand Gecko *Pristurus crucifer* A little (10cm) agama-like diurnal fast-running gecko, with a vertebral stripe. In Kenya, known only from Mandera.

Pemba Day Gecko *Phelsuma abbotti* A 15cm bluish-green day gecko that lives on trees; known only from Pemba.

Dull-green Day Gecko *Phelsuma dubia* A large (15cm) green, red-speckled day gecko with bright orange eyes and big toe pads. On the coast, from Nyali south to Dar es Salaam.

Uluguru Tail-pad Gecko *Urocotyledon wolterstorffi* A small (12cm) forest gecko, with reddish eyes, back mottled grey and brown, tail banded, with adhesive papillae on the tail tip. Known only from Usambara and Uluguru Mountains.

Skinks: Family Scincidae

A family of shiny-bodied lizards; most have small limbs, some have none. Many live underground, and have pointed snouts and tough, smooth scales to assist with their way of life. Some 700 species are known, with about 45 species in East Africa. Most of the burrowing species are secretive and rare, but some skinks of the genus *Mabuya* are common and easily observed.

Short-necked Skink
Mabuya brevicollis

Identification: Up to 32cm. A big, heavily built skink, with a short head. Adult males striped brown and black (right), females (far right) and juveniles brown with darker speckling and crossbars, hatchlings black with yellow spotting.

Habitat and Distribution: Low altitude moist and dry savanna, woodland, semi-desert and coastal thicket, from sea level to about 1,500m. Occurs almost through eastern and northern Kenya, a few records from north-central Tanzania.

Natural History: Diurnal and terrestrial but will climb rocks and fallen timber. Often basks in a prominent place. May live in large groups (possibly colonies). Gives live birth to two or three young. Eats invertebrates.

Speckle-lipped Skink
Mabuya maculilabris

Identification: Up to 30cm. A fairly large, long-tailed, arboreal skink. Brown above, speckled with black, flanks often orange, occasionally darker.

Habitat and Distribution: Forest clearings, woodland, coastal thicket, often near water. Will live on buildings. Occurs along the East African coast, inland on the Rufiji, the Lake Victoria basin and all along the western Rift Valley.

Natural History: Diurnal and arboreal, climbs expertly. Often basks in a prominent place. Lays six to eight eggs. Eats invertebrates.

Rainbow Skink
Mabuya margaritifer

Identification: Up to 30cm. A big rock-dwelling skink. Males (far left) brown, black bars on neck. Females (left) and juveniles striped yellow and black with a blue tail.

Habitat and Distribution: Rocky Hills and outcrops in low to medium altitude savanna, from sea level to 1,600m. From the Tharaka plain south through Ukambani to Tsavo National Park, also occurs around Dodoma and in extreme south-east Tanzania.

Natural History: Diurnal, rock dwelling, often basks in a prominent place. Lives in colonies with a dominant male. Lays three to ten eggs. Eats invertebrates.

Long-tailed Skink
Mabuya megalura

Identification: Up to 25cm. A slim skink with a huge tail. Brown above, sometimes with darker stripes, the flanks have a prominent broad black stripe, lower edge white.

Habitat and Distribution: Grassland and savanna, usually at higher

altitude, but found from sea level to over 3,000m altitude. Known from the Eastern Arc Mountains, high central and western Kenya, Rwanda and Burundi.

Natural History: Diurnal, basks in grass clumps and bushes. Shy and secretive, slides swiftly through grass. Gives live birth to up to 15 young. Eats insects and other arthropods.

Tree Skink
Mabuya planifrons

Identification: Up to 35cm. A big slim, long-tailed skink, grey or brown, with a black flank stripe and a paler (sometimes poorly defined) dorso-lateral stripe, backs and flanks often with lighter speckling.

Habitat and Distribution: Coastal thicket and woodland, semi-desert and savanna. Patchy but widespread in northern and eastern Kenya and north-east and north-central Tanzania, also on Kenya Coast.

Natural History: Diurnal, an expert climber, living in trees and on bushes, will hunt and bask on the ground. Lays eggs. Eats insects and other arthropods.

Five-lined Skink
Mabuya quinquetaeniata

Identification: Up to 25cm. A big rock-dwelling skink. Males brown or grey, black bars and often blue and yellow speckling on neck. Females and juveniles striped yellow and brown or black, with a blue tail.

Habitat and Distribution: Rocky hills, outcrops and lava flows in low to medium altitude savanna, from 200 to 1,600m altitude. Found from Tsavo northward through eastern Kenya, always in rocky places, to rocky north-west Kenya, south-east and north-west Uganda. Also around Sololo in northern Kenya.

Natural History: Diurnal, rock-dwelling, often basks in a prominent place. Lives in colonies with a dominant male. Lays three to ten eggs, communal nests recorded. Eats invertebrates.

Striped Skink
Mabuya striata

Identification: Up to 25cm. A brown or olive skink with conspicuous cream or yellow dorso-lateral stripes, flanks usually speckled, sometimes very bronzy.

Habitat and Distribution: Often in towns, also in semi-desert, savanna

and forest clearings. Probably occurs throughout East Africa, but few records from northern and eastern Kenya and south-west Tanzania.

Natural History: Diurnal, often on buildings, walls and fences, also on trees. Common in suburbia. Gives live birth, up to nine young. Eats insects and other arthropods.

Variable Skink
Mabuya varia

Identification: Up to 18cm. A little skink, very variable in colour, but usually some shade of brown, with some black speckling on the back, with a pale stripe extending from the lips along the lower flanks to the hind limbs.

Habitat and Distribution: Coastal thicket, semi-desert, savanna and woodland, from sea level to over 3,600m altitude. Widespread in Tanzania and central Kenya, sporadic in dry north and eastern Kenya and Uganda.

Natural History: Diurnal, often in rocky areas or on broken ground, may climb trees, hides under rocks in tree holes, etc. Gives live birth, up to ten young. Eats insects and other arthropods.

Peters' Writhing Skink
Lygosoma afrum

Identification: Up to 23cm. A large, shiny-bodied, small-limbed skink, with a short pointed head. Very variable in colour, usually brown, with darker speckling.

Habitat and Distribution: Coastal thicket, semi-desert, savanna and woodland, from sea level to over 2,300m altitude. Widespread in eastern Tanzania and the southern half of Kenya, sporadic in dry northern Kenya, Uganda and western Tanzania.

Natural History: Burrowing, usually found below rocks, under logs and other ground cover. Sometimes on the surface at dusk. Lays four to ten eggs. Eats insects and other arthropods.

Sundevall's Writhing Skink
Lygosoma sundevalli

Identification: Up to 18cm. A shiny-bodied, small-limbed skink, with a short pointed head. Usually brown or grey, uniform or with darker speckling, pale below, sometimes with speckling.

Habitat and Distribution: Coastal woodland and thicket, semi-desert, savanna and woodland, from sea level to about 2,000m altitude. Widespread in Tanzania and Kenya, sporadic in Uganda.

Natural History: Burrowing, usually found below rocks, under logs and other ground cover. Lays two to seven eggs. Eats insects and other arthropods.

Coral Rag Skink
Cryptoblepharus boutonii

Identification: Up to 15cm. The only lizard found in the intertidal zone of the sea coast. A small skink with obvious limbs and very long clawed toes. Eyelids immovable. Dark coloured, with bronzy dorso-lateral stripes, flanks speckled.

Habitat and Distribution: On old coral formations (coral rag) in the intertidal zone on the East African coast, including the islands.

Natural History: Diurnal, quick-moving, foraging on the coral, often just above the waves. Swims well. Lays one or two eggs in crevices above the high water mark. Eats small crustaceans, other arthropods and small fish.

Wahlberg's Snake-eyed Skink
Panaspis wahlbergii

Identification: Up to 14cm. A tiny, thin, small-limbed skink, with a short pointed head and immovable eyelids. The dorsum is usually uniform brown, grey or bronzy, (rarely with fine longitudinal lines), the flanks are striped dark above, lighter below.

Habitat and Distribution: Coastal bush, semi-desert, savanna and woodland, from sea level to about 2,200m altitude. Widespread in eastern Tanzania and south-east Kenya, sporadic elsewhere.

Natural History: Forages on the ground, living in grass tufts, leaf litter and holes. Lays two to six eggs. Eats insects and other arthropods. Believed to live to only 18 months or less.

Percival's Legless Skink
Acontias percivalli

Identification: Up to 23cm. A blunt-snouted legless skink, with a very short blunt tail. Brown or blue-grey above, orange or yellow below.

Habitat and Distribution: Savanna and woodland at low altitude, in south-eastern Kenya and north-eastern Tanzania.

Natural History: Burrowing in sand and soft soil, rarely on surface. Probably eats insects and other arthropods.

Other skink species found in East Africa

Usambara Five-toed Fossorial Skink *Proscelotes eggeli* A thin, round-snouted burrowing skink, up to 21cm. Grey or brown, speckled lighter or darker. Found only in the Usambara Mountains and vicinity.

Four-toed Fossorial Skink *Sepsina tetradactyla* A stout cylindrical burrowing skink, grey or brown, with pink on lower flanks. Up to 14cm. Sporadically recorded from south-eastern and western Tanzania.

Slender Burrowing Skink *Typhlacontias sp* A new striped, limbless blunt-headed burrowing skink, with an orange, black-edged vertebral stripe. Up to 15cm. Recently recorded from Katavi National Park, south-western Tanzania.

Uluguru Fossorial Skink *Scelotes uluguruensis* A small round-headed burrowing skink, with tiny limbs, back reddish-brown, flanks white, black-speckled, tail dark. Up to 17cm. Uluguru and Usambara Mountains only.

Black Limbless Skink *Melanoseps ater* A large (up to 28cm), grey or black legless skink, yellow or white below. Two isolated populations occur on Mt Rungwe and Matengo Highlands, Tanzania.

Udzungwa Mountains Limbless Skink *Melanoseps uzungwensis* A grey, black or pinkish legless skink, white below, up to 21cm long. Udzungwa Mountains only.

Long-tailed Limbless Skink *Melanoseps longicauda* Uniformly black above and below, chin white. Up to 12cm. Known with certainty only from Manga Forest reserve, north-eastern Tanzania.

Loveridge's Limbless Skink *Melanoseps loveridgei* Speckled grey or black above, speckled specimens paler below. Up to 14cm. Widespread in savanna of southern Tanzania.

continued over

Rondo Limbless Skink *Melanoseps rondoensis* Reddish-brown above, paler below, rows of longitudinal dots. Up to 10cm. Occurs in extreme south-eastern Tanzania.

Legless Sand Skink *Scolecoseps acontias* A grey-brown legless skink, with a white chin. Known from a single 15cm specimen from Dar es Salaam.

Litipo Sand Skink *Scolecoseps litipoensis* A recently described, 14cm legless black skink with a white patch on the chin. Recorded from the Litipo Forest in south-eastern Tanzania.

Bayon's Skink *Mabuya bayoni* A stocky skink, up to 17cm long, brown above, with pale flank and dorso-lateral stripes. Found in high grassland and moorland of central and western Kenya.

Boulenger's Skink *Mabuya boulengeri* A big slender skink, up to 30cm long, brown or grey-brown above, lips speckled, a dark stripe between eye and ear. Found in southern Tanzania.

Ukinga Mountain Skink *Mabuya brauni* A small robust skink, up to 15cm long, brown above, with pale vertebral and dorso-lateral stripes, heavily spotted, looks like a Variable Skink. Known only from Ukinga Mountains, south-west Tanzania.

Alpine-meadow Skink *Mabuya irregularis* A big, stocky skink, up to 18cm, black with yellow spotting and a double yellow vertebral line. Known from montane moorlands of the Aberdares, Mt Kenya, the Mau and Mt Elgon.

Red-flanked Skink *Lygosoma fernandi* A big, heavily-built skink, up to 38cm long. Black or brown above, flanks barred black and bright red, tail black with blue bars. Known from forests around Kakamega, Kampala, Entebbe and the Albertine Rift Valley.

Mabuya-like Writhing Skink *Lygosoma mabuiiformis* A large, slim skink, with a very long tail, length up to 37cm, adults are grey, juveniles striped lighter and darker brown. Only known from the Tana Delta area in Kenya.

Pemba Island Writhing Skink *Lygosoma pembanum* A small (12cm) yellow-brown skink, often speckled, snout depressed and wedge-shaped, known from Pemba Island and the Kenya coast.

Mafia Writhing Skink *Lygosoma mafianum* Recently described from Mafia Island; a grey-brown skink, with paler, speckled flanks, length 12cm.

Somali Writhing Skink *Lygosoma somalicum* A small skink (up to 15cm), with a short head, dorsum brown above, with fine stripes, flanks darker, tail orange or pink. Known from Mkomazi and Tsavo National Park.

Tana River Writhing Skink *Lygosoma tanae* A slender skink, up to 15cm long, dorsum brown or grey, upper lips and neck flecked white, throat and lower lips white with brown spots. Known from the Tana Delta in Kenya and near the South Pare Mountains in Tanzania.

Western Serpentiform Skink *Eumecia anchietae* A snake-like skink, with tiny limb buds, striped in shades of brown or black, flanks with dark bars or blotches. Up to 40cm long. Found in the high savanna and grassland of western Kenya and north-west Tanzania.

Uganda Five-toed Skink *Leptosiaphos aloysiisabaudiae* A little skink, up to 14cm, with a short rounded snout. Brown above, becoming reddish posteriorly. Sporadically recorded living in leaf litter in riverine woodland of southern Uganda.

Kivu Three-toed Skink *Leptosiaphos blochmanni* A small skink, up to 14cm long, golden-brown above with fine black speckling, a dark stripe runs from the eye to the shoulder. Known from south-west Rwanda and possibly northern Burundi.

Kilimanjaro Five-toed Skink *Leptosiaphos kilimensis* A smallish skink, up to 18cm, with a short rounded snout. Golden-brown or bronze above, speckled black, flanks pinkish, speckled black and white. Known from the Usambara and Uluguru Mountains in Tanzania, and central highlands of Kenya.

Virunga Four-toed Skink *Leptosiaphos hackarsi* A little skink, up to 14cm, with a short rounded snout. The head is mottled light and dark brown, the dorsum back with scattered yellow spots, flanks and tail orange. Sporadically recorded living in leaf litter in the volcano country of south-west Uganda and north-western Rwanda.

Rwanda Five-toed Skink *Leptosiaphos graueri* A smallish skink, up to 20cm, with a short rounded snout. Metallic yellow-brown to grey above, side of head and flanks white, heavily speckled black. Lives in soil or leaf litter in forests of the Albertine Rift.

Ruwenzori Four-toed Skink *Leptosiaphos meleagris* Up to 20cm long, a thin skink with a short rounded snout. Black above, each scale spotted with white, the throat is mottled black, the belly salmon red. Found only in the Ruwenzori Mountains at around 2,000m altitude.

Udzungwa Five-toed Skink *Leptosiaphos rhomboidalis* A small-limbed skink, brown above, with a cream dorso-lateral stripe, and a dark-brown dorso-lateral band. Recently described from the Udzungwa Mountains in Tanzania.

Blue-tailed Snake-eyed Skink *Panaspis megalurus* A slim skink with a very long tail. Up to 17cm long. Iridescent brown or olive, with a pale, black-edged dorso-lateral stripe. Known from two specimens from the plains of central Tanzania, the male had an orange tail, the female a blue tail.

Ocellated Skink *Chalcides ocellatus* A heavily built, small-limbed skink with a sharp snout. Up to 30cm long. Dorsum brown, with distinctive eyespots, pale dorso-lateral stripes, flanks darker. Recorded from semi-desert in extreme north-western Kenya.

Western Forest Limbless Skink *Feylinia currori* A bluish-grey skink, distinctive as it has no limbs, external ears or eyes. Up to 36cm. Recorded from the shores of Lake Victoria in Tanzania and Uganda, and Toro Game Reserve in Uganda.

Lacertids or Old World Lizards: Family Lacertidae

A family of small to medium-sized slim lizards, with granular rough scales, long tails and well-developed limbs. Most are fast-moving and live on the ground in open country, especially dry savanna and semi-desert. Most are active terrestrial hunters. About 215 species are known, of which 19 occur in East Africa.

Green Keel-bellied lizard
Gastropholis prasina

Identification: Up to 40cm. A slim lizard with a long, prehensile tail. Green above, yellowish-green below, occasionally with fine black speckled flank lines.

Habitat and Distribution: Low-altitude forest and woodland.

Sporadically recorded along the East African coast from the Arabuko-Sokoke Forest to the vicinity of Dar es Salaam.

Natural History: Diurnal, arboreal and secretive, living in tree holes. Males will fight over females or space. They lay up to five eggs. Diet: arthropods.

Blue-tailed Gliding Lizard
Holaspis guentheri

Identification: Up to 12cm. A small lacertid, striped black and cream, with a barred blue and black tail. Able to glide.

Habitat and Distribution: Woodland and forest at medium to low altitude. One subspecies is known from south-

eastern Tanzania and the Usambara Mountains, the other from Budongo Forest in Uganda and Bukoba in Tanzania.

Natural History: Diurnal and arboreal, living mostly on tree trunks, but will descend to ground level. Active agile and fast-moving, they leap between trees if pursued and can glide, using their flattened bodies as aerofoils. They lay two eggs under bark or in leaf litter. Diet: insects and other arthropods.

Jackson's Forest Lizard
Adolfus jacksoni

Identification: Up to 25cm. A medium-sized lacertid, with distinctively spotted flanks. The back may be brown, olive or green, the flanks are brown or grey spotted with white, yellow or blue.

Habitat and Distribution: Woodland, riverine woodland and forest at medium to high altitude. Northern Tanzania, southern and central Kenya, western Uganda, Rwanda and Burundi.

Natural History: Diurnal and arboreal, living mostly on tree trunks, or thick branches above 2m height, but will occasionally descend to ground level. Active and fast-moving. They lay two eggs under bark or in leaf litter. Diet: insects and other arthropods.

Boulenger's Scrub Lizard
Nucras boulengeri

Identification: Up to 18cm. A medium-sized lacertid, brownish above, usually with a yellow vertebral line and longitudinal lines of spots and dashes. Juveniles are more vivid, with red tails.

Habitat and Distribution: Medium to high altitude grassland and savanna. Widespread in central and southern Kenya, north-eastern and south-eastern Tanzania.

Natural History: Diurnal and terrestrial, hunting in open areas, basking in the sun, often seen on roadsides in southern Kenya. Live in holes or under stones. Presumably lay eggs. Diet: insects and other arthropods.

Mozambique Rough-scaled Lizard
Ichnotropis squamulosa

Identification: Up to 23cm. A medium-sized lacertid, coppery-brownish above, with two to five lines of light, dark-edged spots on the back.

Habitat and Distribution: Savanna and woodland of extreme south-eastern Tanzania.

Natural History: Diurnal and terrestrial, hunting in open areas, basking in the sun, may live in small groups and share communal branching burrows. They lay 5–12 eggs. They are annuals in southern Africa, reaching maturity after four to five months, laying eggs and dying. Diet: insects and other arthropods.

Speke's Sand Lizard
Heliobolus spekii

Identification: Up to 18cm. A small lacertid, warm brown with a set of distinctive thin pale longitudinal dorsal lines and short black crossbars. Babies look different, with yellow stripes on a black body and a rufous tail.

Habitat and Distribution: Coastal woodland, dry savanna and semi-desert. Almost throughout northern and eastern Kenya and north-eastern Tanzania.

Natural History: Diurnal, terrestrial and very fast-moving, hunting in open areas, shuttling back and forward between sun and shade. They lay four to six eggs. Diet: insects and other arthropods.

Southern Long-tailed Lizard
Latastia longicaudata

Identification: Up to 40cm. A huge lacertid, with a very long tail, the body marked with a series of pale stripes that may be yellow, green or rufous, clearly cutting across dark or black vertical bars.

Habitat and Distribution: Coastal woodland, semi-desert and savanna. Almost throughout northern and eastern Kenya, patchily distributed in north-eastern Tanzania.

Natural History: Diurnal, terrestrial and very fast-moving, hunting in open areas, shuttling back and forward between sun and shade. Often seen on roads. They run tremendously fast with the tail raised. They lay eggs. Diet: insects and other arthropods.

Other lacertid species found in East Africa

Striped Keel-bellied Lizard *Gastropholis vittata* A large (up to 35cm) striped, long-tailed arboreal lizard. Brown with two dorsal and two lateral white or blue-white lines. Occurs on the coast from Diani (Kenya) south to Dar es Salaam, inland to Kilosa.

Turkana Shield-backed Ground Lizard *Philochortus rudolfensis* A long-tailed, slim lacertid, up to 18cm length. Dorsum bears six white stripes on a brown background, tail rufous. Sporadically recorded from dry northern Kenya.

Multi-scaled Forest Lizard *Adolfus africanus* A slender forest lizard, up to 20cm long. A bronzy stripe with black spots extends from the nose onto the tail, flanks chocolate-brown, lime-green below. Sporadic in forests from Kakamega west to the Albertine Rift.

Alpine-meadow Lizard *Adolfus alleni* A small (max. 18cm) stout lizard, with a long thick tail, brown or olive above with lime-green or light brown dorso-lateral stripes. Lives on montane moorlands of Mt Kenya, Aberdares and Mt Elgon.

continued over

Sparse-scaled Forest Lizard *Adolfus vauereselli* A slender forest lizard, up to 24cm long. A yellow or coppery stripe extends from the nose onto the tail, flanks red-brown, with big light spots. In forests in western Uganda and Rwanda.

Ornate Scrub Lizard *Nucras ornata* A large (up to 27cm) scrub lizard, dark with yellow stripes, fading to rufous brown near the hindlimbs and on the tail. Found on the Rondo Plateau, south-east Tanzania.

Angolan Rough-scaled Lizard *Ichnotropis bivittata* A slender lizard, up to 24cm length, brown above, with a black flank stripe, with white stripes above and below, in breeding males the white head and neck stripes become bright yellow and there is a bright red stripe on the lower flanks. Known only from the Udzungwa Mountains.

Tanzanian Rough-scaled Lizard *Ichnotropis tanganicana* Known from a single specimen from the east coast of Lake Tanganyika; 4cm long without a tail. Bronzy-olive above, with two series of black spots, a black streak from the nostril to the eye, with white black-edged spots on the posterior back.

Neumann's Sand Lizard *Heliobolus neumanni* A small slender lizard, up to 15cm. The front half of the body is brown with yellow stripes, the posterior half and tail are orange-red. Sporadically recorded from the Tana River, eastern Tanzania and near Lake Rukwa.

Peters' Sand Lizard *Pseuderemias striata* A small (up to 16cm) lacertid, cream to buff above with seven brown or black stripes. Recorded from an uncertain locality of the Tana River.

Smith's Sand Lizard *Pseuderemias smithii* Reaches 18cm length, brownish-red in colour with four thin pale body stripes. The tail is rufous. Sporadically recorded from northern Kenya.

Johnston's Long-tailed Lizard *Latastia johnstoni* A medium-sized lacertid (up to 21cm long). Males are reddish-brown with paler stripes, females have a black-edged, yellow vertebral stripe, both sexes have interrupted vertical dark bars, often bright yellow eyespots on the flanks. Occurs in south-central Tanzania, sporadic records elsewhere in Tanzania.

Alpine-meadow Lizard
Adolfus alleni
(see page 55)

Girdled Lizards and their relatives: Family Cordylidae

An African family of lizards containing four genera; these are the grass lizards (*Chamaesura*), the girdled lizards (*Cordylus*), the flat lizards (*Platysaurus*) and the crag lizards (*Pseudocordylus*). All but the last genus occur in East Africa. The latter three genera are mostly rock dwellers and have speciated spectacularly in the ancient exposed rocky landscapes of southern Africa, where there are over 50 species. In East Africa there are three species of girdled lizard, two grass lizards and one flat lizard.

Tropical Girdled Lizard
Cordylus tropidosternum

Identification: Up to 20cm. A brown, rough, spiky lizard, like a pinecone. The back is brown, sometimes with lighter patches and a suggestion of a lighter vertebral line, paler brown on the belly.

Habitat and Distribution: Low-altitude coastal forest and woodland. Known from the Arabuko-Sokoke forest and vicinity, and from the Usambara Mountains south to the Mozambique border, inland to near Dodoma.

Natural History: Diurnal, arboreal and secretive, living in trees, hiding in holes and sheltering under bark. They may have up to five live young. Diet: insects and other arthropods.

Masai Girdled Lizard
Cordylus beraduccii

Identification: Up to 17cm. A brown, rough, spiky lizard, like a pinecone. The back is mottled lighter and darker brown, paler brown on the belly, lower flanks and lips.

Habitat and Distribution: Outcroppings and rocky hills in mid-altitude savanna, from the western slopes of the Ngong Hills south through Kajiado to north-central Tanzania.

Natural History: Diurnal, arboreal and secretive, living in rock cracks. They give live birth. Diet insects and other arthropods.

Highland Grass Lizard
Chamaesaura anguina

Identification: Up to 60cm. A slim, striped, apparently legless lizard (its limbs are minute fleshy spikes) with a very long tail. The number and colour of stripes vary (some specimens appear uniform brown) but there is no similar looking lizard anywhere within its habitat.

Habitat and Distribution: High grassland and grassy savanna of the East African plateau, from 1,200m to over 3,000m, north and west from the Usambara Mountains through to central Uganda and Rwanda.

Natural History: Diurnal and terrestrial, but will climb in grass tufts. They slide through grass like a snake. Between two and nine young are born alive. Diet: arthropods, especially grasshoppers.

Other cordylid species found in East Africa

Ukinga Girdled Lizard *Cordylus ukingensis* A small (14cm) spiky lizard, mottled brown, black and white on the back, upper lips white. Known only from the southern Udzungwa and Ukinga Mountains, Tanzania where it lives in holes and rock crevices.

Spotted Flat Lizard *Platysaurus maculatus* A flat rock-dwelling lizard, reaching 20cm. Males are olive-brown with a pink tail, females are black with five rows of yellow dorsal spots. Known from rock outcrops around Masasi, extreme south-eastern Tanzania.

Zambian Snake Lizard *Chamaesaura macrolepis* A slim, apparently legless lizard, light brown or straw coloured, sometimes with darker dorso-lateral stripes. Grows to 60cm. Found in south-western Tanzania, between Lakes Rukwa, Malawi and the south end of Lake Tanganyika.

Zambian Snake Lizard
Chamaesaura macrolepis

Plated Lizards and their relatives: Family Gerrhosauridae

A family of lizards confined to Africa and Madagascar. There are four African genera in the family, two of which (*Gerrhosaurus*, plated lizards, three species and *Tetradactylus*, seps, a single species) are found in East Africa. The plated lizards are relatively large, with obvious eyes and ears, well-developed limbs, tough squarish scales and a curious skin fold along the lower flanks. The single species of seps has minute limb buds.

Great Plated Lizard
Gerrhosaurus major

Identification: Up to 55cm. A stout, brown lizard with an obvious ear opening and square, obvious scales. The skin fold is easily seen. The throat may be pale, pink, orange or blue. Red-throated phase is shown on the right. The western subspecies (below right) is black and yellow, as are juveniles.

Habitat and Distribution: Woodland, savanna and coastal bush, from sea level to 1,700m. Widely distributed in eastern Tanzania and south-eastern Kenya, the western subspecies (*Gerrhosaurus major bottegoi*) sporadic in northern Kenya and Uganda.

Natural History: Diurnal and terrestrial, living in holes, termite mounds, rock piles and rocky crevices. The males are territorial. Lays from two to six eggs. They are omnivorous, eating fruits, flowers, arthropods, even small verebrates. They make excellent, confiding pets.

Yellow-throated Plated Lizard
Gerrhosaurus flavigularis

Identification: Up to 40cm. Long, slim, striped lizard with hard, tough scales. Skin fold is obvious if viewed carefully. Usually brown above, with a pair of yellow, black-edged dorso-lateral lines. Flanks often barred black and cream or yellow.

Habitat and Distribution: Woodland, savanna and coastal bush, from sea level to 2,000m. Widely distributed in north-eastern Tanzania, most of southern and central Kenya, sporadic in north-west Kenya.

Natural History: Diurnal and terrestrial, living in holes or under ground cover. Secretive and fast-moving, often mistaken for a striped snake. Lays from three to eight eggs. Diet: insects and other arthropods.

Black-lined Plated Lizard
Gerrhosaurus nigrolineatus

Identification: Up to 45cm. A long, striped lizard with hard, tough scales. The skin fold is obvious if viewed carefully. Usually brown above, with a pair of yellow, black-edged dorso-lateral lines. Flanks brown or rufous, speckled white or yellow.

Habitat and Distribution: Savanna, coastal bush and grassland, from sea level to about 1,600m. Widely distributed in eastern Tanzania and south-east Kenya, sporadic in the western half of Tanzania.

Natural History: Diurnal and terrestrial, living in holes or under ground cover. Shy and fast-moving, may be mistaken for a striped snake. Lays from four to nine eggs. Diet: insects and other arthropods eggs.

Other species of plated lizard found in East Africa

Ellenberger's Long-tailed Seps *Tetradactylus ellenbergeri* A small (up to 35cm) snake-like plated lizard with no front limbs and bud-like hindlimbs. Bluish-olive above with a brown vertebral stripe. Known from grassland in southern Tanzania at Tatanda and Songea.

Agamas: Family Agamidae

A family of Old World lizards with big heads, prominent eyes, thin necks and flattened bodies. Their tails are long and thin. Agamas are often highly visible, basking in prominent places. The males of several species are vividly coloured in blues, greens, reds and pinks. Agamas are fast-moving, and several species live in structured colonies under a dominant male. Over 300 species are known; 12 species occur in East Africa. In some areas, they are erroneously believed to be venomous.

Blue-headed Tree Agama
Acanthocercus atricollis

Identification: Up to 37cm. A big, stocky, spiny lizard, males have a big head. Displaying males (top) have a blue or turquoise head and vertebral stripe, the flanks are darker, heavily speckled. Females and juveniles (below) are mottled brown and rufous above, with a black neck patch and a line of paler blotches along the spine.

Habitat and Distribution: Savanna, woodland and forest clearings, from sea level to 2,400m altitude. Found almost throughout western Kenya and southern Uganda, sporadic elsewhere.

Natural History: Diurnal and largely arboreal, but will descend to the ground and utilise rocks and termite hills. They are territorial, living in structured colonies, with the male basking in a prominent place. 4–15 eggs are laid. Diet: insects and other arthropods; fond of ants.

Red-headed Rock Agama
Agama agama

Identification: Males up to 35cm, females smaller. A big, spiny lizard, males (far left) usually have orange heads and blue bodies,

females (above), non-displaying males and juveniles are mottled brown with a vertebral line of pale lozenges.

Habitat and Distribution: Coastal woodland and thicket, savanna and semi-desert, from sea level to over 2,000m but usually below 1,500m. Occurs almost throughout eastern and northern Kenya and central Tanzania.

Natural History: Fast-moving and diurnal, lives on rocks, will utilise buildings and walls, sometimes on trees. They are territorial, living in structured colonies, with the male basking in a prominent place. Four to nine eggs are laid. Diet: insects and other arthropods; fond of ants; will also eat plant material.

Tropical Spiny Agama
Agama armata

Identification: Up to 22cm. A small, brown, rufous or grey ground-dwelling agama, with pale crossbars. The pale double vertebral stripe is a good field character. Displaying males have vivid green or blue on the head.

Habitat and Distribution: Mid-

altitude savanna of south-west Kenya through central Tanzania.

Natural History: Diurnal, lives on the ground, sheltering in holes in open country, may live on sheet rock. Sometimes ascends bushes to bask. May freeze if approached. 9–16 eggs are laid. Diet: insects and other arthropods; fond of ants; possibly eats plant material.

Elmenteita Rock Agama
Agama caudospina

Identification: Males up to 45cm, females smaller. A huge, flattened, spiny lizard; males have a broad tail. Displaying males show various shades of orange or rufous on the chin, neck and chest, non-displaying males shades of brown or grey with a lighter vertebral lines, females are mottled brown with a vertebral line of pale lozenges.

Habitat and Distribution: Endemic to Kenya, lives in the grassland and light woodland of the central Rift Valley, north and west from the Kedong and Muranga to Trans-Nzoia.

Natural History: Secretive, fast-moving and diurnal, living on sheet rock, rocky hills and outcroppings. They are territorial, living in structured colonies, with the male basking in a prominent place. Lay eggs. Diet: arthropods.

Mwanza Flat-headed Agama
Agama mwanzae

Identification: Up to 32cm. A big rock agama. Males have a vivid pink head, back and chest, non-displaying males are mottled grey with a blue vertebral line, females and juveniles are brown with irregular darker cross bars and a vertebral line of light lozenges.

Habitat and Distribution: On rock outcrops in medium to high savanna and grassland. Occurs from the Maasai Mara south and west through north-west Tanzania to eastern Rwanda and Burundi.

Natural History: Diurnal, living on boulders, outcroppings, rocky hills and sheet rock. Wary and fast-moving. They are colonial, displaying males bask in prominent spots. Eggs are laid in a rock fissure or a hole. Diet; arthropods; fond of ants.

Rüppell's Agama
Agama rueppelli

Identification: Up to 28cm. A small brown or rufous ground-dwelling agama, uniform or with darker crossbars and a pale vertebral stripe.

Habitat and Distribution: Dry savanna and semi-desert of eastern and northern Kenya, apparently absent from the extreme north-east.

Natural History: Diurnal, lives on the ground, sheltering in holes in open country, may live on rock. Sometimes ascends bushes to bask. May freeze if approached. No breeding details known. Diet: insects and other arthropods.

Other species of agama found in East Africa

Eritrean Rock Agama *Acanthocercus annectans* A big stocky rock-dwelling agama, up to 34cm, males speckled pink or yellow on black, with blue limbs, females greeny-grey. Recorded only from Dandu and Malka Murri in northern Kenya.

Black-necked Tree Agama *Acanthocercus cyanogaster* Very similar to the blue-headed Tree Agama, males with a blue or turquoise head, females grey with darker crossbars. Sporadically distributed almost throughout East Africa.

Montane Rock Agama *Agama montana* A small, lightly built agama, males are brown or olive, with a blue head and pale vertebral line, females red-brown, sometimes with blue throats. Up to 27cm long, known only from the Usambara and Uluguru Mountains in Tanzania.

Mozambique Agama *Agama mossambica* A big agama, up to 32cm, mottled grey, brown and white, males with a lighter vertebral line, females a row of lighter vertebral patches. Widespread in savanna of south-east Tanzania.

Somali Painted Agama *Agama persimilis* A small agama, up to 16cm, orange, rufous or brown with darker blotches on the back and a pale vertebral line. Sporadically recorded in dry eastern Kenya, from Voi to Mandera.

Malaba Rock Agama *Agama finchi* A new species of agama, recently discovered on rocky hills at Malaba in western Kenya and also observed at Murchison Falls, Uganda. Named after the prominent Kenyan ornithologist Brian Finch, who discovered it. Males have a bright red head, neck and tail, and an indigo body, females are dark with vivid red flank patches.

Chameleons: Family Chamaeleonidae

A family of slow-moving tree lizards, split at present into three genera; the 'typical' long-tailed, usually green chameleons, genus *Chamaeleo*, and two genera of stump-tailed pygmy chameleons, *Rhampholeon* and *Rieppeleon*. Chameleons are unusual lizards; they are mostly arboreal, have independently mobile eyes set in turrets, and excellent vision; their tails cannot be shed and regrown. Their clawed digits are set in opposed bundles for grasping. They can change colour dramatically; they are usually greenest when calm, and become spotted or barred with black when angry. Adapted for life in the trees, they shoot their telescopic tongues at their insect prey. Many people in East Africa have a superstitious fear of chameleons, although they are totally harmless and benefit humanity by eating insect pests. About 135 species are known; most occur in Africa and Madagascar; 42 species are recorded from East Africa.

Side-striped Chameleon
Chamaeleo bitaeniatus

Identification: Up to 15cm. A small chameleon without horns. Colour variable, usually grey or brown, often with two prominent flank stripes (above right). Barred form shown below.

Habitat and Distribution: Medium to high altitude light woodland, savanna and grassland, from 1,000 to over 2,200m. Widespread in the highlands of central and western Kenya, sporadic in northern Tanzania and the Lake Victoria basin.

Natural History: Rarely in large trees, usually in small trees, bushes, tall grass and sedge. Sometimes present in large numbers. They give live birth to from six to 15 young. Diet: insects, especially grasshoppers.

Usambara Three-horned Chameleon
Chamaeleo deremensis

Identification: Up to 30cm. A big chameleon, with a bizarre sail-like dorsal ridge. Males (top) have three horns, females (below) none. Usually green often with yellow spots.

Habitat and Distribution: Forest and high woodland at 1,200 to 2,300m altitude. Sometimes in coffee plantations. Endemic to Tanzania, found only in the Nguru and Usambara Mountains.

Natural History: Lives in trees and bushes. The males fight with their horns. Females lay up to 40 eggs. Diet: insects, especially grasshoppers.

Flap-necked Chameleon
Chamaeleo dilepis

Identification: Up to 43cm, but usually 15 to 25cm. A big chameleon, without horns but with small to large ear flaps. Usually shades of green, with a white flank stripe.

Habitat and Distribution: Coastal forest, woodland, thicket, savanna and semi-desert, from sea level to about 1,500m altitude, sometimes higher. Occurs almost throughout Tanzania and south-eastern Kenya, also in western Kenya from the Mara north to the Kerio Valley.

Natural History: Lives in bushes, shrubs and trees but readily descends to the ground, and often seen crossing roads in the rainy season. Will inflate its body, raise its ear flaps, hiss and bite if threatened. Lays from 20–65 eggs. Eats arthropods.

Montane Side-striped Chameleon
Chamaeleo ellioti

Identification: Up to 18cm. A small chameleon without horns. Usually bright green, blue-green or bluish, with one or two pale flank stripes.

Habitat and Distribution: High moist savanna and grassland, from 1,500 to over 2,800m. Occurs in high western Kenya, along the Lake Victoria shore in Uganda and the Albertine Rift and surroundings in Uganda, Rwanda and Burundi.

Natural History: Rarely in large trees, usually in small trees, bushes and tall grass, often in reedbeds and sedge in swamps areas. Sometimes present in large numbers. They give live birth. Diet: insects, especially grasshoppers.

Usambara Two-horned Chameleon
Chamaeleo fischeri

Identification: Up to 40cm. A big chameleon; males (top) have two blade-like horns, females (below) none. Usually green, sometimes brown.

Habitat and Distribution: Forest and high woodland from 400 to 2,400m altitude. Endemic to Tanzania, found only in the East Usambara, West Usambara and Uluguru Mountains.

Natural History: In any suitable habitat, from low bushes to high trees, tolerant of urbanisation, will live in hedges and gardens. The males are territorial and fight with their horns. Females lay

from 18–27 eggs. Diet: insects, especially grasshoppers.

Slender Chameleon
Chamaeleo gracilis

Identification: Up to 25cm, sometimes larger. A big chameleon, without horns, usually without ear flaps. Usually shades of green, with a white shoulder patch and flank stripe, and an orange gular pouch.

Habitat and Distribution: Moist and

dry savanna and semi-desert, often where there are acacia trees. Occurs in a savanna belt from north-eastern Tanzania north around Mt Kenya and across central Uganda. Also known from extreme north-east Kenya.

Natural History: Lives in bushes, shrubs, trees and grass clumps but will descend. May be seen crossing roads in the rainy season; it can run surprisingly fast. Will inflate its body, hiss and bite if threatened. Usually lays from 10–25 eggs (but up to 44 recorded). Eats arthropods.

Von Höhnel's Chameleon
Chamaeleo hoehnelii

Identification: Up to 18cm. A small chameleon without horns but a prominent raised casque. Quite variable in colour, shades of olive, green, yellow, even orange, but nearly always has two prominent paler flank stripes.

Habitat and Distribution: An East

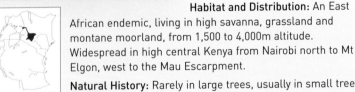

African endemic, living in high savanna, grassland and montane moorland, from 1,500 to 4,000m altitude. Widespread in high central Kenya from Nairobi north to Mt Elgon, west to the Mau Escarpment.

Natural History: Rarely in large trees, usually in small trees, bushes and tall grass, thicket and reedbeds. Sometimes present in large numbers. They give live birth. Diet: insects, especially grasshoppers. They can supercool where they live above the frost line, for example on the Aberdares.

Jackson's Chameleon
Chamaeleo jacksoni

Identification: Males up to 38cm, females smaller. A big chameleon, males (top) have three long horns, females (below) may have one or three short horns, or none. Males usually shades of green, females mottled black, dull green or brown and white.

Habitat and Distribution: Mid-altitude woodland, forest and agriculture, including gardens and plantations, from 1,600 to 2,300m altitude. Occurs east of the Rift Valley in Kenya, from Nairobi north to Mt Kenya, the Nyambeni Hills and Ol Donyo Lessos, also on Mt Meru in Tanzania.

Natural History: Lives in trees and bushes. The males fight with their horns. Females give live birth from seven to 28 young. Diet: insects and other arthropods.

Ruwenzori Three-horned Chameleon
Chamaeleo johnstoni

Identification: Up to 30cm. A big chameleon, males have three horns, females none. Usually green, often with yellow or scarlet splotches.

Habitat and Distribution: Forest and high woodland, from 1,800 to 2,500m altitude. Occurs in the high country of western Uganda, Rwanda and Burundi.

Natural History: Lives in forest trees and bushes. The males fight with their horns. Females lay between 14–20 eggs. Diet: arthropods.

Smooth Chameleon
Chamaeleo laevigatus

Identification: Up to 25cm. A fairly large chameleon, without horns or ear flaps. Usually shades of green, greenish brown or yellow-brown.

Habitat and Distribution: Moist savanna from 1,000 to 1,500m altitude. Occurs in extreme western

Tanzania, along Lake Tanganyika north to Burundi and Rwanda, also in north-west and south-east Uganda.

Natural History: Lives in bushes, shrubs and trees but readily descends to the ground, and often seen crossing roads in the rainy season. Will inflate its body, raise its ear flaps, hiss and bite if threatened. Lays from 15–60 eggs. Eats arthropods.

Spiny-flanked Chameleon
Chamaeleo laterispinis

Identification: Up to 14cm. Unmistakable: a spiny, mottled white, grey, black and brown chameleon, with spines on the sides and on the back.

Habitat and Distribution: Forest and woodland of the Udzungwa Mountains.

Natural History: Poorly known, usually in thicket and understory rather than in big trees. Its superb camouflage - it looks like a lichen-covered stump - makes it almost impossible to detect. Gives live birth, up to 16 young. Eats arthropods.

Giant One-horned Chameleon
Chamaeleo melleri

Identification: Up to 55cm. A huge chameleon, the biggest in Africa, with a fin-like undulating dorsal crest, and an annular horn or a fleshy rostral process. Colour very variable, but the impression is of broad vertical darker and lighter bars.

Habitat and Distribution: Well-wooded savanna and woodland, from sea level to around 1,200m. Found in eastern Tanzania, from near the Kenya border south to Mozambique, inland at Morogoro and Kilosa.

Natural History: Often in big trees, up to 10m above ground, but will also descend to the ground. Inflates the body, puts up the ear flaps and hisses when angry. The males are territorial and fight with their horns. Females lay from 38–91 eggs. Diet: insects and other arthropods.

Ruwenzori Side-striped Chameleon
Chamaeleo rudis

Identification: Up to 17cm. A small robust chameleon without horns. Usually green, occasionally bluey-grey or brown, with two flank stripes, the upper one more prominent.

Habitat and Distribution: Medium to high altitude savanna and grassland, from 1,000 to over 4,000m. Widespread in the highlands of northern Tanzania, also in the Albertine Rift.

Natural History: Rarely in large trees, usually in small trees, bushes, tall grass and sedge. Sometimes present in large numbers. Can survive sub-zero temperatures by supercooling; in the Ruwenzori Mountains they live above the frost line. They give live birth, eight young recorded. Diet: insects, especially grasshoppers.

Usambara Soft-horned Chameleon
Chamaeleo tenue

Identification: Up to 15cm. A small chameleon, males have a small scaly horn on the nose, females have an even smaller horn or a few raised scales. Quite variable in colour, usually green but may be grey, live or red-brown.

Habitat and Distribution: An East African endemic, living in woodland and forest from 100 to 1,400m altitude. Known from the Shimba Hills, in Kenya and Magrotto Hill and the Usambara Mountains in Tanzania.

Natural History: Almost unknown. Males may fight with their horns. Lays from three to five eggs. Diet: arthropods.

Other *Chamaeleo* chameleons found in East Africa

Ituri Chameleon *Chamaeleo adolfifriderici* A small (up to 15cm) dull green or brown chameleon with no horns or ear flaps. Lives in forests of the Albertine Rift and western Uganda.

Angola Chameleon *Chamaeleo anchietae* A medium-sized (20cm) chameleon without horns, very similar to the Slender Chameleon. Found in low-altitude grassland, sporadic records from the Udzungwa Mountains, north-western Tanzania and eastern Rwanda and Burundi.

Carpenter's Chameleon *Chamaeleo carpenteri* A fairly big chameleon, up to 27cm, males have a tall blade-like casque and a short horn, females hornless. Lives in forest over 2,000m in the Ruwenzori Range.

Mt Kenya Hornless Chameleon *Chamaeleo excubitor* A medium-sized chameleon, up to 24cm, with no horns. Usually green, barred dark when irritated. A Kenyan endemic, known only from evergreen woodland on the eastern and north-eastern side of Mt Kenya, between Embu and Meru.

Poroto Three-horned Chameleon *Chamaeleo fuelleborni* Grows to about 22cm long, males have three short horns, females have a stout nose horn and two tiny horns in front of the eyes. Endemic to Tanzania, on the Ngosi Volcano, Poroto Mountains and Kungura Mountains, in south-west Tanzania.

Goetze's Chameleon *Chamaeleo goetzei* A small chameleon, up to 20cm, without horns but has small ear flaps. Usually brown or grey. Known from highlands in southern Tanzania, from just north of Lake Rukwa across to the western Udzungwa Mountains.

Ukinga Hornless Chameleon *Chamaeleo incornutus* Reaches a length of 18cm, a chameleon without horns but with large ear flaps. Known only from Ukinga, Poroto and Rungwe Mountains.

Ituri Forest Chameleon *Chamaeleo ituriensis* A large (up to 25cm) slender chameleon, no horns but has a prominent pointed casque. Recorded in Uganda from Bwamba Forest and Kibale.

Mt Marsabit Chameleon *Chamaeleo marsabitensis* A small chameleon, up to 18cm. The males have a small nose horn, the females a little cone on the nose. Recorded only from rainforest on Mt Marsabit, Kenya.

Mt Kulal Chameleon *Chamaeleo narraioca* Recently described small (max 17cm) chameleon from the montane forests of Mt Kulal, northern Kenya. Virtually identical to Von Hohnel's chameleon, with similar side-stripes.

Malagasy Giant Chameleon *Furcifer oustaleti* A huge (up to 69cm) chameleon with a high, raised casque. A species from Madagascar, introduced into the Ngong Road Forest on the south-west of Nairobi, but not seen for some years.

Uluguru One-horned Chameleon *Chamaeleo oxyrhinum* A small chameleon, up to 15cm. Males have a single, long, bladelike horn; females have no horns. Known from forests of the Uluguru and Udzungwa Mountains.

Mt Kenya Side-striped Chameleon *Chamaeleo schubotzi* A small hornless chameleon, very similar in appearance to the Ruwenzori Side-striped Chameleon. Known only from the alpine zone of Mt Kenya, at altitude over 3,000m.

Rosette-nosed Chameleon *Chamaeleo spinosum* A tiny (up to 9cm) chameleon with a club-like, spiky soft horn on the end of its long snout, and a short tail. Found only in the Usambara Mountains.

Mt Kilimanjaro Two-horned Chameleon *Chamaeleo tavetanus* Up to 24cm. Has two blade-like horns and resembles the Usambara Two-horned Chameleon. Known from hill woodland of south-east Kenya and north-east Tanzania.

Tubercle-nosed Chameleon *Chamaeleo tempeli* Up to 24cm, a chameleon with a small horn-like lump on the snout and small ear flaps. Known from the mountains of southern Tanzania, from the southern Udzungwa Mountains to the Kipengere Range.

Eldama Ravine Chameleon *Chamaeleo tremperi* Recently described and of doubtful status, up to 14cm long, a chameleon without horns or ear flaps. Known from the vicinity of Eldama Ravine, western Kenya.

Hanang Hornless Chameleon *Chamaeleo uthmoelleri* A thickset chameleon, without horns, with a curious scooped-out snout. Grows to 23cm. Northern Tanzania only, in the woodlands of Hanang and Oldeani Mountains and the Ngorongoro Crater.

Werner's Three-horned Chameleon *Chamaeleo werneri* Males have three horns, females have one, both sexes have a big occipital lobe that overlies the neck like a short cape. Reaches 24cm. Known only from forests of the Udzungwa and Uluguru Mountains, Tanzania.

Strange-horned Chameleon *Chamaeleo xenorhinus* A distinctive chameleon; males have a big, rounded, rostral projection and a tall, elevated casque; females have a tiny casque. Males reach 27cm, females 18cm. Known only from high woodland and forest of the Ruwenzori Mountains.

African Pygmy or Leaf Chameleons: Genera *Rhampholeon* and *Rieppeleon*

These little chameleons differ from typical chameleons (genus *Chamaeleo*) in that, among other things, they have short non-prehensile tails and are usually shades of brown. Originally placed in the genus *Brookesia*, which included Madagascan examples; the African forms were then moved to the genus *Rhampholeon*, and recent work has split *Rhampholeon* into two genera, *Rhampholeon* and *Rieppeleon*. They are well camouflaged, resembling dead leaves. When picked up, some species vibrate or buzz, by exhaling small amounts of air, this is a defence against predators. Eight species are so far known from East Africa but there are probably several undescribed species.

Boulenger's Pygmy Chameleon
Rhampholeon boulengeri

Identification: Up to 8cm. A small brown or grey chameleon with a little, soft horn on the snout and a prominent spiky crest above each eye. Male (above) usually has a thick tail, female (below) has a thin one.

Habitat and Distribution: Medium to high-altitude forest and woodland, from 1,400 to over 2,000m. Known from forests in western Kenya, Mpumu Forest in central Uganda and the forests of the Albertine Rift.

Natural History: Lives around clearings and along streams, living in the leaf litter or on low plants. If

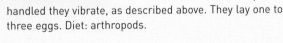

handled they vibrate, as described above. They lay one to three eggs. Diet: arthropods.

Beardless Pygmy Chameleon
Rieppeleon brachyurus

Identification: Up to 6cm. A small brown or grey chameleon with a short head.

Habitat and Distribution: Low to medium-altitude forest, woodland and bushed grassland, from sea level to 1,200m. Found from the

Usambara Mountains south along the Tanzanian coastal strip, extending inland in south-east Tanzania.

Natural History: Lives mostly on the ground, in grass or leaf litter, will climb on low plants. If handled they inflate themselves and then vibrate, as described in the introduction. They lay up to 14 eggs. Diet: arthropods.

Bearded Pygmy Chameleon
Rieppeleon brevicaudatus

Identification: Up to 9cm. A small brown, rufous, pinkish or grey chameleon with a tiny chin tuft.

Habitat and Distribution: Evergreen forest and coastal thicket, from sea level to 1,200m. Found from the Shimba Hills in Kenya to the

Usambara Mountains, thence south along the Tanzanian coastal strip, extending inland in the Rufiji River area.

Natural History: Lives mostly on the ground, in grass or leaf litter, moving slowly, will climb on low plants. If handled they vibrate, as described in the introduction. They lay up to nine eggs. Diet: arthropods.

Kenya Pygmy Chameleon
Rieppeleon kerstenii

Identification: Up to 9cm. A small, brown, rufous, pinkish or grey chameleon with little spiky scales and scale clusters on the chin, the prominent raised eyebrows and face.

Habitat and Distribution: Coastal woodland and thicket, savanna and semi-desert, from sea level to 1,400m altitude. Occurs in extreme north-east Tanzania, south-east Kenya and north-east Kenya between the Nyambeni Hills and Malka Murri.

Natural History: Lives mostly on the ground, in bush and grass; hides in thickets. Active by day, although will shelter in the shade to avoid the midday heat. If handled they vibrate, as described on p74. They lay eggs. Diet: arthropods.

Other species of pygmy chameleon found in East Africa

Moyer's Pygmy Chameleon *Rhampholeon moyeri* A small (up to 6.5cm) brown chameleon with a small, soft, floppy horn. Recently described from the Udzungwa Mountains.

Pitless Pygmy Chameleon *Rhampholeon nchisiensis* A small brown or grey chameleon with a tiny, soft horn. Maximum length 8cm. Usually has two or three thin dark oblique flank stripes. Occurs in the mountains just north of the north end of Lake Malawi.

Usambara Pitted Pygmy Chameleon *Rhampholeon temporalis* Brown or grey, with a short nose horn. Known only from the Usambara Mountains.

Uluguru Pygmy Chameleon *Rhampholeon uluguruensis* A tiny (5cm) pygmy chameleon, may be brown, grey or dull green, with three very short horns on the eyebrows and the nose. Recorded only from the Uluguru Mountains.

Pitless Pygmy Chameleon
Rhampholeon nchisiensis

Monitor Lizards: Family Varanidae

Monitors are the world's largest lizards. About 50 species are known, with the majority from Australasia. The world's largest lizard, the Komodo Dragon *Varanus komodoensis*, is a monitor. Monitors have tough leathery skin with bead-like scales, a forked tongue and a long flexible neck. Their tail cannot be shed. They are dangerous lizards to handle; they can bite hard, lash with their tails and scratch with their claws. Five species are known from Africa; four occur in East Africa.

White-throated Savanna Monitor
Varanus albigularis

Identification: Up to 1.6m. A big, heavily built monitor lizard, dull grey or brown, with a rounded snout, dark and light crossbars on the tail and bands of lighter spots on the body.

Habitat and Distribution: Coastal woodland and thicket, dry and moist savanna and semi-desert, from sea level to about 1,500m altitude. Widespread almost throughout Tanzania and eastern Kenya below 1,500m, sporadic in northern Kenya, eastern Uganda only.

Natural History: Diurnal, mostly terrestrial but will climb trees and rocks, often to a considerable

height. Shelters in holes, rock and tree crevices and hanging beehives. Can be truculent if cornered, hissing and lashing with the tail. Clutches up to 50 eggs recorded, although 10–30 are more usual. They eat any living thing they can overpower, including mammals, birds, reptiles and invertebrates.

Nile Monitor
Varanus niloticus

Identification: Up to 2.5m, possibly larger. A big monitor lizard, yellow-striped or spotted on a green, greeny-grey or black background.

Habitat and Distribution: Usually near freshwater sources, from sea level to around 1,600m, liable to occur anywhere in East Africa meeting those conditions.

Natural History: A diurnal, versatile lizard, will hunt on the ground, in trees, on waterside rocks or in water. The Nile Monitor can run fast, climb well and swim superbly. Shelters in holes, in rock or tree crevices but may also simply rest on a branch, provided it is near water. Clutches of 20–60 eggs are laid. Nile Monitors are opportunistic carnivores; they eat a lot of aquatic invertebrates, especially crabs and mussels, but will take any suitable invertebrate or small vertebrate they can catch and overpower; they also take carrion and will dig up buried reptile eggs.

Other species of monitor found in East Africa

Western Savanna Monitor *Varanus exanthematicus* A relatively small (up to 90cm) monitor lizard, grey or brown, with cross markings of light spots on the back, tail barred light and dark, large cobblestone-like scales on the neck. May occur in extreme north-west Uganda.

Forest Monitor *Varanus ornatus* Virtually identical to Nile Monitor, but has fewer crossbands of spots (only four to six) on back. Possibly in western Burundi and Rwanda and south-west Uganda.

Western Savanna Monitor
Varanus exanthematicus

Worm-lizards or Amphisbaenians
Sub-order Amphisbaenia

A strange group of burrowing animals, the least known of East African reptiles. Despite the common name, they are neither worms nor lizards, but a distinct group of reptiles modified for underground life. They are usually pale or pink, and the East African species have no legs or external ears. Some have eyespots below the skin, others do not. No East African species is larger than 30cm. They have smooth rectangular scales arranged in external rings or annuli, and a wedge-or keel-shaped head. Their skin is only loosely attached to the muscles below, and this, coupled with their head shapes, enable the head to be used as a ram for burrowing. They have large strong teeth with which they seize their invertebrate prey, which is then usually ripped to shreds before being consumed. They lay eggs but in some cases these are retained in the body and the female produces live young. About 155 species are known worldwide; 65 species are found in Africa, and ten species in East Africa; nine of these are endemic to East Africa and eight endemic to Tanzania. They are very hard to identify to species level without the use of a key and a binocular microscope. Many species have not been seen or collected in the last 40 years. Anyone finding a worm-lizard should take it to a museum; almost nothing is known of their distribution, lifestyle or variation.

Voi Wedge-snouted Worm-lizard
Geocalamus acutus

Identification: Up to 30cm. A pinkish or yellowish worm lizard with a distinctive wedge-shaped snout; turns brown in preservative. Paler below, sometimes with mottling on the tail segments.

Habitat and Distribution: Dry savanna at medium to low altitude. It is endemic to East Africa, but has a somewhat disjunct distribution in the dry east; it occurs in south-east Kenya (Samburu, Voi, Galana Ranch), and north-east and central Tanzania (Dodoma). Most records are from dry sandy soil areas.

Natural History: Little known. Terrestrial, burrowing, probably diurnal. Has been dug up by ploughs. Presumably lays eggs; feeds on invertebrates.

Liwale Round-snouted Worm-lizard
Loveridgea ionidesi

Identification: Up to 19cm. A small worm-lizard with a rounded snout, brown in colour, with the centre of each segment slightly darker. Unusually, it has a discrete ocular shield, through which the eye is visible.

Habitat and Distribution: Sometimes associated with river floodplains, in areas that have been seasonally flooded in low-altitude moist savanna in south-east Tanzania.

Natural History: Terrestrial, burrowing, probably diurnal. Most specimens collected between December and May. A female contained two embryos, suggesting that this species might give live birth. Diet: invertebrates. Preyed on by a range of burrowing snakes, especially purple-glossed snakes (*Amblyodipsas*) and burrowing asps (*Atractaspis*). Its prescence can sometimes be detected by small casts of damp soil, like worm casts.

Swynnerton's Round-headed Worm-lizard
Chirindia swynnertoni

Identification: Up to 15cm. A small worm-lizard with a round head, pink or pinkish-grey in colour. Looks like an earthworm.

Habitat and Distribution: Low-altitude moist savanna in southern Tanzania; known from Mikindani and Tunduru.

Natural History: Little known. Burrowing, living in loose soil; takes cover below stones, in and below rotting logs and other ground cover. Writhes wildly when handled. A single elongate egg recorded in one female. Diet: probably invertebrates, especially termites. Preyed on by a range of burrowing snakes.

Other species of worm-lizard found in East Africa

Mpwapwa Wedge-snouted Worm-lizard *Geocalamus modestus* Grows to 28cm, a violet to grey-white worm-lizard, with white grooves between the segments. Sporadically recorded from central Tanzania, from the Dodoma region and Ushora. Has not been collected in over 60 years.

Ujiji Round-snouted Worm-lizard *Loveridgea phylofiniens* A round-snouted worm-lizard reaching 20cm. A Tanzanian endemic, but nothing is known about it, and its colour is undescribed. Known only from Ujiji, Lake Tanganyika; not collected in over 100 years.

Ewerbeck's Round-headed Worm-lizard *Chirindia ewerbecki* A round-headed worm-lizard, up to 15.5cm, pink in colour. Known only from extreme south-east Tanzania, where it hides in soil beneath large logs. The females are known to lay a single large egg.

Mpwapwa Round-headed Worm-lizard *Chirindia mpwapwaensis* Reaches 20cm, probably pink in colour but no living specimens have been described. Recorded only from Mpwapwa, in moist savanna in east-central Tanzania. Nothing is known of its biology.

Rondo Round-headed Worm-lizard *Chirindia rondoensis* Reaches 15cm length, and bright pink in colour. A Tanzanian endemic, this species is only known from the woodland and moist savanna of the Rondo and Makonde Plateaux in south-west Tanzania, where it lives in sandy and laterite soils.

Barker's Sharp-snouted Worm-lizard *Ancylocranium barkeri* A sharp-snouted worm-lizard; if viewed from above the head has a distinct point. Probably pinkish-brown in colour, but the colour of a living specimen has never been described. Little else known; recorded from the Makonde Plateau and Mbemkuru, southern Tanzania. Two subspecies are known.

Ionides' Sharp-snouted Worm-lizard *Ancylocranium ionidesi* A worm-lizard with an enormous rostral scale, compressed to a cutting edge, which it presumably uses to shove through soil. Two subspecies are known, one from Kilwa and the other from the Rondo Plateau, in extreme south-east Tanzania.

Crocodiles
Order Crocodylia

An order of unmistakable reptiles of an ancient lineage, all crocodiles are relatively large, aquatic carnivores. They are advanced reptiles, with a four-chambered heart (most reptiles have three), meaning they can keep moving much longer.

Twenty-three species are known, three of which occur in East Africa.

All crocodiles are to some extent endangered by humanity; some are very close to extinction. They are persecuted for their skins and their largely undeserved reputation as predators on humans and livestock. In reality, only two species regularly take humans. One is the largest living crocodile, the Estuarine or Salt-Water Crocodile, *Crocodylus porosus*, of South-east Asia and Australia, which reaches at least 6.5m. Unfortunately, the other species that regularly takes humans is the Nile Crocodile *Crocodylus niloticus*.

Nevertheless, crocodiles are worthy of protection; fossil crocodiles from the time of the dinosaurs are little different from present day species, and thus crocodiles offer us a modern glimpse of the magnificent giant reptiles that once ruled the earth.

Slender-snouted Crocodile
Crocodylus cataphractus

Identification: Up to 3m. A big crocodile with a long slender snout.

Habitat and Distribution: In our area known only from Lake Tanganyika.

Natural History: Secretive and shy, avoids humans. Basks in the daytime in secluded spots. A fast and agile swimmer. It lays clutches of 12 to 30 eggs in a nest that the female makes of vegetation. They eat mostly fish; they may opportunistically take swimming birds, reptiles and amphibians, but they are not known to ambush creatures coming to the brink to drink and are thus no danger to humans.

Nile Crocodile
Crocodylus niloticus

Identification: Up to 5m, possibly slightly more, may weigh up to 1,000kg. A big, thickset crocodile with a fairly broad snout, usually brown (top), grey (bottom) or tan (opposite page), juveniles mottled to a greater or lesser extent with black.

Habitat and Distribution: Widespread throughout East Africa in suitable waters (rivers, lakes, dams and springs) below 1,600m. Absent from the lakes of the high central Rift Valley in Kenya.

Natural History: May bask or swim during the day, usually in the water at night. Small crocodiles tend to be

secretive, hiding in backwaters and basking in sunlight patches, but big adults bask openly. The large males are territorial. Nile Crocodiles are superb, fast swimmers, and can also run fast on land, with their limbs beneath them. They will walk across country to escape drying-up pools. Nile Crocodiles have excellent sight, hearing and taste.

Females dig a hole on an elevated sandbank, above flood level, and lay from 20 to 95 (usually 30 to 50) hard-shelled white eggs. The incubation temperature determines the sex of the hatchlings. The female also assists the youngsters at hatching; clearing sand from the nest site and transporting the babies to water in her mouth. They have a varied diet; babies take insects and frogs, but they soon begin to take fish, which form the major part of the diet of all size classes. They are opportunistic carnivores, seizing smaller swimming creatures, and will also snatch animals (including humans) coming down to the water's edge. A crocodile may wait at a suitable spot, concealed in the water with just eyes and nose showing, or may cruise and watch for a prey item on the bank, which is then carefully stalked. If the prey is a short distance back from the water, the crocodile may jump or rush out of the water with a tail-propelled lunge and seize its prey, serving as a caution to anyone approaching a crocodile-infested water body.

Other species of crocodile found in East Africa

Dwarf or Broad-fronted Crocodile *Osteolaemus tetraspis* A small thickset broad-snouted crocodile, dark brown or black, reaching a length of 1.2m. In East Africa known only from small rivers near Lake George, Uganda.

Dwarf Crocodile
Osteolaemus tetraspis

Snakes
Order Squamata
Suborder Serpentes

Around 200 species of snake occur in East Africa, of which 45 are dangerously venomous. Snakes have a very long spine and many ribs to support their rounded body. They have no eyelids, external ears or legs, although a few have a vestigial pelvic girdle and spur-like vestigial legs. All are carnivores, eating their prey whole, and consequently have special adaptations (unfused lower jaw bones and highly extensible skin) to enable them to swallow large prey items. They usually lay eggs; a few species retain the eggs internally until they are about to hatch. There is no parental care. Non-venomous snakes kill large prey by constricting the victims in their coils, which prevents circulation and breathing; smaller prey items may be swallowed alive.

Some snakes have evolved specialised teeth (fangs) to transfer venom. Venom kills prey rapidly, thus reducing the risk to the snake and enabling rapid location; it also aids digestion. The dangerous snakes in East Africa are the vipers or adders (particularly the Puff Adder and the North-east African Carpet Viper) with long, hinged, poison fangs, and the elapids (garter snakes, mambas, cobras and their allies). Some rear-fanged snakes (with poison fangs set back in the upper jaw, usually around the level of the eye) are also dangerously venomous. Although venom is not designed for defence, a snake under threat may bite. Humans are at risk from snake-bite in East Africa, particularly in the more remote areas. Nevertheless, snakes are an important part of food webs, and many eat rodents, so they should not be killed needlessly.

Blind Snakes: Family Typhlopidae

Over 240 species of blind snake are known; three genera and 20 species are so far recorded from East Africa. Blind snakes live underground, in soft substrates or in holes, but occasionally appear on the surface, especially during the rainy season. They are easily identified. They have a blunt, often rounded head, to aid with burrowing, their shiny body scales are all the same size and the tail does not taper evenly but is short, fat and usually ends with a little spike. Their eyes range from dark spots, visible beneath the scales, to largely invisible, although one species has a pupil and iris. They eat invertebrates, usually eggs and larvae of ants and termites. They have teeth only in the upper jaw. The taxonomy (classification) of these snakes is changing: some species are poorly defined, and there is overlap in some of the characteristics that define them. In addition, they are secretive and poorly represented in museums, hence the distribution and status of several species is not well known.

Wedge-snouted Blind Snake
Typhlops cuneirostris

Identification: Up to 19cm long. A small, wedge-snouted blind snake, reddish-brown above. Close up, it appears reticulated owing to the lighter centres of the scales.

Habitat and Distribution: Semi-desert and savanna at low altitude.

An isolated record from near Kibwezi, and between Wajir and Mandera in north-east Kenya.

Natural History: Burrowing, lives in soft sand and soil, usually found in holes or under ground cover. Lays eggs but no details known.

Gierra's Blind Snake
Typhlops gierrai

Identification: Up to 48cm long. A big, dark-coloured blind snake, blue-grey above, darker on the flanks, orange or yellow below.

Habitat and Distribution: Forest and woodland of the Eastern Arc Mountains, in Tanzania, from the Usambara Mountains to the Udzungwa Mountains.

Natural History: Burrowing, lives in soft soil, usually found in holes or under ground cover.

Spotted Blind Snake
Typhlops punctatus

Identification: Up to 66cm long. A big blind snake, brown or grey above, each scale with a lighter spot, another colour phase has dark blotches on a lighter (usually yellow) background.

Habitat and Distribution: Guineo-Congolian rainforest-grassland mosaic of central, western and south-western Uganda.

Natural History: Burrowing, lives in soft soil, usually found in holes or under ground cover. Nocturnal. Eats invertebrates, especially termites. Lays eggs.

Angola Blind Snake
Typhlops angolensis

Identification: Up to 62cm long. A big blind snake, dark to reddish-brown in our area, reddish below.

Habitat and Distribution: Forest, woodland and savanna. Known from the forests around Mt Kenya, Kakamega, central and western

Uganda, the Albertine Rift, Rwanda and Burundi.

Natural History: Burrowing, lives in soft soil, usually found in holes or under ground cover. Nocturnal. Eats invertebrates, especially termites. Lays eggs.

Lineolate Blind Snake
Typhlops lineolatus

Identification: Up to 64cm long. A big blind snake, black, brown or grey above, each scale with a lighter spot; these combine to make this snake look finely striped light and dark.

Habitat and Distribution: Coastal

thicket and woodland, savanna, woodland and forest, from sea level to over 2,000m altitude. Distribution oddly disjunct, not known from dry northern Kenya and north-east Uganda, or central Tanzania but widespread elsewhere.

Natural History: Burrowing, lives in soft soil, usually found in holes or under ground cover. Nocturnal. Eats invertebrates, especially termites. Lays eggs.

Zambezi Blind Snake
Rhinotyphlops mucroso

Identification: East Africa's biggest blind snake, up to 82cm long. A big blind snake, distinctly marked with brown or grey blotches on a lighter background.

Habitat and Distribution: Coastal thicket, woodland and savanna, from sea level to over 2,000m altitude. Widespread in central and south-eastern Tanzania and coastal Kenya.

Natural History: Burrowing, lives in soft soil, usually found in holes, termitaria or under ground cover. Nocturnal. Eats invertebrates, especially termites. Lays eggs.

Yellow-striped Blind Snake
Rhinotyphlops unitaeniatus

Identification: Up to 40cm long. A slim blind snake, black or brown above, with a distinctive yellow stripe in the centre of the back.

Habitat and Distribution: Coastal thicket, woodland and savanna, from sea level to about 1,600m altitude. Occurs in extreme north-east Tanzania, south-east Kenya and up the Tana River to the Nyambene Range.

Natural History: Burrowing, lives in holes or soft soil, usually found under ground cover. May emerge at night and crawl around on the surface, or even in the day during rainstorms. Has been found in houses on the Kenya Coast. Eats invertebrates, especially termites. Lays eggs.

Other species of blind snake found in East Africa

Tanga Blind Snake T*yphlops platyrhynchus* A small blind snake, up to 25cm, with a prominent rounded snout, pale reddish-yellow above. Recorded only from Tanga.

Uluguru Blind Snake *Typhlops uluguruensis* Reaches 23cm in length, flesh-pink in colour. Known from Nyange in the Uluguru Mountains.

Blotched Blind Snake *Typhlops congestus* A big blind snake, growing to 63cm, usually yellowish with large black blotches. Found in southern, west and north-west Uganda.

Usambara Blind Snake *Typhlops usambaricus* Yellow or yellowish pink above, with large, black blotches, reaches a length of 61cm. Known only from the Usambara Mountains.

Rondo Plateau Blind Snake *Typhlops rondoensis* Grows up to 37cm, black with a yellow spot on each scale, giving the impression of being finely striped. Recorded from extreme south-east Tanzania.

Tanganyika Blind Snake *Typhlops tanganicus* A small blind snake, up to 39cm long. Its scales are brown with yellow centres. It resembles the Lineolate Blind Snake. Occurs in south-east Tanzania, in Kilwa and Liwale districts.

Angle-snouted Blind Snake *Rhinotyphlops brevis* Reaches a length of 70cm. A stocky blind snake, it is brown but the pigment is less regular on the side, giving a serrated appearance. Sporadically recorded from dry eastern and northern Kenya.

Somali Blind Snake *Rhinotyphlops ataeniatus* A slim blind snake, reaching 45cm. Regarded by some as a subspecies of the Yellow-striped Blind Snake. Brown or black, with a short orange stripe on the head. Recorded from Malka Murri in northern Kenya.

Zanzibar Blind Snake *Rhinotyphlops pallidus* A small blind snake, reaching 27cm. As its specific name suggests, it is colourless. Occurs on the East African coast, from the Tana Delta to Tanga, and on Pemba and Zanzibar.

Worm-like Blind Snake *Rhinotyphlops lumbriciformis* Grows to 45cm long. Each body scale has a brown spot at the centre. Found on the coast, from the Tana Delta south to Tanga, also on Zanzibar.

Slender Blind Snake *Rhinotyphlops gracilis* Grows to a length of 47cm. Appears finely striped or colourless. Known from south-west Tanzania (between Lakes Rukwa and Tanganyika) and the Uluguru Mountains.

Lake Tanganyika Blind Snake *Rhinotyphlops graueri* An unpigmented blind snake, reaching a length of 36cm. Occurs on the north-eastern shores of Lake Tanganyika and extreme western Uganda.

Flowerpot Blind Snake *Ramphotyphlops braminus* A small blind snake, less than 20cm. Thin and shiny black or pinkish black in colour. Sporadically recorded from the East African coast and Dodoma.

Worm Snakes: Family Leptotyphlopidae

A family of primitive burrowing snakes. Over 100 species of worm snake are known; eight species are so far recorded from East Africa. They are thin (much thinner than blind snakes) but have similar shiny scales, a rounded head and tail. They are sometimes called 'bootlaces', 'thread snakes' or 'two-headed snakes', or mistaken for worms. Like blind snakes, they live underground, in soft substrates or in holes, but occasionally appear on the surface, especially during the rainy season. The colour of individual worm snakes varies a lot; depending on the state of their skin, they can look black one day and pinkish the next. Their eyes are mostly just dark eye spots, visible beneath the scales, although one species has a fairly large eye. They mostly eat small insects, usually eggs and larvae of ants and termites; they also eat fleas and have been found in birds' nests, eating bird fleas, indicating they can climb. They have teeth only in the lower jaw. They lay eggs.

Peters' Worm Snake
Leptotyphlops scutifrons

Identification: Up to 25cm, but usually much shorter. A thin black snake, looks like a pencil lead, close up it appears reticulated or spotted black and grey, due to the light edging of the scales.

Habitat and Distribution: Coastal thicket, savanna, woodland and high grassland, from sea level to nearly 2,000m. Widespread in Tanzania, southern Kenya and western Uganda, sporadic records elsewhere.

Natural History: Burrowing, lives in holes and soft soil, usually found under ground cover. Lays from two to seven eggs.

Hook-snouted Worm Snake
Leptotyphlops macrorhynchus

Identification: Up to 23cm. A long, thin red-brown worm snake, close up it looks reticulated owing to the light edging of the scales.

Habitat and Distribution: Savanna and semi-desert, sporadically recorded in northern and eastern

Kenya and north-east Tanzania.

Natural History: Burrowing, lives in holes, in sand and soft soil, usually found under ground cover. Lays eggs.

Emin Pasha's Worm Snake
Leptotyphlops emini

Identification: Up to 19cm. A thin dark brown or black snake, looks like a pencil lead, close up it appears reticulated or spotted black and grey owing to the light edging of the scales.

Habitat and Distribution: Mostly in medium to high-altitude savanna,

but also known from coastal thicket and woodland and high grassland, from sea level to nearly 2,400m. Sporadic records from all over East Africa, including a number from south-western Uganda and south-eastern Tanzania.

Natural History: Like other worm snakes; burrowing, lives in holes and soft soil, usually found under ground cover. Lays from two to seven eggs.

Other species of worm snake known from East Africa

Lamu Worm Snake *Leptotyphlops boulengeri* Reaching 23cm, a flesh-pink worm snake, known only from Manda and Lamu Islands.

Drewes' Worm Snake *Leptotyphlops drewesi* A small worm snake, 14.3cm long, known from one specimen from the type locality, 10km south of Isiolo, Kenya. It is bicoloured, striped brown along the centre of the back, lighter brown below, ventrals creamy-white, a pale collar on the neck.

Large-eyed Worm Snake *Leptotyphlops macrops* Reaching 30cm, a big, uniform dark brown or black worm snake, occurs on the coast from Malindi area south to the Rufiji Delta. Some problematic records from the Kenya Highlands.

Pemba Worm Snake *Leptotyphlops pembae* A dark brown or black worm snake, with white chin patches, reaching 22cm, known only from Pemba Island.

Long-tailed Worm Snake *Leptotyphlops longicaudus* Grows to about 13cm in East Africa (larger elsewhere), pale brown to red-brown above, white below. Occurs along the coast south from the Tana Delta to the Mozambique border, inland in south-east Tanzania.

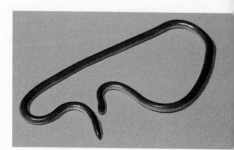

Long-tailed Worm Snake
Leptotyphlops longicaudus

Pythons: Family Pythonidae

A family of Old World and Australasian snakes, many pythons are very large, and the family includes the world's biggest snake, the Reticulated Python *Python reticulatus* of South-east Asia, which grows to more than 8m. Pythons have the remains of a pelvic girdle in the form of minute limb bones and small spur-like claws on either side of the cloaca. They kill by constriction. Originally three species of python, the African Rock Python, the Royal Python and the Anchieta's Dwarf Python *Python anchietae* were known from Africa. Recent (and somewhat controversial) work has split the African Rock Python into two species: a southern form, the Southern African Rock Python and the Central African Rock Python. Large adult rock pythons can deliver a savage bite; they are big enough to consider small humans as prey, and thus a few people have been killed by rock pythons, including delayed deaths resulting from rupture of internal organs by squeezing. Thus pythons should be treated with care.

Southern African Rock Python
Python natalensis

Identification: Up to 5.5m, but usually 2–4m. Unmistakable if seen clearly, a huge thickset snake with a subtriangular head, patterned in a mixture of brown, tan, yellow, grey and black (top). Darkens with age, big adults can be almost black (below).

Habitat and Distribution: Coastal thicket, savanna, woodland and high grassland, from sea level to 2,200m, but rarely over 1,500m. Widespread in Tanzania and southern Kenya.

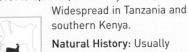

Natural History: Usually nocturnal, but will bask and hunt opportunistically during the day. Mostly terrestrial, but juveniles will climb trees, or up on rocks. Hides in holes, in thickets, reedbeds, or in rock crevices, sometimes under water. They are superb swimmers. They will strike and bite freely if cornered, and often remain bad-tempered if kept in captivity. Diet: usually birds and mammals, but recorded taking fish, amphibians, lizards and crocodiles. They kill by constriction. Large adults will take prey up to the size of antelope such as impala and goats; even porcupines have been taken. They lay eggs, clutches of 16–100 recorded, and the female coils around the eggs to protect them.

Central African Rock Python
Python sebae

Identification: Probably about the same size as the Southern African Rock Python, but there are reports of much larger specimens (up to 9.8m) from West Africa; this is scarcely credible but there is a more credible report of a 7.5m specimen. Recorded to 6m in Kenya. Unmistakable if seen clearly, a huge thickset snake with a subtriangular head, patterned in a mixture of brown, tan, yellow, grey and black (top). Darkens with age, big adults can be almost black (below), but usually more brightly coloured than the southern form.

Habitat and Distribution: Much the same as for the southern form. Sporadically distributed in Tanzania, Kenya

Coast and Tana River, western Kenya, Lake Victoria basin and Uganda and Rwanda.

Natural History: As for the Southern African Rock Python.

Other species of python found in East Africa

Royal Python *Python regius* A small python with a fat body and pear-shaped head, growing to about 1.5m, boldly marked in black, yellow and brown. Known only from extreme north-west Uganda.

Royal Python
Python regius

Boas: Family Boidae

A family that includes the giant boas of the Americas (e.g. Green Anaconda *Eunectes murinus*, Boa Constrictor *Boa constrictor*) but in our area represented by a single small burrowing boa of the subfamily Erycinae, the sand boas.

Kenya Sand Boa
Eryx colubrinus

Identification: Up to about 90 cm. A stout little snake, with a short bullet-shaped head, marked with darker blotches (brown, grey or black) on a lighter background (white, yellow, orange or grey).

Habitat and Distribution: Desert, semi-desert and dry savanna, from sea level to around 1,500m. Widely distributed in northern and eastern Kenya and extreme north-east Tanzania.

Natural History: Burrowing, probably nocturnal. May emerge to bask. Lives in holes or buried in soft soil or sand, in areas of hard soil it may live in dry sandy riverbeds.

Diet: usually small rodents and lizards. They give live birth, from 4–20 young. Although harmless, sand boas are greatly feared in parts of their range, possibly a result of confusion with some vipers.

Colubrid or 'Typical' Snakes: Family Colubridae

A large, successful family of 'ordinary' snakes. Most have no fangs, only solid teeth, but a number have grooved poison fangs set towards the rear of the upper jaw; these snakes are conveniently called back-fanged or rear-fanged snakes. The venom of most rear-fanged snakes has little effect on humans, although bites from the larger species should be avoided. However, three rear-fanged snakes (the Boomslang and the two vine snakes) occurring in East Africa have been shown to have deadly venoms.

Brown House Snake
Lamprophis fuliginosus

Identification: Usually 50 to 80cm, max 1.2m. A medium-sized, fairly slim harmless snake, its head is shaped like a python's. Colour very variable: almost any shade of brown, may also be orange, yellow, black, grey or olive. Usually a pair of lines on each side of the head, these may be any thickness (or absent) and may extend down the body. Some juveniles have spotted necks, these spots (and sometimes the lines) fade with age.

Habitat and Distribution: Forest, woodland, savanna and semi-desert, from sea level to over 2,400m, although rare over 2,000m. Probably East Africa's most common snake, it is recorded throughout our area, apart from montane areas over 2,500m, seemingly absent from much of dry northern Kenya.

Natural History: Nocturnal and terrestrial, emerging at dusk to hunt. Shelters during the day in holes or under ground cover. Harmless but bites fiercely. Lays from 2–16 eggs. Juveniles eat mostly lizards, adults mostly small mammals.

Olive House Snake
Lamprophis olivaceus

Identification: Up to 90cm. A medium-sized, fairly slim harmless snake, head shaped like a python's. Black, brownish or grey above, the dark flank colour encroaching on the lighter ventrals. The eye is distinctly red or rufous.

Habitat and Distribution: Forest, riverine forest, forest/savanna mosaic and deforested areas, from 600m to over 2,000m altitude. Sporadic records from the southern half of Uganda, also found along the Albertine Rift from Burundi and Rwanda north to Lake Albert.

Natural History: Nocturnal and terrestrial, emerging at dusk to hunt. Supposedly common near water sources. Shelters during the day in holes or under ground cover. Harmless and good natured. Lays eggs. Juveniles take frogs and lizards, adults mostly small mammals.

Cape Wolf Snake
Lycophidion capense

Identification: Up to 60cm. A small, harmless snake with a flat head. Several subspecies occur in East Africa, the colour is quite variable, most are grey or brown, the scales light-edged. Has long teeth, hence the name.

Habitat and Distribution: High grassland, moist and dry savanna, from sea level to about 2,400m. Widespread in Uganda, Rwanda and Burundi, most of Tanzania (records lacking from north-west) and southern Kenya.

Natural History: Slow-moving, nocturnal and terrestrial, emerging at dusk to hunt. Shelters during the day in holes or under ground cover. Harmless. Lays three to eight eggs. Diet: mostly lizards, occasionally small snakes.

Flat-snouted Wolf Snake
Lycophidion depressirostre

Identification: Up to 48cm. A small harmless snake with a flat head. Looks dark grey with light speckling.

Habitat and Distribution: Semi-desert, dry and moist savanna, rarely woodland, from sea level to 2,000m. Widespread in eastern Tanzania, and northern Kenya, plus one record (Kampala) from Uganda.

Natural History: Slow-moving, nocturnal and terrestrial, emerging at dusk to hunt. Shelters during the day in holes or under ground cover. Harmless. Lays eggs. Diet: presumably mostly lizards.

Forest Wolf Snake
Lycophidion ornatum

Identification: Up to 60cm. A small, harmless snake with a flat head, reddish or red-brown in colour, sometimes with dark spots and a distinctive pale snout band.

Habitat and Distribution: Forest, woodland and deforested areas, from 700 to 2,700m altitude. Known from Ngorongoro Crater in Tanzania, highland forest from Nairobi north to the Nyambeni Hills in eastern Kenya, recorded from Kakamega area, sporadically distributed in forests of central Uganda and along the Albertine Rift from Burundi to Lake Albert.

Natural History: Slow-moving, nocturnal and terrestrial, emerging at dusk to hunt. Shelters during the day in holes or under ground cover. Harmless. Lays two to six eggs. Diet: presumably mostly lizards.

Cape File Snake
Mehelya capensis

Identification: Up to 1.6m. A big, slow-moving, dark snake with a triangular body, the vertebral ridge is raised, rough and obvious. The body scales don't overlap, unlike most other snakes, the skin is visible between them. Grey, black or brown above, southern specimens have a white vertebral line.

Habitat and Distribution: Savanna, woodland and forest, not usually in arid areas, from sea level to over 2,000m altitude, although rarely above 1,600m in Kenya and Tanzania. Sporadic records from Tanzania, widespread in south-east Kenya, central Uganda, Rwanda and Burundi.

Natural History: Slow-moving, nocturnal and terrestrial, (will sometimes climb after prey) emerging at dusk to hunt. Shelters during the day in holes or under ground cover. Harmless and good natured but restless in the hand. Lays 5–13 eggs. Diet: mostly amphibians and reptiles, including highly dangerous snakes.

Dwarf or Black File Snake
Mehelya nyassae

Identification: Up to 65cm. A small dark file snake with a triangular body and enlarged scales on the vertebral ridge. Black or grey in colour, the skin between the scales pink, white or grey.

Habitat and Distribution: Low savanna, coastal thicket and woodland, from sea level to about 1,200m altitude. Sporadically distributed along the East African coastline, extends inland up the Tana River, to Voi and in south-east Tanzania.

Natural History: Slow-moving, nocturnal and terrestrial. Shelters during the day in holes or under ground cover. Harmless. Lays up to six eggs. Diet: mostly small lizards, might take small snakes.

Forest File Snake
Mehelya poensis

Identification: Up to 1.4m. A big file snake with a triangular body and enlarged scales on the vertebral ridge, with a very long tail. Olive-grey or grey-brown in colour, the skin between the scales visible light grey or pinky-grey.

Habitat and Distribution: Forest and forest islands, from 700 to 2,200m altitude. Sporadically recorded from central, western and south-western Uganda.

Natural History: Slow-moving, nocturnal and terrestrial, although its long tail suggests that it climbs. Shelters during the day in holes or under ground cover. Harmless. Lays up to eight eggs. Diet in West Africa seems to be mostly lizards.

Other harmless snakes found in East Africa

Red-and-black Striped Snake *Bothropthalmus lineatus* A red and black striped snake, with a pale head. Reaches 1.3m length. Known from forests on the Uganda Lake Victoria shore and the Albertine Rift.

Lake Tanganyika Water Snake *Lycodonomorphus bicolor* A grey or brown (sometimes yellow-brown) water snake, reaching 70cm, with a small round pupil, found only in Lake Tanganyika.

Whyte's Water Snake *Lycodonomorphus whytei* A brown or olive water snake, up to 75cm in length, with dark markings on the belly scales, sporadically recorded from southern Tanzania.

Mozambique Wolf Snake *Lycophidion acutirostre* A little wolf snake, reaching 31cm, blackish-brown with a white snout band, recorded only from Liwale in southern Tanzania.

Western Forest Wolf Snake *Lycophidion laterale* A spectacular wolf snake, banded grey, orange and brown, reaching 48cm long. Recorded from the Bwamba Forest, extreme western Uganda.

Speckled Wolf Snake *Lycophidion meleagre* A grey-spotted wolf snake with a black tail, grows to 35cm, recorded from the Arabuko-Sokoke Forest, Kenya, the Uluguru and Usambara Mountains and their vicinity in Tanzania.

Pemba Wolf Snake *Lycophidion pembanum* Small wolf snake, grows up to 45cm, dark brown or black, with pale, dark-spotted head, found only on Pemba Island.

continued over

Taylor's Wolf Snake *Lycophidion taylori* Grows to 51cm, a grey speckled wolf snake, often has a white collar, known from dry country around Mt Kilimanjaro in Tanzania and from Kakuma in north-west Kenya.

Red-snouted Wolf Snake *Lycophidion uzungwense* Reaches 61cm, shiny black colour, each scale white-tipped, so it appears grey, with a distinctive scarlet or orange V-shape on snout. Known from the southern Udzungwa Mts.

Ituri Banded Snake *Chamaelycus fasciatus* A little, brown, terrestrial snake, up to 35cm long, sometimes with narrow dark crossbars, recorded from the Bwamba Forest in extreme western Uganda.

Yellow Forest Snake *Hormonotus modestus* A yellow, yellow-brown, pinky-brown or grey-brown snake with a broad pear-shaped head, grows to 85cm long, sporadically recorded from forests in western Kenya and Uganda.

Small-eyed File Snake *Mehelya stenophthalmus* A little (up to 76cm) file snake, usually glossy black or olive-brown. Known from forest areas in western Uganda.

Mocquard's Lesser File Snake *Gonionotophis brussauxi* Grows to 45cm length, a small dark brown or grey file snake, with a subtriangular body and enlarged scales along the centre of the back. Known only from the Budongo Forest, north-central Uganda.

Mole Snake
Pseudaspis cana

Identification: Up to 1.8m, but usually 1–1.3m. A big stout snake with a short head, pointed snout and small eye. Colour variable, brown, olive, red-brown, orange or grey. Juveniles are brown with black crossbars and white spots.

Habitat and Distribution: Grassland, moist and dry savanna, from 1,200 to 2,600m altitude. A curiously disjunct distribution in East Africa; southern Tanzania, Rwanda and Burundi, the Arusha-Moshi area, high central rift valley in Kenya, Nyeri-Nanyuki and Kitui.

Natural History: Diurnal but secretive and terrestrial, spending much time hunting prey in rodent burrows or buried in soil. When threatened, it hisses loudly and makes lunging strikes. Harmless. Males fight in the breeding season. Gives live birth, up to 95 young. Diet: mostly rodents, especially mole rats; juveniles will eat lizards.

Slug-eater
Duberria lutrix

Identification: Up to 45cm. A stout little brown snake with a very short head, usually in high grassland. Shades of brown or rufous above, often with a darker flank stripe and a thin vertebral line.

Habitat and Distribution: High grassland and moist savanna, from 1,000 to 2,600m altitude, possibly higher. A curiously disjunct distribution in East Africa; southern, north-eastern and northern Tanzania and the crater highlands, Rwanda, Burundi and south-west Uganda, high central and western Kenya.

Natural History: Diurnal but secretive and terrestrial, foraging in grass and vegetation. When inactive hides under ground cover, in grass tufts, vegetation heaps and in holes. Gentle and slow-moving, never tries to bite. In other areas of Africa it rolls up in a flat spiral when threatened. It gives live birth up to 12 young. Diet: slugs and thin-shelled snails. Sometimes abundant, especially in fruit farms.

Smyth's Water Snake
Grayia smythii

Identification: Up to 1.7m, but usually 1–1.3m. A big robust water snake, banded when young. Colour variable, adults various shades of brown or black, juveniles have dark half bands on a lighter background.

Habitat and Distribution: Associated with lakes and larger rivers, in waterside vegetation in savanna or woodland, at altitude between 600 and 1,200m. Occurs all around Lake Victoria, the Victoria Nile, Lakes Kyoga, Albert, Edward and the Albert Nile.

Natural History: Diurnal and aquatic, swims readily, shelters in waterside vegetation, holes and man-made waterside constructions. Harmless and fairly placid. Lays 9–20 eggs. It eats fish but will also take amphibians.

Thollon's Water Snake
Grayia tholloni

Identification: Up to 1.1m. A fairly large, banded snake, brown or grey-brown, lightening down the flanks, the body faintly banded, the lip scales black-edged.

Habitat and Distribution: In lakes, rivers and streams in moist savanna

and woodland, at altitudes of 500 to 1,500m in East Africa. Occurs around the northern and western shores of Lake Victoria, north-western Uganda and eastern Rwanda and Burundi, possibly Lake Tanganyika.

Natural History: Diurnal, aquatic and terrestrial, swims readily, shelters in waterside vegetation. Harmless. Lays eggs. It eats fish and amphibians.

Smith's Racer
Platyceps brevis smithii
(formerly *Coluber smithii*)

Identification: Up to 70cm. A slim little snake, brown or rufous, often barred, with a big eye.

Habitat and Distribution: Dry savanna and semi-desert, from 100m altitude to 1,300m. Widely but

sporadically distributed in north-western and south-eastern Kenya.

Natural History: Diurnal and terrestrial, but will climb into low bushes. Secretive and fast-moving. Lays up to three eggs. Diet: small lizards.

Semi-ornate Snake
Meizodon semiornatus

Identification: Up to 80cm. A slim, harmless little snake with a big eye. Usually olive, brown or grey, occasionally black. Juveniles are lighter, with a series of dark crossbars on the front half of the body, this fades in adults (top) from the top down; some adults are uniform black (below).

Habitat and Distribution: Coastal thicket and woodland, semi-desert, savanna and woodland, from sea level to 2,200m altitude. Sporadic records from northern Kenya, widespread in south-east Kenya and north-east Tanzania.

Natural History: Fast-moving and terrestrial, usually diurnal but also active at dusk. When inactive, hides under ground cover, occasionally small aggregations have been found under tree bark. Secretive and rare. Lays up to three eggs. Diet: small lizards, frogs and rodents.

Prince Ruspoli's Shovel-snout
Prosymna ruspolii

Identification: Up to 30cm. A small, shovel-nosed snake, scales brown or grey with white edging, giving a speckled effect, some specimens have a black head and collar.

Habitat and Distribution: Dry savanna and semi-desert usually below 1,500m altitude. Sporadically distributed in dry eastern and northern Kenya and northern Tanzania.

Natural History: A nocturnal burrowing snake, spending its time in holes or under ground cover, but may prowl on the surface, especially in the rainy season. They lay 3–4 eggs. Diet: snake and lizard eggs.

East African Shovel-snout
Prosymna stuhlmanni

Identification: Up to 30cm. A small, shovel-nosed snake, light to dark grey, with a single or double row of white spots down the centre of the back, the snout is distinctly yellow or orange.

Habitat and Distribution: Dry and moist savanna and semi-desert usually below 1,800m altitude. Known from south-eastern Kenya and eastern and southern Tanzania, a few sporadic records elsewhere.

Natural History: A nocturnal burrowing snake, spending its time in holes or under ground cover, but may prowl on the surface, especially in the rainy season. They lay three to four eggs. Diet: snake and lizard eggs. This snake has a curious threat display, lifting up the front half of the body and flattening its neck like a cobra, while flicking the tongue in and out.

Angolan Green Snake
Philothamnus angolensis

Identification: Up to 1.2m. A long, thin, green tree snake with a big eye and a golden iris, there is a pale spot on the lower edge of the body scales.

Habitat and Distribution: Moist savanna and woodland, near water sources, from sea level to nearly 2,000m. Known from southern Tanzania and the Albertine Rift from Burundi and Rwanda north to Lake Albert; a few sporadic records elsewhere.

Natural History: Arboreal and diurnal, spending the day hunting in waterside vegetation. A fast-moving, secretive and graceful climber. Swims well. Hisses, inflates neck and body, exposing the white spots and strikes if cornered. It lays from 4–16 eggs. May lay eggs in a communal nest, usually a suitable damp hole. Diet: usually frogs, occasionally nestling birds.

Battersby's Green Snake
Philothamnus battersbyi

Identification: Up to 90cm. A fairly large thin green tree snake with a big eye and a golden-brown iris, there is a bluish or white spot on the lower edge of the body scales.

Habitat and Distribution: Moist savanna and woodland, near water sources, from sea level to nearly 2,400m. Known from south-eastern Uganda, very common in high western and central Kenya and northern Tanzania, sporadic reports elsewhere include Mt Marsabit.

Natural History: Arboreal and diurnal, spending the day in waterside vegetation, waiting for prey to pass or actively hunting. A fast-moving, secretive and graceful climber. When resting it may show a 'shimmy', a series of sinuous neck waves. Swims well and may hunt under water. Hisses, inflates neck and body, exposing the white spots and strikes if cornered. It lays from 3–11 eggs. May lay eggs in a communal nest, usually a suitable damp hole. Diet: usually frogs and fish, occasionally lizards.

Thirteen-scaled Green Snake
Philothamnus carinatus

Identification: Up to 85cm. A slim, barred green tree snake with a very big eye and a golden-brown iris. Green, blue-green or olive green, marked with dark crossbars, dorsal scales edged turquoise.

Habitat and Distribution: Forest, forest islands and well-wooded savanna, from 600 to 2,300m altitude. Recorded from western Kenya, Mt Elgon and all along the Albertine Rift from the Mahale Peninsula on Lake Tanganyika north to Lake Albert.

Natural History: Arboreal and diurnal. A genuine forest-dwelling green tree snake, not tied to water sources. Inflates the body when angry, exposing the bars and turquoise spots. Lays eggs. Diet: presumably frogs.

Slender Green Snake
Philothamnus heterolepidotus

Identification: Up to 1m. A large, very slim, green tree snake with a very big eye and a golden-brown or yellow iris, the lips and chin are yellow, skin between the scales black. No light spots on dorsal scales (a good field character).

Habitat and Distribution: Moist savanna and woodland, near water sources, from 600 to 2,000m. Extreme western Kenya, southern and northern Uganda, all along the Albertine Rift to north-west Tanzania.

Natural History: Arboreal and diurnal, climbs and swims well, usually found near water sources. Lays three to five eggs. Eats frogs.

South-eastern Green Snake
Philothamnus hoplogaster

Identification: Up to 95cm. A fairly large, vivid green tree snake with a short head, eye pupil golden-brown. The snout is sometimes yellow or orange, the lower flanks blue, interstitial skin black.

Habitat and Distribution: Coastal forest, thicket and moist savanna, from sea level to about 1,800m altitude, often near water sources. Found in coastal Kenya, coastal and south-east Tanzania, sporadic records elsewhere including around the top of Lake Tanganyika.

Natural History: Arboreal and diurnal, but will also hunt on the ground, climbs and swims well. Lays three to eight eggs. Eats frogs. Does not inflate the neck like other green tree snakes.

Speckled Green Snake
Philothamnus punctatus

Identification: Up to 1.2m. A large, slim, green or turquoise-blue tree snake, most specimens distinctly spotted black. Has a very big eye and a golden-yellow iris, with a raised 'eyebrow' (supraocular scale).

Habitat and Distribution: Coastal forest, woodland and thicket, savanna and semi-desert, from sea level to about 1,200m. Found in coastal Kenya and south-eastern Tanzania, sporadic records from eastern and northern Kenya.

Natural History: Fast-moving, arboreal and diurnal, climbs well using its keeled belly scales. Unlike other green-snakes is not tied to water sources. Inflates neck and strikes if cornered. Lays three to six eggs. In keeping with its willingness to live in dry country, it eats mostly lizards, but will take other small vertebrates.

Spotted Bush Snake
Philothamnus semivariegatus

Identification: Up to 1.3m. A large, slim green tree snake, usually with black crossbars, a big eye and a golden-brown iris, with a raised 'eyebrow' (supraocular scale). Various shades of green, in southern parts of its range it becomes bronzy towards the tail.

Habitat and Distribution: Coastal forest, woodland and thicket, savanna and semi-desert, will utilise forest clearings. Occurs from sea level to about 1,500m. Although seemingly uncommon, it is found throughout Tanzania, southern Uganda and south-east Kenya, sporadic records elsewhere.

Natural History: Fast-moving, arboreal and diurnal. Climbs superbly well using its keeled belly scales; has been seen to climb concrete walls. Unlike other green tree snakes is not tied to water sources. Inflates neck and strikes if cornered. Lays 3–12 eggs. Diet: mostly lizards, but will take other small vertebrates.

Emerald Snake
Hapsidophrys smaragdina

Identification: Up to 1.1m. A slim, green, tree snake with a bright yellow belly and a dark stripe through the eye.

Habitat and Distribution: Woodland, forest and deforested areas, occurs all along the western shore of Lake

Victoria and southern Uganda, across to the Ruwenzori and Lake Albert.

Natural History: Diurnal and arboreal, a fast-moving climber. Basks in clearings. Lays from three to four eggs. Eats lizards and frogs.

Jackson's Tree Snake
Thrasops jacksoni

Identification: Up to 2.3m. Unmistakable if seen clearly, a big, jet-black, shiny, tree snake with a large dark eye and short head. Smells strongly of liquorice if recently sloughed. Juveniles are vividly marked, the head and neck green, the body chequered black and yellow or orange, darkening to the adult colour between 50 and 90cm length.

Habitat and Distribution: Forest, forest islands, woodland and riverine forest, from 600 to over 2,400m altitude. Forests of the eastern escarpment of the rift valley, Mt Kenya and the Nyambeni Hills in eastern Kenya, western Kenya, southern Uganda and Rwanda.

Natural History: Diurnal and arboreal, climbs superbly well, ascending to 30m or more in forest trees. If pursued, it will jump, even from high branches. Inflates its neck and strikes if cornered. Lays 7–12 eggs. Eats lizards (especially chameleons), small mammals and birds.
Note well: adults are almost identical to the black colour form of a very dangerous snake, the Boomslang.

Hook-nosed Snake
Scaphiophis albopunctatus

Identification: Up to 1.6m.
A big, stocky snake, the head
short and blunt with a big
projecting rostral scale. May
be grey, pinky-grey, brown or
orange with a grey vertebral stripe, juveniles blue-grey
speckled white.

Habitat and Distribution: Coastal thicket and forest, savanna
and woodland, from sea level to about 1,500m. Occurs in
south-east Kenya, north-central Tanzania, around Lake
Rukwa in Tanzania and the Victoria Nile in Uganda.

Natural History: Lives in holes, occasionally emerges and moves about
in cover, probably diurnal. If threatened, it opens the mouth, exposing
the black interior, raises the forepart of the body, hisses and makes big
lunging strikes. Lays eggs, up to 48 recorded. Eats mammals, which it
catches in holes.

Other harmless snakes found in East Africa

Flowered Racer *Platyceps florulentus* A slim, brown or rufous, diurnal
snake, reaching a length of 1m, known from the Lake Baringo-Lokori area in
Kenya and Nimule in northern Uganda.

Tana Delta Smooth Snake *Meizodon krameri* A slim, olive-brown snake,
reaching 50cm length, recorded only in the Tana River delta area in Kenya

Black-headed Smooth Snake *Meizodon plumbiceps* A small, slim, diurnal
snake, growing to 55cm , pink or red with black dots and a black head or
neck. Recorded only from Malka Murri in northern Kenya.

Eastern Crowned Snake *Meizodon regularis* A small, grey, diurnal snake,
juveniles have a black head with light crossbars, known from Chemilil in
Kenya and north-west Uganda.

Angolan Shovel-snout *Prosymna ambigua* A little, speckled grey or brown
snake with a sharp snout, reaching 36cm, sporadically recorded from the
area around Lake Victoria and in northern Uganda.

Speckled Shovel-snout *Prosymna meleagris* A small (to 36cm), speckled,
grey snake with a dark spot on the neck, known from just beyond the
borders of north-west Uganda.

Ornate Shovel-snout *Prosymna ornatissima* This snake is vividly banded red
and black, with a pointed snout, grows to about 30cm. Known only from the
Uluguru Mountains, Tanzania.

continued over

Pitman's Shovel-snout *Prosymna pitmani* A small snake, reaching 31cm, dark purple-brown above, each scale with a small, pale spot. Recorded from south-east Tanzania.

Banded Shovel-snout *Prosymna semifasciata* A short, grey shovel-snout with blue spots and black crossbars, grows to 26cm, recorded only from the eastern Usambara Mountains and nearby coastal forests.

Uganda Green Snake *Philothamnus bequaerti* A slender green-snake, reaching 90cm uniform green, scales with a white dot on the lower edge. Sporadically recorded from mid-altitude localities in Uganda.

Forest Green Snake *Philothamnus heterodermus* Grows to about 75cm, green in colour, body scales with a concealed light dot, chin and throat yellow. A few sporadic records from Uganda and Tanzania.

Hughes' Green Snake *Philothamnus hughesi* Grows to 93cm. Never seen alive but presumably green with black and white spots forming half-rings on the body. Recorded at Sango Bay, Lake Victoria shore, Uganda.

Usambara Green Snake *Philothamnus macrops* Grows to about 90cm. Very variable in colour; various shades of green, dull red or brown, with or without darker spots, crossbars or blotches. Dull red with turquoise crossbars seems to be the most common phase. Found in coastal eastern Tanzania and Zanzibar.

Loveridge's Green Snake *Philothamnus nitidus* An emerald to blue-green snake with a white throat; grows to about 90cm. Sporadic records from western Kenya, Uganda, Rwanda and Burundi.

Stripe-backed Green Snake *Philothamnus ornatus* Grows to 80cm; green with a yellow-edged, red-brown vertebral stripe. Recorded from Tatanda, extreme south-west Tanzania.

Rwanda Forest Green Snake *Philothamnus ruandae* Reaches just under 1m; very variable in colour, may be shades of green or brown or black, with or without fine or broad yellow crossbars. Occurs along the Albertine Rift from south-west Uganda down to the shores of Lake Tanganyika.

Black-lined Green Snake *Hapsidophrys lineata* Grows to 1.1m. Slim and green with fine black stripes along body, very large eye and short head. Recorded in forests of western Kenya, northern Lake Victoria shore and south-west Uganda.

Large-eyed Green Tree Snake *Rhamnophis aethiopissa* A big (1.3m maximum), slim, tree snake with a large eye. Colour green with black barring, yellow chin and underside. Sporadic records from forests of western Kenya and Tanzania, southern Uganda, Rwanda and Burundi.

Ethiopian Hook-nosed Snake *Scaphiophis raffreyi* A stocky snake, up to 1.3m, with a distinctive pointed snout. Dull grey, brown or red-brown. Known from Moroto in Uganda, and possibly around Lake Baringo.

Pale-headed Forest Snake
Buhoma depressiceps

Identification: Up to 44cm. A small, dark snake with a short head and fairly small eyes, brown with a pale collar, body sometimes with fine black lines.

Habitat and Distribution: Forest between altitudes of 1,000 and 2,200m. Recorded from south-western Uganda.

Natural History: Terrestrial and apparently diurnal. Slow-moving, gentle and non-aggressive. Lays eggs. Diet includes frogs.

Blanding's Tree Snake
Boiga blandingii

Identification: Up to 2.8m. A big, robust, broad-headed tree snake with a thin neck, body subtriangular in section. Males are glossy black above, yellow below; females may be brown, grey or yellow-brown. Juveniles are brown with diamond-shaped black crossbars.

Habitat and Distribution: Forest, woodland, forest-savanna mosaic and riverine woodland, from 700 to about 2,200m altitude. Recorded from western Kenya, southern and western Uganda, and the Mahale Peninsula and Rubondo Island in Tanzania.

Natural History: Arboreal, an expert climber and nocturnal. Rests in leaf clumps, hollows in trees, bird nests and other refuges. Inflates the body and strikes vigorously if cornered. Lays 7–14 eggs. Eats a range of prey: birds and their eggs, lizards, frogs, arboreal rodents and bats.

Venom: Rear-fanged, its venom might be dangerous to humans, and is very toxic in laboratory studies.

Powdered Tree Snake
Boiga pulverulenta

Identification: Up to 1.25m. A broad-headed tree snake with big eyes, colour pinkish or rufous brown, dusted with fine dark specks, with dark, light-centred crossbars.

Habitat and Distribution: Forest and woodland at medium to high altitude. Recorded from western Kenya, central and western Uganda.

Natural History: Arboreal, an expert climber and nocturnal. Shelters in holes and cracks in trees, creeper and epiphyte tangles and bird nests. Lays eggs. Diet: rodents and arboreal lizards.

Large-eyed Snake
Telescopus dhara

Identification: Up to 1.3m but usually 50-80cm. A broad headed snake with big prominent eyes and a subtriangular body, colour very variable, usually brown, rufous, grey or black, sometimes with narrow lighter crossbars.

Habitat and Distribution: Semi-desert, dry savanna and coastal thicket, from sea level to about 1,400m. Widespread in northern and eastern Kenya and extreme north-east Tanzania. One record from eastern Uganda (Amudat).

Natural History: Nocturnal and semi-arboreal, will hunt on the ground or in bushes and low trees. Shelters under cover or down holes by day, sometimes in bird nests. It will flatten its head, hiss and strike if cornered; if restrained bites slowly and deliberately. Lays 5–20 eggs. Diet: small mammals, lizards, bats and birds.

Tiger Snake
Telescopus semiannulatus

Identification: Up to 1m. A broad-headed snake with big, prominent, orange eyes and a subtriangular body, orange in colour with black, brown or dull rufous saddles on the back.

Habitat and Distribution: Dry and moist savanna, coastal thicket and woodland, from sea level to about 1,700m altitude. Occurs almost throughout Tanzania, and along the Kenya coast, recently recorded from the Masai Mara Reserve, sporadic inland records in eastern Kenya.

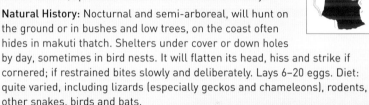

Natural History: Nocturnal and semi-arboreal, will hunt on the ground or in bushes and low trees, on the coast often hides in makuti thatch. Shelters under cover or down holes by day, sometimes in bird nests. It will flatten its head, hiss and strike if cornered; if restrained bites slowly and deliberately. Lays 6–20 eggs. Diet: quite varied, including lizards (especially geckos and chameleons), rodents, other snakes, birds and bats.

Yellow-flanked Snake
Crotaphopeltis degeni

Identification: Up to 60cm. A small, broad-headed snake. Black or blue-black above, the belly is vivid orange or yellow, this colour extends up onto the flanks to a greater or lesser extent.

Habitat and Distribution: Moist savanna, usually near water, at altitudes between 600 and 2,700m. Widespread in high western Kenya and central Uganda on lakes Victoria, Kyoga and Albert.

Natural History: Slow-moving, nocturnal and terrestrial, active in damp areas, hides by day under ground cover. Threatens by flattening the head to a triangle, flaring the lips and striking with a loud hiss. Lays up to six eggs. Diet: amphibians, possibly small fish.

White-lipped Snake/White-lip
Crotaphopeltis hotamboeia

Identification: Up to 90cm. A small, broad-headed, rear-fanged snake. Black, grey or olive above, lips usually white. Usually has a series of crossbars, consisting of fine white dots. Olive specimens have a black patch on the side of the head.

Habitat and Distribution: Moist savanna and woodland, usually near water, from sea level to 2,500m altitude. One of East Africa's most widespread and common snakes, occurs virtually throughout Rwanda, Burundi, Uganda and Tanzania, and southern and western Kenya, absent from most of dry northern and eastern Kenya.

Natural History: Nocturnal and terrestrial, active in damp areas, hides by day under ground cover. Slow-moving but has a distinctive threat display: it flattens the head to a triangle, flares the lips, elevates the front of the body and strikes with a loud hiss. Lays 6–19 eggs. Diet: amphibians.

Cross-barred Tree Snake
Dipsadoboa flavida

Identification: Up to 63 cm. A small, slender snake with a broad head and prominent yellow eyes. Brown to red-brown above, the front half of the body extensively marbled or barred with yellow.

Habitat and Distribution: Coastal thicket, woodland and low-altitude savanna. Occurs along the length of the East African coast, inland in the Galana River area and in south-eastern Tanzania.

Natural History: Slow-moving, nocturnal and partially arboreal, hides by day under ground cover, under bark or in crevices. Threatens by flattening the head, raising the body and striking. Lays eggs. Diet: geckos and frogs.

Günther's Green Tree Snake
Dipsadoboa unicolor

Identification: Up to 1.3cm. A medium-sized, broad-headed tree snake. Juveniles are brown or grey, at about 40cm length the adults become green or turquoise.

Habitat and Distribution: Medium to high altitude forest and woodland,

from 500 to 3,000m. Occurs along the Albertine Rift from the Ruwenzori Mountains south to the Mahale Peninsula on Lake Tanganyika, also Mabira and Budongo Forest in Uganda.

Natural History: Slow-moving, nocturnal and partially arboreal, hides by day under ground cover. Active even on nights as cold as 7°C. Lays eggs. Diet: frogs.

Boomslang
Dispholidus typus

Identification: Up to 1.85m. A big, back-fanged, highly venomous tree snake, with a huge eye, short head and keeled dorsal scales. Very

variable in colour, males (right) are usually green, females (far right) brown or grey. Other colours include green with black-edged scales (characteristic of woodland), brown with a rufous head, striped black and grey-white, yellow or tan with white spots. Juveniles have a grey or brown, blue-spotted vertebral stripe, the head is dark brown above and white below, the eye emerald green.

Habitat and Distribution: Semi-desert, savanna and woodland, from sea level to 2,200m. Found almost throughout East Africa, although absent from parts of high central Kenya and records sporadic in northern Kenya.

Natural History: Diurnal and arboreal, although it will descend to cross open areas. It has binocular vision and can spot motionless prey. If cornered, it inflates the front half of the body and flicks the tongue up and down. Boomslangs lay 8–25 eggs. Diet: mostly arboreal lizards such as chameleons and agamas but may also take birds and frogs.

Venom: Has a deadly, slow-acting venom, causing a general bleeding tendency. However, bites are rare: this snake is non-aggressive.

Savanna Vine Snake
Thelotornis mossambicanus

Identification: Up to 1.4 m. A thin grey tree snake, with a keyhole-shaped pupil. The top of the head is green, often black speckled, body also speckled on grey or grey-brown.

Habitat and Distribution: Coastal thicket, woodland and savanna, sea level to 1,500m. Coastal Kenya, inland to Voi, south-eastern Tanzania, shores of Lake Tanganyika and Lake Eyasi area.

Natural History: Diurnal and arboreal. It has binocular vision and can spot motionless prey. Superbly camouflaged. If cornered it inflates the front half of the body and flicks the red and black tongue up and down. Lays 4–13 eggs. Diet: mostly arboreal lizards, sometimes takes birds, frogs and snakes, ambushed from a low branch.

Venom: A non-aggressive snake, but the venom is potent, causing a general bleeding tendency. No antivenom is produced.

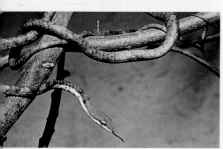

Forest Vine Snake
Thelotornis kirtlandii

Identification: Up to 1.6 m. A very thin grey tree snake, with a keyhole-shaped pupil. Head green or grey-green above, body grey or grey-brown, speckled.

Habitat and Distribution: Forest and woodland, from 600 to 2,200m

altitude. North and western shore of Lake Victoria in Uganda, the Budongo Forest and the forests of the Albertine Rift, plus two isolated Tanzanian records; Mahale Peninsula and Udzungwa Mountains.

Natural History: Diurnal and arboreal. It has binocular vision and can spot motionless prey. Superbly camouflaged. If cornered it inflates the front half of the body and flicks the red and black tongue up and down. Lays 4–12 eggs. Diet: as for the savanna vine snake.

Venom: Like the savanna vine snake, the venom is potent, causing a general bleeding tendency. No antivenom is produced.

Other rear-fanged snakes found in East Africa

Uluguru Forest Snake *Buhoma procterae* A small, brown or grey, striped or spotted snake, with a round pupil, reaching 50cm length. Only in the Uluguru and Udzungwa Mountains.

Usambara Forest Snake *Buhoma vauerocegae* A small, brown snake, with a dark V-shape on the neck, a fine dark vertebral stripe, and a round pupil, reaching 41cm length. Only in the Uluguru and Usambara Mountains.

Tana Herald Snake *Crotaphopeltis braestrupi* A small, dark snake, very like a white lip but without the white spots, and the lips sometimes have dark speckles. Reaches a length of 67cm. Occurs on the Kenya coastal plain from Malindi north to the Somali border.

Tornier's Cat Snake *Crotaphopeltis tornieri* A small, dark snake, grey to black above, with a broad head and a distinctive red eye. Length up to 65cm. Known from the Eastern Arc mountains in Tanzania.

Marbled Tree Snake *Dipsadoboa aulica* A slender snake, reaching 70cm, with a large head and prominent eyes. Red-brown or pinkish, with light crossbars, spots and dashes, which fade with age. Known only from extreme south-central Tanzania.

Shreve's Marbled Tree Snake *Dipsadoboa shrevei* A slender snake with a large head and prominent eyes, shiny black above, (juveniles are grey-brown), lips cream or yellow. Grows to just over 1m in length. Two subspecies occur: one on the southern slopes of Kilimanjaro, the other on the Rondo Plateau, extreme south-east Tanzania.

Laurent's Green Tree Snake *Dipsadoboa viridis* A slender snake with a broad head, never described alive but might be green or brown. Grows to 1.25m in length. Known from Rwanda and Burundi and the Semliki River near the Uganda border.

Black-tailed Green Tree Snake *Dipsadoboa weileri* A slender snake with a broad head, reaching a length of 96cm. Colour apparently unknown, might be dark green, brown or grey. Known from Nyanda in Rwanda and the Mabira Forest in Uganda, also recorded from the Semliki River near the Uganda border.

Werner's Tree Snake *Dipsadoboa werneri* A slender snake, reaching 1.2m, with a large head and prominent yellow eyes, yellow-brown or grey above, each scale with a lighter edging. Known only from the Usambara Mountains in Tanzania.

Usambara Vine Snake *Thelotornis usambaricus* A slender vine snake, length 1.3m, top of the head bright green, body mottled brown, green and grey with light and dark speckling, recorded in the southeast corner of Kenya and Usambara Mountains.

Uluguru Dagger-tooth Snake *Xyelodontophis uluguruensis* Recently described, a snake reaching 1.3m, with a brown head, the front half is barred black and yellow. Known only from the Uluguru Mountains.

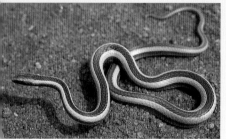

Striped Bark Snake
Hemirhagerrhis kelleri

Identification: Up to 40cm. A small, fast-moving striped snake, with a brown vertebral stripe, (sometimes this is very faint) a yellow or fawn dorsolateral stripe, brown on the flanks.

Habitat and Distribution: Semi-desert, dry savanna and coastal thicket, from sea level to about 1,500m altitude. Widespread in eastern Kenya and north-east Tanzania in suitable habitat.

Natural History: Diurnal, partially arboreal, climbing low trees and bushes. Fairly quick-moving, liable to be mistaken for a sand snake. Lays eggs. Diet: lizards, especially geckos and gecko eggs.

Bark Snake
Hemirhagerrhis nototaenia

Identification: Up to 50cm. A small, fast-moving grey snake, with a small head and raised eyebrows. Usually some shade of mottled grey or grey-brown, with a dark zigzag vertebral stripe, that may go all the way to the tail or break up into crossbars (or disappear).

Habitat and Distribution: Semi-desert, savanna and coastal thicket, from sea level to about 1,600m altitude. Widespread in northern and eastern Kenya and eastern Tanzania in suitable habitat, sporadic records in western Tanzania.

Natural History: Diurnal, partially arboreal, climbing low trees and bushes, often found climbing the bark of trees (hence the name). Fairly quick moving, liable to be mistaken for a sand snake, but may freeze when approached. Lays two to eight eggs. Diet: lizards, especially geckos and gecko eggs.

Kenyan Striped Skaapsteker
Psammophylax multisquamis

Identification: Up to 1.4m but usually 60 to 90cm. A distinctly striped rear-fanged snake, with a round pupil. Colour: usually a thin light, dark-edged vertebral line, on a broad central grey, fawn or brown dorsal stripe, with a darker flank stripe.

Habitat and Distribution: High grassland, moorland and moist savanna, from 600 to over 3,300m altitude. Widespread in high central and western Kenya and in the high country around Mt Kilimanjaro, sporadic records elsewhere from Rwanda and Tanzania.

Natural History: Diurnal and terrestrial, shelters under ground cover, in holes, rotting logs and so on. Might be nocturnal to some extent, as often under cover during the day. Quick-moving, but sometimes shams death if seized. May bask in a curious kinked fashion. Lays 4–16 eggs, the females coil around the eggs to protect them. Diet: lizards, amphibians, rodents and small snakes.

Rufous Beaked Snake
Rhamphiophis rostratus

Identification: Up to 1.6m. A big, stocky, rear-fanged snake, with a short pointed head. A dark line runs through the eye. Colour variable, may be grey, brown, pinkish or almost white, in darker specimens the scales towards the tail have light centres, the snake looks speckled.

Habitat and Distribution: Semi-desert, savanna, coastal thicket and woodland, from sea level to about 1,500m altitude. Widespread in northern and eastern Kenya and northern and eastern Tanzania, sporadic in south-western Tanzania.

Natural History: Diurnal and terrestrial, although it will climb low bushes. Very secretive, spends much time in holes. When moving, it jerks its head from side to side. If threatened, it can spread a small hood, it may hiss loudly and bite. Lays 4–15 eggs. Eats a wide range of prey: other snakes, lizards, frogs and rodents, possibly invertebrates. Males have been reported neck-wrestling.

Red-spotted Beaked Snake
Rhamphiophis rubropunctatus

Identification: Up to 2.5m. A big, slim, rear-fanged snake, with a large dark eye. Grey in colour, with a rufous head, juveniles are heavily spotted red on a cream background.

Habitat and Distribution: Near-desert, semi-desert, savanna, coastal thicket and woodland, from sea level to about 1,200m altitude. Widespread in south-eastern Kenya and north-eastern Tanzania, sporadic in northern Kenya.

Natural History: Diurnal and terrestrial, although it will climb low bushes. Fast-moving. Very secretive, spends much time in holes. Lays eggs. Diet known to include squirrels and smaller rodents and lizards.

Olive Sand Snake/Hissing Sand Snake
Psammophis mossambicus

Identification: Up to 1.7m. A big brown rear-fanged snake, with a rounded snout. Brown or grey above. All the dorsal scales, (or just the central ones) may be black-edged, giving a finely striped appearance. Yellow or cream below, sometimes with faint or dark ventral stripes.

Habitat and Distribution: Savanna, woodland and riverine areas in semi-desert, from sea level to over 2,500 m. Within East Africa, absent only from dry northern and eastern Kenya.

Natural History: Diurnal and partially arboreal, fast moving and alert, dashing noisily away if scared. Often mistaken for more dangerous species. Lays from 8–30 eggs. Diet: mostly lizards, sometimes small snakes, rodents, frogs and birds.

Venom: Not life threatening, but known to cause local pain, swelling, nausea and intense local itching.

Dwarf Sand Snake
Psammophis angolensis

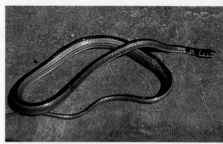

Identification: Up to 50cm. A small, striped snake, very small for a sand snake, brownish in colour, with a darker vertebral stripe, the head is black with fine light crossbars.

Habitat and Distribution: Savanna and grassland, from sea level to about 2,000m. Occurs almost throughout Tanzania, although not recorded on the islands.

Natural History: Diurnal, terrestrial and secretive. Rarely bites even if picked up. Lays 2–5 eggs. Diet: lizards, skink eggs and frogs.

Eastern Stripe-bellied Sand Snake
Psammophis orientalis

Identification: Up to 1.25m. A slim, fast-moving, rear-fanged snake, with a long head, pointed nose and big eye. Usually light brown above (sometimes dark), with faint striping, like a washed-out version of the Northern Stripe-bellied Sand Snake. There are two distinct black stripes underneath, with yellow between them and white or yellow outside.

Habitat and Distribution: Coastal thicket, savanna and woodland, from sea level to 1,300m. Occurs along the East African coast, inland on the Rufiji River and in south-east Tanzania.

Natural History: Diurnal, partially arboreal, fast-moving and alert. Lays from 2–10 eggs. Diet: mostly lizards but will take small snakes and other vertebrates. A common snake on the East African coast, and very variable in colour.

Northern Stripe-bellied Sand Snake
Psammophis sudanensis

Identification: Up to 1.2m. A slim, fast-moving, rear-fanged snake, with a long head, pointed nose and big eye. Brown above, with two yellow dorso-lateral stripes and often a fine, light, dotted, vertebral line. There are two distinct black stripes underneath, with yellow between them and white outside.

Habitat and Distribution: Coastal thicket, savanna and woodland, from sea level to 2,000m, sometimes higher. Occurs in north-central Tanzania, central Kenya, north-west Kenya and north-east Uganda. Sporadic records elsewhere.

Natural History: Diurnal, partially arboreal, fast moving and alert. Quite common in some areas. Lays from four to ten eggs. Diet: mostly lizards but will take small snakes and other vertebrates.

Speckled Sand Snake
Psammophis punctulatus

Identification: Up to 1.9m. A big, slim, striped snake. Grey (smaller specimens) to yellow (large specimens), with three distinct black stripes, lower flanks and ventrals heavily spotted, head orange, eye large with a round yellow iris.

Habitat and Distribution: Dry savanna and semi-desert, from sea level to around 1,400m. Found in extreme north-east Tanzania, almost throughout eastern and northern Kenya.

Natural History: Diurnal and partially arboreal. Probably the fastest snake in Africa. Hunts both by ambush and by prowling. Sleeps under ground cover, in holes or out on a branch. Lays 3–12 eggs. Diet: mostly lizards and snakes, but will take other vertebrates as well.

Venom: A bite from a large specimen caused intense local itching, swelling and pain.

Link-marked Sand Snake
Psammophis biseriatus

Identification: Up to 1m. A slim, grey, rear-fanged snake, with a long head, pointed nose and big eye. Speckled grey, with a broad olive or brown vertebral stripe, edged with dark bars; the scales on the vertebral row are light yellow-brown.

Habitat and Distribution: Coastal thicket, dry savanna and semi-desert, from sea level to about 1,300m altitude. Occurs throughout northern and eastern Kenya, sporadic records in northern and eastern Tanzania.

Natural History: Diurnal, partially arboreal, living in thornbush country where its excellent camouflage makes it hard to see. Lays from two to four eggs. Diet: mostly lizards.

Venom: A prolonged bite caused swelling, pain and local haemorrhaging.

Tanganyika Sand Snake
Psammophis tanganicus

Identification: Up to 1m. A slim, rufous and grey, rear-fanged snake, with a long head, pointed, slightly bulbous nose and big eye. Flanks rufous on light grey, with a broad dark grey vertebral stripe, edged with dark bars; the scales on the vertebral row are lighter rufous.

Habitat and Distribution: Dry savanna and semi-desert, from sea level to about 1,300m altitude. Sporadically recorded throughout central and northern Tanzania and eastern and northern Kenya.

Natural History: Diurnal, partially arboreal, living in thornbush country where its excellent camouflage makes it hard to see. Seems to prefer hunting on the ground. Lays eggs. Diet: mostly lizards.

Other rear-fanged snakes found in East Africa

Striped Olympic Snake *Dromophis lineatus* To 1.2 m, a slim brown or olive snake, uniform or with three thin yellowish stripes. Resembles a sand snake. Belly edged with distinctive short transverse dark dashes. Near water sources in western East Africa.

Southern Striped Skaapsteker *Psammophylax tritaeniatus* Grows to 90cm. Closely resembles the Kenya Striped Skaapsteker, but nose slightly more pointed. Occurs in southern Tanzania.

Grey-bellied Skaapsteker *Psammophylax variabilis* A grey or olive-brown skaapsteker, uniform or with a light dorsal stripe and darker brown flank stripe, grey below. Known from Rwanda, Burundi, north and north-east of Lake Tanganyika.

Striped Beaked Snake *Rhamphiophis acutus* Small striped snake, like striped skaapsteker with pointed snout. Up to 1 m. Two subspecies: one from Murchison Falls, Uganda, other sporadically recorded from western Tanzania.

Western Beaked Snake *Rhamphiophis oxyrhynchus* A big brown, grey or orange snake, with a large eye and a pointed snout. Reaches 1.5m. Sporadic records from eastern to western Uganda.

Beautiful Sand Snake *Psammophis pulcher* A rare, tiny sand snake, reaching 43cm, striped orange, fawn/grey and black, white below. Only two records, Voi and Mwingi, eastern Kenya.

Lake Rukwa Sand Snake *Psammophis rukwae* Looks like a large Northern Stripe-bellied Sand Snake. Identified by fine dark ventral lines. Sporadically recorded from central and north-western Tanzania, western Kenya and eastern Uganda.

Olive Marsh Snake
Natriciteres olivacea

Identification: Up to 55cm. A small, harmless snake, with a short head, round pupil and distinctive black barring on the lips. Colour variable, usually brown or green, with a vertebral stripe of a different colour.

Habitat and Distribution: Coastal bush and savanna, from sea level to 2,200m. Usually near water sources, and occurs in quite dry country in the vicinity of water, for example at Lake Baringo. Found all around the Lake Victoria basin, southern and eastern Tanzania and the north Kenya coast, sporadic records elsewhere.

Natural History: Terrestrial and diurnal, crepuscular (active at dawn and dusk) in some areas. Slow-moving, hunting among waterside vegetation for the amphibians and fish that it eats. Lays four to 11 eggs. The tail is easily broken and not regenerated.

Montane Egg-eater
Dasypeltis atra

Identification: Up to 1.1m. A small, harmless snake, with a bullet-shaped head, small but prominent eyes and strongly keeled scales. Colour variable, may be black, rufous, pink, or brown with or without darker markings along the spine and flanks.

Habitat and Distribution: High-altitude savanna, grassland, woodland and forest, from 500m (sometimes lower) to 2,800m. Known from high forests on either side of the Rift Valley in Kenya, southern Uganda, Rwanda and Burundi, one record from Moshi in northern Tanzania.

Natural History: Hunts on the ground and in trees and bushes. Nocturnal, shelters under ground cover or in tree holes during the day. Eats only birds eggs. From 7–14 eggs laid. If threatened, may shift the body in a series of C-shaped coils and rub the coils against each other, producing a hissing sound, and strike with open mouth.

Rufous Egg-eater
Dasypeltis medici

Identification: Up to 1m. A slim, harmless snake, with a bullet-shaped head, small but prominent eyes and strongly keeled scales. Colour variable, may be pink, orange, red, grey, fawn or brown. Two subspecies occur: the northern subspecies (*D. m. lamuensis*, found north and west of Mombasa) usually mono-coloured red, orange or pink; the southern subspecies (*D. m. medici*, south of Mombasa) usually brown or orange with three to seven distinct V-shapes on the neck, dark and light blotches along the spine, dark bars on flanks.

Habitat and Distribution: Coastal bush and savanna, from sea level to about 1,000m altitude. Found along the East African coast, inland in Tsavo National Park and on the Rufiji River.

Natural History: Semi-arboreal, hunting on the ground and in trees and bushes. Nocturnal, shelters under ground cover, in holes or recesses in trees during the day. Eats only birds' eggs. Lays from 6–28 eggs. Some specimens show the C-coil threat described for the Montane Egg-eater.

Common Egg-eater
Dasypeltis scabra

Identification: Up to 1.1m. A slim, harmless snake, with a bullet-shaped head, small but prominent eyes and strongly keeled scales. Colour variable; usually brown or grey with dark or faint rhombic markings all along the back and dark flank bars, mono-coloured

reddish, grey or brown specimens occur, sometimes with fine white dots along the back.

Habitat and Distribution: Semi-desert, savanna, woodland and forest, from sea level to over 2,600m altitude. Probably occurs throughout East Africa, but records sporadic for northern Kenya.

Natural History: Semi-arboreal, hunting on the ground and in trees and bushes. Nocturnal, shelters under ground cover, in holes or recesses in trees during the day. Eats only birds' eggs. Lays from 6–28 eggs. Often shows the C-coil threat, as described for the Montane Egg-eater, and closely resembles the very dangerous North-east African Carpet Viper.

Other harmless snakes found in East Africa

Forest Marsh Snake *Natriciteres sylvatica* A small, dark olive or grey-black snake, with a dark vertebral stripe, reaches about 40cm. Resembles the Olive Marsh Snake, found in southern Tanzania.

Pemba Marsh Snake *Natriciteres pembana* A small, dark olive-coloured snake, grows to 30cm, found only on Pemba Island.

Western Forest Egg-eater *Dasypeltis fasciata* A big, brown or yellow-brown egg-eater, growing to 1.1m, known only from extreme western Uganda.

Western Forest Egg-eater
Dasypeltis fasciata

African Burrowing Snakes: Family Atractaspididae

A family of small burrowing snakes; most have small, short heads and small eyes. Most have grooved rear-fangs, apart from the dangerous burrowing asps, which have front fangs, and the Western Forest Centipede-eater, which has no fangs. Twenty-six species, in six genera, occur in East Africa.

Cape Centipede-eater
Aparallactus capensis

Identification: Up to 30cm. A tiny, slim, rear-fanged snake, with a black head and a brown body, the body often with fine dark stripes.

Habitat and Distribution: Coastal thicket and moist savanna, from sea level to 1,600m altitude. Occurs along the Tanzanian coast, inland to Mt Kilimanjaro, along the Rufiji River and along the southern border. Sporadic records from the west.

Natural History: Lives underground, in holes and cracks, root clusters, soft soil, and termite hills. Sometimes on the surface on wet nights. They lay two to four eggs. Diet: centipedes.

Black Centipede-eater
Aparallactus guentheri

Identification: Up to 50cm. A tiny, slim, rear-fanged snake. Adults grey or black, juveniles have two distinct light neck crossbars.

Habitat and Distribution: Coastal thicket, moist savanna and evergreen hill forest, from sea level to 1,200m altitude. Sporadic records from eastern Tanzania and south-east Kenya.

Natural History: Lives underground, in holes and cracks, root clusters, soft soil, and termite hills. Sometimes on the surface on wet nights. Lays eggs. Diet: centipedes.

Jackson's Centipede-eater
Aparallactus jacksoni

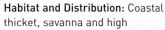

Identification: Up to 28cm. A tiny, slim, rear-fanged snake. Brown with a black head and usually a yellow collar. Sometimes tiny black dots on the back.

Habitat and Distribution: Coastal thicket, savanna and high

grassland, from sea level to 2,200m. Widespread in north-eastern Tanzania and central Kenya, sporadic records elsewhere.

Natural History: Lives underground, in holes and cracks, root clusters, soft soil, and termite hills. Sometimes on the surface on wet nights. Gives live birth, to two or three youngsters. Diet: centipedes.

Plumbeous Centipede-eater
Aparallactus lunulatus

Identification: Up to 50cm. A small, slim, rear-fanged snake. Adults usually lead-grey or brown, often with a yellow or tan head and a broad black collar, some juveniles have dark crossbars on the neck.

Habitat and Distribution: Coastal thicket, moist and dry savanna and

semi-desert, from sea level to 2,200m altitude. Widespread but sporadic throughout East Africa.

Natural History: Lives underground, in holes and cracks, root clusters, soft soil, and termite hills. Sometimes on the surface on wet nights. Lays two to four eggs. Diet: centipedes.

Christy's Snake-eater
Polemon christyi

Identification: Up to 50cm. A small, dark, rear-fanged snake, with a stubby head and a short tail that ends in a spike. Black, grey or brown in colour.

Habitat and Distribution: Forest, woodland and wooded savanna, from 600 to 1,700m altitude. Occurs in western Kenya (Kakamega area), southern Uganda, Rwanda and Burundi. Sporadic records from south-west Tanzania and Budongo Forest in Uganda.

Natural History: Lives underground, in holes and cracks, may hide in leaf litter. Sometimes on the surface on wet nights. Slow-moving and inoffensive. Lays eggs. Eats other snakes, even its own kind.

Pale-collared Snake-eater
Polemon graueri

Identification: Up to 85cm. A small, rear-fanged snake. Adults dark grey or bluish-black, with a broad white head bar. Scales sometimes white-edged.

Habitat and Distribution: Forest and high woodland, from 800 to 1,800m altitude. Occurs along the Albertine Rift from Burundi to just south of Lake Albert, sporadic records in north-central Uganda.

Natural History: Lives underground, in holes and cracks, may hide in leaf litter. Sometimes on the surface on wet nights. Slow-moving and inoffensive. Lays eggs. Eats other snakes, especially blind snakes.

Mpwapwa Purple-glossed Snake
Amblyodipsas dimidiata

Identification: Up to 50cm. A small, rear-fanged snake, iridescent blackish-brown or purple-brown above, with a vivid chrome-yellow flank stripe and a long, sharp snout.

Habitat and Distribution: Dry savanna of central Tanzania, in the Dodoma-Mpwapwa area.

Natural History: Poorly known, but lives underground, its sharp snout suggests it pushes through soil and sand. Sometimes on the surface on wet nights. Slow-moving and inoffensive. Probably lays eggs and eats worm lizards.

Common Purple-glossed Snake
Amblyodipsas polylepis

Identification: Up to 70cm. A small, stout, rear-fanged snake with a rounded snout and a short blunt tail. Purple, black or pinkish-brown above, with the distinct purple gloss on the scales that give it its name.

Habitat and Distribution: Coastal woodland and thicket, savanna and evergreen hill forest, from sea level to about 1,500m. Occurs in south-west Tanzania, right along the East African coast, sporadic records inland including the highlands of northern Tanzania, and Chuka and the Nyambeni Hills in Kenya.

Natural History: Lives underground or in leaf litter, may hide under logs and rocks. Nocturnal, sometimes on the surface after rain. Nervous and quite quick-moving; will bite furiously if handled. Lays eggs. Diet: smaller snakes, skinks and caecilians.

Two-coloured Snake
Micrelaps bicoloratus

Identification: Up to 33cm. A small, rear-fanged snake, variable in colour. Usually brown above, flanks and ventrals white or cream, sometimes the flanks have a stripe of black, white-edged scales. Specimens from the low country around Mt Kilimanjaro have a yellow vertebral stripe. This form was recently named as a new subspecies, *M. b. moyeri*.

Habitat and Distribution: Coastal bush, savanna and high grassland, from sea level to 2,000m altitude. Widespread in north-east Tanzania and south-east Kenya; one record from Laikipia.

Natural History: Poorly known, but lives underground, active at night, hides under ground cover during the day. Lays eggs. Diet unknown but other *Micrelaps* eat snakes.

Desert Black-headed Snake
Micrelaps vaillanti
(formerly *boettgeri*)

Identification: Up to 50cm. A little grey snake, speckled white, the head is black, some specimens uniformly dark brown or purple-brown above.

Habitat and Distribution: Semi-desert, dry and moist savanna, from 200 to 1,700m altitude. North-eastern Tanzania, south-east Kenya, sporadic records from northern Kenya and eastern Uganda.

Natural History: Poorly known. Lives underground, active at night, hides under ground cover during the day. Lays up to six eggs. Diet: small snakes and burrowing skinks.

Bibron's Burrowing Asp
Atractaspis bibronii

Identification: Up to 70 cm. A slim dark dangerous front-fanged snake, snout prominent, tail short, ending in a spike. Dark brown or grey-black, sometimes with a purplish sheen. The light belly colour may extend slightly up the flanks.

Habitat and Distribution: Coastal bush, woodland and savanna, from sea level to 1 800 m altitude. Southern Rwanda, Burundi, eastern and northwestern Tanzania, coast and Kitui in Kenya.

Natural History: Lives in holes or soft soil, hides under ground cover. Sometimes active on the surface on wet nights. Quite fast moving. If molested or restrained, may point the head at the ground, forming an inverted U. If held, they stab backwards with their long fangs. Lays 4-7 eggs. Diet: other snakes, lizards, worm lizards and small mammals.

Venom: Not usually deadly but can cause swelling, pain, local necrosis and swollen lymph nodes. N.B. Burrowing asps cannot be held safely by hand, due to their long fangs, short head and ability to jerk upwards if held by tail.

Variable Burrowing Asp
Atractaspis irregularis

Identification: Up to 66 cm. A slim dark dangerous front-fanged snake with a short tail that ends in a spike. Shiny black or blackish-grey, the scales are iridescent.

Habitat and Distribution: Moist savanna, woodland and forest, from 600 to 1,800 m altitude. Highlands of central and western Kenya, western Uganda and down the Albertine Rift to north-west Tanzania.

Natural History: Burrowing, living in holes or soft soil, may shelter under ground cover. May emerge on wet nights. Quite fast moving. If molested and restrained, may point head at ground forming an inverted U. If held, stab backwards with their long fangs. Lays up to 6 eggs. Diet: other snakes, lizards, small mammals.

Venom: As for the previous species. Human fatalities are known. Burrowing asps cannot be held safely, as described above.

Small-scaled Burrowing Asp
Atractaspis microlepidota

Identification: Up to 1.1m. A
relatively large, dangerous, front-
fanged snake, big adults can be stout,
with a broad blunt head and short
tail that ends in a spike. Usually
shiny black, grey, brown or purple-
brown, sometimes darkens towards
the head. The scales are iridescent.

Habitat and Distribution: Coastal bush and thicket, savanna
and semi-desert, from sea level to 1,800m but most
common below 1,000m. Occurs in extreme north-east
Tanzania and east and south-east Kenya, sporadic records in
northern Kenya, and the Mara-Serengeti area.

Natural History: Burrowing, living in holes or soft soil, can
be found under rocks, logs and other ground cover. May prowl on the surface
on wet nights. Quite fast-moving. Points the nose like other burrowing asps.
Lays up to eight eggs. Eats other snakes, lizards, and small mammals.

Venom: Causes swelling, pain, occasional local necrosis and swollen lymph
nodes. Human fatalities are known. N.B. Burrowing asps cannot be held
safely by the hand. See the venom note for Bibron's Burrowing Asp.

Other burrowing snakes found in East Africa

Western Forest Centipede-eater *Aparallactus modestus* A small, grey or
grey-brown snake (juveniles have a white head bar), reaching 65cm length.
Sporadically recorded from forest and woodland of central and western
Uganda.

Malindi Centipede-eater *Aparallactus turneri* A very small, slim, brown
snake, with a black head and a black collar, reaching 20cm length.
Sporadically recorded from the Kenya Coast, from Mkonumbi near Lamu
south to Diani Beach. Endemic to Kenya.

Usambara Centipede-eater *Aparallactus werneri* A small, brown snake, top
of head darker, with a black collar. Has the usual stubby tail. Grows to 36cm.
Sporadically recorded from coastal and hill forests of eastern Tanzania.

Fawn-headed Snake-eater *Polemon collaris* A little, grey or grey-brown
snake, top of head pale fawn or fulvous. Grows to 86cm. Recorded from
extreme western Uganda.

Yellow-necked Snake-eater *Polemon fulvicollis* A little snake, reaching
50cm, iridescent black with a fawn patch on the nape or a yellow collar.
Only known from the Bwamba Forest, western Uganda.

continued over

Gabon Snake-eater *Polemon gabonensis* A small, grey-brown snake with a short, stubby tail. Greyish-blue above, with a light reddish-brown stripe very low on the sides. Sometimes with a yellow collar. Reaches 80cm. Known only from the Bwamba Forest.

Butler's Black-and-yellow Burrowing Snake *Chilorhinophis butleri* A slender, black and yellow striped snake, with a black head and tail tip. Grows to 36cm. Known from extreme south-east Tanzania.

Gerard's Black-and-yellow Burrowing Snake *Chilorhinophis gerardi* A slender, black and yellow striped snake, with a black head with fine yellow crossbars, and a black tail tip. Grows to 57cm. Sporadic records from the shores of Lake Tanganyika.

Ionides' Purple-glossed Snake *Amblyodipsas katangensis* A slim, sharp-nosed snake, black above, sometimes chequered black and white below. Length to 40cm. Known from south-eastern Tanzania.

Taita Hills Purple-glossed Snake *Amblyodipsas teitana* A small, dark snake, black above, some white under the chin. Known from a single 43cm specimen from the Taita Hills.

Western Purple-glossed Snake *Amblyodipsas unicolor* A stocky, snake with a blunt tail. Dark grey, purple-grey or black above and below with the characteristic purple gloss. Grows to 1.1m. Sporadic records from the Kerio Valley and north-central Uganda.

Slender Burrowing Asp *Atractaspis aterrima* A slender burrowing asp, reaching 70cm, black or blackish-grey. Sporadically recorded from south-east Tanzania (in hill woodland) and north-west Uganda.

Engdahl's Burrowing Asp *Atractaspis engdahli* A small burrowing asp, growing to 66cm. May be blue-black, black or red-brown in colour. Recorded only from Wajir Bor in north-east Kenya.

Western Forest Centipede-eater
Aparallactus modestus
(see page 137)

Cobras, Mambas and Relatives: Family Elapidae

A family of dangerous snakes with short, erect, immovable poison fangs at the front of the upper jaw. There are over 200 species worldwide, mostly in Australasia. There are over 30 species of elapid in Africa; 14 species in five genera occur in East Africa; one is endemic. They range in size from the Black Mamba, which reaches over 3.5m, to the little garter snakes, mostly smaller than one metre. All are venomous; the mambas and cobras are among East Africa's most dangerous snakes and kill a number of people every year.

In the field, the size (most are large) and behaviour are useful aids to elapid identification. Mambas have a distinctive, 'coffin-shaped' head. Cobras spread a hood, but bear in mind that a cobra with a spread hood is an angry snake. A cobra that hasn't spread its hood can look like a nondescript, harmless snake. Several elapids will actively defend themselves if they feel threatened; their large size, alertness, speed of movement and venom make them very dangerous snakes. Several cobras can spit venom; if this enters the eyes, it causes agonising pain and can do permanent damage. A bite from an elapid (apart from the garter snakes) is a major medical emergency. Hence elapids should be approached only if strictly necessary, and with considerable caution.

Boulenger's Garter Snake
Elapsoidea boulengeri

Identification: Up to 75cm. A small, glossy snake, with a short head. Juveniles (far right) are banded black and white; these bands fade with age to irregular white rings and then disappear, leaving a uniformly black adult (above).

Habitat and Distribution: Moist savanna, from sea level to about 1,500m. Known within Tanzania from Kibondo in the north-west, Lake Rukwa area and the south-east corner.

Natural History: Burrowing, living in holes or soft soil, can be found under rocks, logs and other ground cover. May prowl on the surface on wet nights. Lays from four to eight eggs. Eats other snakes, lizards, frogs and small rodents. Not at all aggressive; if molested may hiss and inflate the body but rarely tries to bite.

Venom: A neurotoxin but not life-threatening, known to cause swelling, pain and nasal congestion.

East African Garter Snake
Elapsoidea loveridgei

Identification: Up to 65cm. A small, glossy banded snake (far left), with a short head. Ground colour black, with

19–36 narrow white, white and pink, yellow or white-edged grey-brown bands. These bands sometimes darken at the centre, to become two white rings (left), but rarely disappear.

Habitat and Distribution: Mid-altitude woodland, moist savanna and grassland, from 600–2,200m. Found in north-central Tanzania, highlands on both sides of the Rift Valley in Kenya, most of southern Uganda, Rwanda and northern Burundi.

Natural History: Terrestrial and slow-moving. Lives in holes or under ground cover during the day, sometimes prowls on the surface at night, especially after rain. Lays eggs. Eats other snakes, lizards, reptile eggs, frogs and small rodents. Gentle and non-aggressive, but some specimens, if molested, may flatten and inflate the body, elevate the head and neck and jerk from side to side.

Venom: Details unknown. No fatalities recorded; known symptoms include local pain, swelling and swollen lymph glands.

Usambara Garter Snake
Elapsoidea nigra

Identification: Up to 60cm. A small, glossy banded snake. Juveniles (far left) are grey, with black, white-edged bands and an orange head,

fading when adults (above) to fine white rings on a black body.

Habitat and Distribution: Forest, woodland and moist savanna, from 300 to 1,900m. Known from north-east Tanzania (Usambara, Uluguru and North Pare Mountains, Magrotto Hill), and the Shimba Hills in Kenya.

Natural History: Terrestrial and slow-moving. Lives in holes or under ground cover during the day, sometimes prowls on the surface at night, especially after rain. Lays two to five eggs. Eats caecilians. Gentle and non-aggressive, but may lash about if molested.

Venom: No details known.

Banded Water Cobra
Boulengerina annulata

Identification: Up to 2.7m. A big, heavy-bodied snake. Lake Tanganyika specimens are brown, darkening to grey and then black on the tail, with two to seven black rings on the neck. Elsewhere, specimens are brown with black rings.

Habitat and Distribution: In East Africa only definitely recorded from Lake Tanganyika.

Natural History: An aquatic snake, hunts fish in the water, by day and by night. Moves ponderously on land, but a superb, fast swimmer. Hides in waterside rocks formations, root cluster, also in the rocks of jetties. Non-aggressive, but spreads a broad hood if cornered. Diet: fish. Lays eggs.

Venom: No details known, probably neurotoxic; potentially dangerous.

Egyptian Cobra
Naja haje

Identification: Up to 2.5m. A big, thick-bodied cobra. Usually some shade of brown or rufous above, yellow or cream below (this may extend up onto the flanks), usually with a broad, dark throat bar. Juveniles may be tan or rufous, with fine dark bars.

Habitat and Distribution: Moist and dry savanna, woodland and grassland, from 1,000 to 1,600m altitude. Found from Nairobi south to north-central and north-western Tanzania, and in most of north-east Uganda, sporadic records elsewhere.

Natural History: Terrestrial, active by day and by night. Lives in termite holes, rock fissures and holes. Clumsy but quick-moving. If molested, it rears up, spreads a broad hood, may rush forward and strike. Lays up to 20 eggs. Eats a wide range of prey: amphibians, eggs, small mammals, snakes.

Venom: A potent neurotoxin, causing flaccid paralysis. Fatalities not uncommon; bites must be treated as a medical emergency.

Forest Cobra
Naja melanoleuca

Identification: Up to 2.7m. A big, thick-bodied cobra. Those from western East Africa usually glossy black above, cream below, with black throat bars and blotches; those from the east usually speckled brown, yellow or tan below, with heavy dark mottling.

Habitat and Distribution: Forest, woodland, coastal thicket, moist savanna and grassland, from sea level to 2,500+m altitude. Found in western Kenya, most of Rwanda and Uganda (except the north-east). Also found along the East African coast, north to the Sabaki River mouth. Sporadic records elsewhere in forests.

Natural History: Terrestrial, and semi-arboreal, climbs well. Quick-moving and alert. Active by day and night. Shelters in holes, rock crevices, vegetation piles. If molested, it rears up to a considerable height and spreads a long narrow hood; if cornered, may rush forward and strike. Lays from 15–26 eggs. Eats a wide range of prey: amphibians, fish, snakes, lizards and small mammals.

Venom: A potent neurotoxin. Fatalities are known; bites must be treated as a medical emergency.

Mozambique Spitting Cobra
Naja mossambica

Identification: Up to 1.5m. A relatively small cobra. Brown or pinkish above, the scales sometimes black edged so it appears finely barred, the neck and throat strongly blotched and barred black.

Habitat and Distribution: Coastal forest, thicket and moist savanna, at low altitude below 1,000m. Occurs in south-east Tanzania, Pemba and Zanzibar.

Natural History: Mostly terrestrial, but climbs well. Quick-moving and alert. Adults usually active by night, juveniles often by day. Shelters in holes, rock crevices, vegetation piles. If molested, it rears up, spreads a broad hood and spits venom. Lays from 10–22 eggs. Eats a wide range of prey; fond of amphibians, but also takes snakes, lizards and small mammals.

Venom: As for the Black-necked Spitting Cobra (see next species).

Black-necked Spitting Cobra
Naja nigricollis

Identification: There are two forms; the brown one reaches 2.7m, the pink-necked form 2m. A thick-bodied cobra. One form (top) is brown-olive or grey above, lighter below, with brown speckling and a deep, darker throat bar. The smaller form (bottom) is black, grey or coppery, the throat is banded black and pink or orange, sometimes yellow. Sometimes the head and neck are black, the body is grey.

Habitat and Distribution: Coastal thicket, semi-desert, moist and dry savanna and open woodland, from sea level to about 1,800m altitude. Occurs almost throughout East Africa in that altitudinal range, but few records from northern Kenya and southern and western Tanzania. The brown form is more abundant at lower altitudes.

Natural History: Largely terrestrial, but climbs readily. Quick-moving and alert. Usually nocturnal, juveniles often active by day. Hides in termite hills, holes, rock fissures and so on. If threatened, it will rear up, spread a hood and accurately spit venom, to a distance of over 3m, usually aiming for the eyes.
These snakes lay 8–22 eggs. Diet: amphibians, birds and their eggs, small rodents, snakes and lizards.

Venom: Cytotoxic in effect, but neurological effects have been noted. Bites known to cause swelling, pain and necrosis. Fatalities are known; bites must be treated as a medical emergency. However, venom in the eye is the common result of an encounter with a spitting cobra, in which case the eyes should be gently washed out with copious quantities of water (or other bland fluids like milk) and the victim taken for a medical check-up.

Red Spitting Cobra
Naja pallida

Identification: Up to 1.5m. A relatively small cobra. Usually red, orange or pink above (occasionally grey or yellow), with a black throat band. Adults become dull red-brown, and the throat band fades.

Habitat and Distribution: Dry savanna and semi-desert, from sea level to about 1,200m altitude. Occurs throughout northern and eastern Kenya, and dry north-east Tanzania.

Natural History: Mostly terrestrial, but can climb. Quick-moving and alert. Adults usually active by night, juveniles often by day. Shelters in holes and termitaria, or under rocks, inside old logs, etc. If molested, rears up, spreads a narrow hood and spits venom. Lays from 6–15 eggs. Eats wide range of prey: fond of amphibians, but also takes small mammals, lizards and birds.

Venom: Little known, not usually regarded as deadly, probably similar to that of other spitting cobras. Venom in the eye is the common result of an encounter with a Red Spitting Cobra; see the venom notes for Black-necked Spitting Cobra.

Gold's Tree Cobra
Pseudohaje goldii

Identification: Up to 2.7m. A big, shiny thin-bodied tree cobra with a very short head and a huge dark eye. Glossy black above, yellow below, scales on the junction yellow with black edging.

Habitat and Distribution: Forest at medium altitude, 600–2,000m (although reported from urban areas elsewhere). Known from Nandi and Kakamega Forests in Kenya, Mabira Forest, some lakeshore forests and forests of northern Albertine Rift in Uganda.

Natural History: A quick-moving, active arboreal snake, although it will descend to the ground. Has been found in squirrel traps in Kenya. Apparently diurnal. Known to eat amphibians and fish, might take small mammals. Lays 10–20 eggs.

Venom: A potent neurotoxin, but no known bite cases.

Green Mamba
Dendroaspis angusticeps

Identification: Up to 2.3m. Big and slender, bright uniform green above, sometimes a few yellow scales.

Habitat and Distribution: Coastal bush and forest, moist savanna and evergreen hill forest, from sea level to 1,700m, although usually below 500m altitude. Occurs from the Tana Delta south along the entire East African coastal plain, inland to the Usambara Mountains, up the Rufiji River and south-eastern Tanzania. Isolated reports from Kibwezi, Meru National Park and Nyambeni Hills (Kenya) and the Arusha-Moshi area (Tanzania).

Natural History: A fast-moving, diurnal, secretive tree snake. Climbs expertly, and sleeps up in the branches. Relatively abundant in some coastal and lowland forests. Not aggressive. Lays up to 17 eggs. Diet includes birds, nestlings, rodents and bats.

Venom: A potent neurotoxin, causing neurological symptoms. Not as dangerous as the Black Mamba, but bites must be treated as a medical emergency.

Jameson's Mamba
Dendroaspis jamesoni

Identification: Up to 2.7m. A big, slender snake with a long head and a small eye. Dull green above, neck and throat yellow, tail scales yellow-edged black, becoming black posteriorly. Head scales often black-edged.

Habitat and Distribution: Forest, woodland, forest-savanna mosaic and deforested areas, from 600 up to 2,200m altitude. Known from the Kakamega area in Kenya (possibly in other western Kenyan forest), the northern lakeshore in Uganda and forests of the Albertine Rift.

Natural History: A fast-moving, diurnal, secretive tree snake. Climbs expertly. Not aggressive but may occasionally flatten the neck if cornered. Lays eggs. Diet includes birds, nestlings and rodents.

Venom: Little is known, but probably a potent neurotoxin, as possessed by other mambas.

Black Mamba
Dendroaspis polylepis

Identification: Up to 3.2m, possibly larger. A long, slender snake, with a distinct 'coffin-shaped' head. Colour olive, brownish, yellow-brown or grey, sometimes very dark but never really black, despite the name. Sometimes heavily speckled black towards the tail, some snakes have rows of lighter and darker scales,

giving the impression of oblique dark and light bars. Scales sometimes with a distinct purple bloom.

Habitat and Distribution: Coastal bush and forest, moist and dry savanna and woodland, from sea level to about 1,600m, although usually below 1,200m altitude. Often in areas with big trees or rocky hills. Occurs almost throughout Tanzania, southern Kenya, eastern Uganda and low eastern Rwanda. Absent from high central and western Kenya, and records sporadic in northern Kenya.

Natural History: A very fast-moving, alert, diurnal snake, equally at home on the ground or climbing trees or rocks. May shelter, often for several months, in holes, termitaria, rock fissures, tree beehives or even roof spaces. Has an undeserved reputation for aggression, but can be truculent if threatened; may rear up, spread a narrow hood, open the black-lined mouth, hiss and shake the head. Lays from 6–17 eggs. Males indulge in combat, neck wrestling while intertwined. Diet includes small mammals, birds, nestlings and snakes.

Venom: A potent, fast-acting neurotoxin and cardiotoxin, causing paralysis. Many bites are fatal; a Black Mamba bite must be treated as a major medical emergency, and large quantities of antivenom may be needed.

Another elapid and a sea snake found in East Africa

Central African Garter Snake *Elapsoidea laticincta* A stout little snake, reaching 56cm, with 8–17 pale brown or rufous bands on a black body; in adults these fade to white double rings. Recorded from Nimule on the northern Uganda border.

Yellow-bellied Sea Snake *Pelamis platurus* A long-headed sea snake, with a laterally compressed body, reaching 90cm. Black above, yellow below, the tail spotted yellow and black. The only sea snake found off the East African coast; sporadically recorded between Kilwa and Malindi. Highly venomous but no known bite cases.

Vipers or Adders: Family Viperidae

A family of dangerous snakes with long, tubular, folding poison fangs at the front of the upper jaw. There are around 50 species of viper in Africa; 21 species in seven genera occur in East Africa; six are endemic. They range in size from the Puff Adder, reaching nearly 2m, to the tiny 35cm Kenya Montane Viper. All vipers are venomous, some dangerously so. The Puff Adder and the North-east African Carpet Viper probably cause more bites than any other dangerous East African snake.

Many of the East African vipers are readily identifiable in the field (the names viper and adder are interchangeable). Most have the top of the head covered with small scales (except the night adders). A fat-bodied snake with a subtriangular head, that lies quietly when approached, is probably a viper or adder. Any snake with rectangular, subrectangular or triangular markings on its back or sides, or rows of semi-circular markings along the flanks, is probably a viper. Most bush vipers are a mixture of greens, blacks and yellows, with broad heads and thin necks, and are usually in a bush or low tree. A snake that forms C-shaped coils and rubs them together, making a noise like water falling on a hot plate, will be either a carpet viper (dangerous) or an egg-eater (harmless). Vipers are not as large and mobile as the elapids, but they can strike very quickly, often to a good distance. Most have highly potent cytotoxic venoms, causing swelling, pain and tissue destruction. Vipers should therefore be treated with caution; do not be fooled by their apparent immobility.

Snouted Night Adder
Causus defilippii

Identification: Up to 40cm. Small and stout with short head. Brown, grey or pinkish-grey, with black V-shape on head, white-edged dark blotches down back and dark oblique bars on flanks.

Habitat and Distribution: Moist and dry savanna, coastal thicket and woodland from sea level to about 1,800m. Occurs along the Kenya coast from Malindi southwards, widespread in south-eastern Tanzania.

Natural History: Terrestrial, active by day and by night. Hides in holes and under ground cover.Inflates itself and hisses loudly if molested. Diet: amphibians. Lays 3–9 eggs.

Venom: Little known, no known fatalities. Bites characterised by swelling, pain and inflamed lymph glands.

Rhombic Night Adder
Causus rhombeatus

Identification: Up to 95cm. A small, stout viper with a short head. Brown, grey or pinkish-brown in colour, with a black V-shape on the head, white-edged dark blotches down the back and dark oblique bars on the flanks.

Habitat and Distribution: Moist savanna, grassland and woodland from 600 to about 2,200m altitude. Occurs in high central and western Kenya, the southern half of Uganda and western Tanzania, sporadic records elsewhere include hilly areas around Mt Kilimanjaro.

Natural History: Terrestrial, active by day and by night. Hides in holes and under ground cover. Inflates itself and hisses loudly if molested. Diet: amphibians. Lays 3–9 eggs.

Venom: No known recent fatalities. Symptoms include pain and minor swelling.

Velvety-green Night Adder
Causus resimus

Identification: Up to 75cm. A small, stout viper with a short head. Vivid green in colour, sometimes with a black V-shaped outline on the head and scattered black blotches down the back and on the flanks. The hidden margin of the flank scales is a vivid blue.

Habitat and Distribution: Coastal savanna and thicket, savanna and woodland, from sea level to over 2,000m altitude, usually near water sources. Occurs on the Kenya coast and all around the Lake Victoria basin, western Uganda, Rwanda and Burundi. Sporadic records elsewhere.

Natural History: Terrestrial, active by day and by night. Sometimes basks. Hides in holes and under ground cover. Inflates itself and hisses loudly if molested. Diet: amphibians. Lays 4–12 eggs.

Venom: Little known; no documented bite cases.

Forest Night Adder
Causus lichtensteini

Identification: Up to 70cm. A small, relatively slim viper with a rounded head. Adults are green, with a white V-shape on the neck and black speckling; juveniles are brown.

Habitat and Distribution: Forest and woodland, usually in swampy areas. From 500 to 2,100m altitude. Forests of western Kenya, central Uganda and the Albertine Rift.

Natural History: Terrestrial and secretive, active by day. Hides in holes and under ground cover. Swims well. If molested inflates itself, hisses loudly. Diet: amphibians. Lays 4–8 eggs.

Venom: Little known; no documented bite cases.

Puff Adder
Bitis arietans

Identification: Usually from 0.7–1m, may reach 1.9m. Largest specimens found in northern Uganda, northern and eastern Kenya. A big viper with a broad triangular head. Brown, grey, (above) yellow (far right) or orange above, with light, dark-edged V-shapes along back. The short dark dashes on the outer belly, and light line between eyes, aids identification.

Habitat and Distribution: All habitats save closed forest, sea level to around 2,400m altitude, although usually below 1,700m.

Natural History: Terrestrial and nocturnal, sometimes active by day during rain. Hides in holes, under ground cover or in thick vegetation, sometimes barely hidden but perfectly camouflaged. It also freezes when approached, so liable to be trodden on by the unwary walker. Usually slow moving, creeping forward in a straight line, but can wriggle if agitated. If molested it inflates itself, hisses loudly and draws up the body, ready for a rapid strike. Males neck-wrestle in combat. Usually hunts from ambush. Gives live birth, usually 10 to 50, but one Kenyan snake had 156 young. Diet: mostly small mammals, also other small vertebrates.

Venom: Potent, causing swelling, pain, bruising, blistering and necrosis, fluid and blood leaks into tissues. Many fatalities are known; it is Africa's most dangerous snake. Treat puff adder bites as medical emergencies.

Gaboon Viper
Bitis gabonica

Identification: Up to 1.75m. A fat viper with a broad head. The back has a series of pale, sub-rectangular blotches, interspaced with dark, yellow edged hourglass markings, flanks marked with fawn or brown rhomboidal shapes.

Habitat and Distribution: Coastal thicket, forest, woodland and well-wooded savanna, from sea level to 2,100m altitude. Coastal and south-east Tanzania, forests of western Kenya, central Uganda and the Albertine Rift Valley.

Natural History: A slow-moving, terrestrial, placid, nocturnal viper, hides in leaf litter or thick vegetation, waiting to strike at passing prey. Sometimes active on wet nights. Usually 10–30 live young are produced, but up to 60 recorded. Diet: mostly small mammals, occasionally birds, lizards and amphibians.

Venom: Rarely bites but the venom is deadly; local effects similar to a Puff Adder bite and must be treated as a medical emergency.

Rhinoceros Viper
Bitis nasicornis

Identification: Up to 1.2m. A fat viper with a triangular head, usually with long horn-like scales on the nose. Head has a black arrow-shape, back marked with butterfly shapes, the flanks with bars and triangles, in green, black and maroon.

Habitat and Distribution: Forest, woodland and forest-savanna mosaic, from 600 to 2,400m altitude. Forests of western Kenya, central Uganda and the Albertine Rift, from Lake Albert south to Rwanda. One record from north-eastern Tanzania.

Natural History: A slow-moving, terrestrial nocturnal viper, sometimes climbs. Hides in vegetation and leaf litter, hunts by ambush. Swims well. Sometimes bad-tempered, hissing loudly if molested. Strikes rapidly. They give live birth, from 6–38 young. Diet: mostly small mammals, occasionally amphibians and fish. Juveniles seek out newborn mammals to eat.

Venom: Poorly known but probably similar to puff adder venom; treat bites as medical emergencies.

Kenya Horned Viper
Bitis worthingtoni

Identification: Up to 50cm. Small, stout viper with horns above eyes, grey with a pale dorsolateral line and black blotches on back and flanks.

Habitat and Distribution: High grassland and savanna from 1,600–2,700m. Found only in the

high central Rift Valley of Kenya, from the Kedong Valley and Naivasha north to Njoro, out of the Rift Valley to Kipkabus and Eldoret, on valley walls on the Kinangop and Ndabibi. Usually on broken rocky ground.

Natural History: Terrestrial, nocturnal and slow-moving. Hunts from ambush but may also prowl. Hides under ground cover, in holes and in leaf litter, sometimes climbs into low bushes. Often associated with Leleshwa (*Tarchonanthus camphoratus*) bushes. Gives live birth, 7–12 young. Eats mostly small mammals and lizards.

Venom: Unlikely to be dangerous. One bite case involved pain and mild swelling.

North-east African Carpet Viper
Echis pyramidum

Identification: Up to 70cm. Small snake, head pear-shaped, neck thin. Rufous, grey or brown above, light crossbars becoming triangles on the flanks.

Habitat and Distribution: Near desert, semi-desert and dry savanna, from 250 to 1300m altitude. Widespread in northern Kenya, from Samburu Game Reserve and Lake Baringo north to Lake Turkana and Marsabit District, isolated records from Wajir and Garissa areas.

Natural History: Terrestrial and nocturnal, hides in holes, under ground cover, partially buried or among vegetation. Quick moving. When angry it shifts a series of C-shaped coils against each other, making a hissing sound, while striking vigorously and continuously, and moving back or forwards. 4–20 eggs laid. Diet: invertebrates, and small vertebrates. Sometimes very common; near Laisamis over 7000 were collected in 4 months.

Venom: A potent, slow-acting anticoagulant; causing systemic internal bleeding, initial symptoms local pain and swelling. Treat bites as medical emergencies; monitor coagulation times.

Horned Bush Viper/Usambara Bush Viper
Atheris ceratophorus

Identification: Up to 55cm. Small bush viper with broad head and tuft of small, horn-like scales above each eye. Colour variable: black and yellow, (at times almost entirely yellow with a few black speckles, or yellow with green bars on tail), uniformly black or dark brown, or olive-green. Hatchlings black with yellow tail.

Habitat and Distribution: Around clearings in forest and woodland, from 700 to 2,000m altitude. Endemic to Tanzania and known only from the Usambara and Udzungwa Mountains.

Natural History: A slow-moving tree viper, probably opportunistically active at any time; known to bask and move in the daytime. Most active during the warmer months of the year. Male combat has been observed. They give live birth to 5–7 young. Diet: amphibians, possibly small mammals and lizards.

Venom: Unlikely to be life threatening; one documented bite caused local pain and discoloration.

Mt Kenya Bush Viper
Atheris desaixi

Identification: Up to 70cm. A thick-bodied bush viper with a broad head, black and yellow in colour, the yellow forming festoons on the flanks.

Habitat and Distribution: Around clearings in forest and woodland, between 1,500 and 1,700m altitude.

Endemic to Kenya and known only from the forest west of Chuka, south-east Mt Kenya and at Igembe in the Nyambeni Hills. Might be more widespread in central Kenya.

Natural History: Slow-moving tree viper, probably opportunistically active at any time; known to bask and move by day. May ascend 15m plus. They form C-shaped coils and rub them together to make a hissing noise, like Carpet Vipers. They give live birth; one clutch was 13 young. Diet: probably small mammals.

Venom: Unlikely to be life threatening; one documented bite caused pain and swelling.

Rough-scaled Bush Viper
Atheris hispida

Identification: Up to 74cm. A long, slender bush viper with bizarrely long scales. Males (right) usually olive or brownish-green, females (far right) tan or olive-brown, both sexes with some black speckling on the neck.

Habitat and Distribution: Forest, woodland and thicket, sometimes waterside vegetation, from 900 to 2,400m altitude. Sporadic records from forests around the Lake Victoria basin (Kakamega in Kenya, Minziro in Tanzania) and along the Albertine Rift Valley.

Natural History: Arboreal, living in tall grass, papyrus, creepers, bushes and small trees. Probably opportunistically active at any time; known to bask and move in the daytime. They form C-shaped coils and rub them together to make a hissing noise, like Carpet Vipers. They give live birth to 2–12 young. Diet: small mammals and amphibians.

Venom: Nothing known but unlikely to be life threatening.

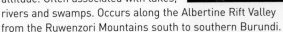

Great Lakes Bush Viper
Atheris nitschei

Identification: Up to 75cm. A stout bush viper, green with black speckling and blotching.

Habitat and Distribution: Moist savanna, woodland and montane forest, from 1,000 to 2,800m altitude. Often associated with lakes, rivers and swamps. Occurs along the Albertine Rift Valley from the Ruwenzori Mountains south to southern Burundi.

Natural History: Arboreal, living in papyrus and reedy swamp vegetation, elephant grass, bushes, small trees and bamboo. Probably nocturnal but opportunistically active at any time; known to bask and move in the daytime. Will slide quickly downward or drop off its perch if disturbed. Known to hunt from ambush on the ground. They form C-shaped coils and rub them together to make a hissing noise, like Carpet Vipers. They give live birth to 4–13 young. Diet: small mammals, lizards (including chameleons) and amphibians.

Venom: Nothing known, but a relatively large snake, so bites could be serious.

Green Bush Viper
Atheris squamiger

Identification: Up to 80cm. A fairly stout bush viper. Usually green in East Africa, with faint turquoise crossbars and yellow-edged scales.

Habitat and Distribution: Forest and well-wooded savanna, from 700 to 1,700m altitude. Found in the

forests of western Kenya, in Uganda known from the lakeshore forests, Budongo and Mt Elgon forests, sporadic records from the Albertine Rift.

Natural History: Arboreal, usually nocturnal but opportunistically active at any time, known to bask. They live in bushes and small trees but known to descend to ground level. They form C-shaped coils and rub them together to make a hissing noise, like Carpet Vipers. They give live birth. Hunt from ambush, taking small mammals, lizards, frogs and snakes.

Venom: Nothing known, but one fatality recorded: the victim showed massive swelling and incoagulable blood.

Mt Rungwe Bush Viper
Atheris rungweensis

Identification: Up to 65cm. A fairly stout bush viper. Usually green, with yellow, or black and yellow, festoon-like dorsolateral lines.

Habitat and Distribution: Moist savanna, woodland and hill forest, between 800 and 2,500m altitude.

Sporadically recorded from western and south-western Tanzania.

Natural History: Arboreal, probably opportunistically active at any time, living in bushes and small trees but known to descend to ground level. They give live birth. Diet: amphibians.

Venom: Nothing known.

Kenya Montane Viper
Montatheris hindii

Identification: Up to 35cm. A slim little viper, males (right) are brown, females (far right) grey, both sexes with a paired series of dark blotches down the back, and dark blotches along the flanks, sometimes a faint dorsolateral line is present.

Habitat and Distribution: Known only from the montane moorlands over 2,700m, of the Aberdare Mountains and Mount Kenya.

Natural History: Terrestrial and diurnal. Hides under ground cover and in grass tussocks, emerges on sunny days to bask and then hunts. Gives live birth to two or three young. Diet: lizards (including chameleons) and small frogs, probably small mammals.

Venom: Nothing known, unlikely to be life-threatening.

Other vipers known from East Africa

Two-striped Night Adder *Causus bilineatus* A small (up to 65cm) night adder, usually with distinct light dorsolateral stripes and black bars on the back, recorded from north-east Rwanda, might be in south-west Tanzania.

West African Night Adder *Causus maculatus* A small, stout night adder, up to 70cm long, brown or olive above with faint markings, resembles a faded rhombic night adder, sometimes with a slightly darker broad vertebral stripe, recorded from western Uganda.

Barbour's Short-headed Viper/Udzungwa Viper *Adenorhinos barbouri* A small (37cm maximum) viper, brown to dark olive in colour, with a pair of yellow zig-zag dorsolateral stripes. Known only from the Udzungwa and Ukinga Mountains. Never photographed alive.

Acuminate Bush Viper *Atheris acuminata* A small, slim bush viper, looks identical to a green Rough-scaled Bush Viper, with an H-shaped dark marking on the crown. Known only from Kyambura Game Reserve, near Lake George, western Uganda.

Floodplain Viper *Proatheris superciliaris* A robust little viper, grows to 60cm. Grey-brown with two yellow dorsolateral stripes, black oval saddles along the back and black semi-circular blotches along the flanks. Known from the floodplain at the north end of Lake Malawi, in Tanzania.

Frogs and Toads
Order Anura

Carolus Linnaeus, the father of modern classification, had
a low opinion of amphibians. In 1758, he wrote:

*'These foul and loathsome animals are abhorrent because
of their…pale colour…filthy skin, fierce aspect…offensive
smell, harsh voice…and terrible venom; and so their creator
has not exerted his powers to make many of them.'*

Glance at our pictures of East African frogs, and admire
their colours. Few of our frogs smell; those that do, smell
largely pleasant. Admittedly, many have harsh voices, but
some are highly melodic, evocative of the African night.
Some have toxic skin secretions, but unless one chooses
to lick them, they are of no danger to humans. Few look
threatening, and many, especially the tree frogs, are
appealing looking animals. Nearly 4,000 species of frog are
known; about 200 occur in East Africa. Good zoologist that
he was, Linnaeus was misinformed about amphibians.

The humble *chura* (Swahili for frog) is an important
component of our fauna. Although they need water to
breed, frogs have radiated throughout the East African
landscape in a remarkable way, from the coastal lowlands
to high montane moorlands, from the wettest swamps into
arid deserts. In dry country they live an astonishing life,
adapted to breed rapidly in temporary pools that appear
after rainstorms, spending much of their life aestivating,
buried deep in the soil, waiting for rain. Frogs have also
proved to be environmental indicators, their porous skins
rendering them sensitive to pollution. At present, they
seem to be declining worldwide. Worrying though this is,
amphibians may be providing the service of naturally
occurring early warning systems, giving vital clues to the
health of our planet. Frogs also eat a great many insect
pests. Amphibians are considerably more useful and
significant to humanity than most people realise.

Squeakers: Family Arthroleptidae

The squeakers are a poorly understood group of leaf litter frogs that usually live in forest or woodland, although some can tolerate urbanisation in moist gardens. About ten cryptically coloured species, in two genera (*Arthroleptis and Schoutedenella*, the latter sometimes called litter frogs) occur in East Africa. Unusually, they lay direct-developing eggs in hollows in moist leaf litter; there is no free-living tadpole stage. Species of a third genus, *Cardioglossa*, found in West and Central Africa, are usually brightly coloured (aposematic) and retain the normal frog breeding strategy of deposition of eggs in or near water, tadpole stage and metamorphosis. All squeakers in East Africa are strictly terrestrial; their toe discs, if expanded, are only slightly so. Webbing between fingers and toes is usually reduced, as you might expect with a species living in leaf litter. The third finger in males may be very much longer than other fingers, especially within the genus *Schoutedenella*. The calls vary in nature and may easily be mistaken for a chirping insect. Because of their inconspicuous habits and colours, and their unremarkable vocalisations, members of the genus are often overlooked.

Genus *Arthroleptis*: Squeakers

Small to medium-sized frogs, usually varying shades of grey, brown, or reddish-brown, often with an hourglass-shaped pattern on the back. They have a thin, median skin fold (raphe) always present down the centre of the back; snout blunt, head and body broad and robust, distinguished from litter frogs (*Schoutedenella*) in much larger size and head usually as wide or wider than the body across the shoulders and from puddle frogs (*Phrynobatrachus*) by absence of a tarsal tubercle. In breeding males the third finger has minute spike-like structures on the underside; the third finger may be expanded in length up to nearly one-quarter the length of the body from snout to vent (see *Schoutedenella* on page 160). *Arthroleptis* individuals are much larger than specimens of *Schoutedenella*. There are presently five species of the genus *Arthroleptis* described for East Africa; most of these are extremely difficult to separate; moreover, some authors consider litter frogs (*Schoutedenella*) to be members of this genus as well. Treatment of the three species below should allow readers to at least recognise members of the genus *Arthroleptis* from those of *Schoutedenella*.

Common Squeaker
Arthroleptis stenodactylus

Identification: Males to 33mm SVL, females to 44mm. First finger equal in length to or slightly longer than second; toes not webbed. Skin various shades of brown; a semi-hourglass pattern common on the dorsum; side of head between snout and tympanum always darker than head and body colouration.

Habitat and Distribution: Forested areas of Kenya and Tanzania, from the coast inland. Widespread in southeast Tanzania, sporadic elsewhere, present in Uganda at Bwindi Impenetrable National Park at higher elevations, but evidently absent in lower western Uganda forests such as Kibale.

Natural History: This species is most frequently heard or encountered after rainstorms. Male advertisement call is a very high-pitched *peep-peep-peep*, frequently heard during daylight hours, especially after rainfall.

Tanner's Squeaker
Arthroleptis tanneri

Identification: Males to 44mm; females to 55mm. May be easily distinguished by size (females are the second-largest known members of the genus) and very stout appearance. Colour pattern often an indistinct chain of markings. The ground colour has been described as claret-brown or dark maroon, with hands and feet pinkish; undersides are light in colour; foot webbing absent, toe tips blunt but not expanded; upper part of iris bright gold.

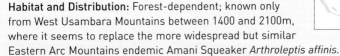

Habitat and Distribution: Forest-dependent; known only from West Usambara Mountains between 1400 and 2100m, where it seems to replace the more widespread but similar Eastern Arc Mountains endemic Amani Squeaker *Arthroleptis affinis*.

Natural History: Found under or within holes in rotten logs, under leaf litter and debris on forest floor. Nothing is known of its reproduction, but direct development, like other members of the genus is assumed. The male advertisement call is unrecorded.

Amani Squeaker
Arthroleptis affinis
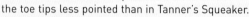

Identification: Females to about 44mm. Similar to Tanner's Squeaker, but smaller. Often has a double-diamond dorsal pattern. The ground colour is shades of light and darker brown rather than dark maroon; the hand and feet are not pinkish. Dark in colour ventrally; the toe tips less pointed than in Tanner's Squeaker.

Habitat and Distribution: Known only East Usambara Mts.

Natural History: Lives on the forest floor, a leaf litter species similar to Tanner's squeaker. Breeding unknown, presumably similar to other members of the genus. Male advertisement call is unrecorded.

Genus *Schoutedenella*: Litter Frogs

These are very small frogs, similar to *Arthroleptis* in presence of median skin fold and absence of tarsal tubercle but they differ in internal structures such as reduced number of vertebrae; the head is more slender (narrower than width across shoulders). In breeding males of most species the third finger may reach a length of nearly half that of the total body from snout to vent and bears minute spike-like structures. (Compare with *Arthroleptis* on pages 158–159.)

Albertine Rift Litter Frog
Schoutedenella schubotzi

Identification: Males to about 13mm, females to 20mm. Similar to squeakers (*Arthroleptis*) but smaller, head somewhat narrower and snout more pointed. Third finger of breeding males strikingly long. Cryptically coloured; very dark, hour glass pattern and other dorsal markings may be present or absent.

Habitat and Distribution: Forests of middle to higher elevation along the Albertine Rift in Uganda and Rwanda.

Natural History: Calling male and female of this species found in association with 12 large eggs deposited in a small declivity in the bank of a roadside cut about 1.5m above ground in Bwindi Impenetrable National Park. The male call is undescribed.

Other squeakers and litter frogs found in East Africa

Eastern Forest Squeaker *Arthroleptis adolfifriderici* A large squeaker (females to 49mm); similar in pattern and habitus to the Amani Squeaker, but with a marbled dorsal pattern. Widespread in forests of high rainfall and medium elevation (800m+) of Rwanda, Burundi, Kenya, Tanzania and Uganda. Known for certain from the Rugege and Bugoya Forests of Rwanda, Mubwindi Swamp, Bwindi Impenetrable National Park, Uganda and Mlanje Mountain in southern Malawi.

Reiche's Squeaker *Arthroleptis reichei* Up to 34mm length, red-brown in colour with the typical hourglass pattern on the back. Known from the Poroto Mountains in southern Tanzania, and from northern Malawi.

Rubeho Mountains Squeaker *Arthroleptis nikeae* A big squeaker, up to 57mm, recently described from the Rubeho Mountains, Tanzania. Brown above, with darker V-shapes on the back, flanks darker, heavily mottled.

Mottled Squeaker *Arthroleptis poecilonotus* A small squeaker, reaches about 30mm, variable in colour, the back is reddish, or brown and tan with a dark hour-glass pattern. Known from central Uganda.

Plain Litter Frog *Schoutedenella xenochirus* A small squeaker, 24mm maximum, reddish, tan or grey above, usually without pattern, found in southern Tanzania.

Strange-toed Litter Frog *Schoutedenella xenodactyla* A small (up to 26mm) squeaker, red-brown above; known only from the Usambara Mountains in Tanzania.

Common Litter Frog *Schoutedenella xenodactyloides* Grows to 25mm snout–vent length. A small dark, slender frog with smooth skin and reddish thighs and groin, sometimes with a dark hourglass marking on the back. In wooded highlands in southern Kenya, south through Tanzania.

Plain Litter Frog
Schoutedenella xenochirus

Toads: Family Bufonidae

Toads are a diverse group. Some species are very common; most people will have seen a 'typical' toad (*Bufo*), and heard their deep booming calls, but there are many other kinds of toad in East Africa. Most toads have a fairly rough skin and most have an enlarged swollen gland behind each eye, the parotid gland. These, and sometimes other skin glands, can produce powerful poisons. If a toad is taken into the mouth of a predator, these poisons produce intense irritation, and can kill the predator if the toad is swallowed.

Toads vary a lot in colour. Most of the toads of the genus *Bufo* are some shade of brown or tan, often with darker paired blotches down the back, but some toads are bright blue, red, green or yellow. The most familiar species are often relatively large, but other members of the family are small to tiny, and inconspicuous. The males of the genus *Bufo* produce loud, deep, raucous advertisement calls that annoy many a householder at night. Some of the smaller toads have a metallic *pink, pink* call. Other small toads appear to have no hearing apparatus and may not vocalise; just how the males of these forms attract females in the breeding season is a complete mystery.

Reproduction in toads varies considerably. Many follow the typical amphibian pattern, where terrestrial adults return to water to reproduce, the females producing thousands of eggs which are externally fertilised by the males. These eggs then hatch into larvae (tadpoles), the tadpoles metamorphose into adults. However, some toads deposit their eggs in pockets of water in snail shells in the forest and the tadpoles have to survive under these difficult circumstances. One group of toads found in East Africa, the forest toads, *Nectophrynoides*, are live bearers; the fertilisation is internal, the female retains the fertilised eggs in her oviducts and gives birth to tiny toadlets.

Six genera in the family Bufonidae occur in East Africa: *Bufo*, *Churamiti*, *Mertensophryne*, *Nectophrynoides*, *Schismaderma* and *Stephopaedes*.

Genus *Bufo*: Bufo Toads

A large genus of many species with a very wide range of size, from very large to very small. About 24 species occur in East Africa. The skin tends to be rough with 'warts' on the back. The colour pattern of the back is cryptic, involving symmetrical arrangement of dark blotches of brown, olive and grey on a lighter background. They have a parotid gland behind each eye and many have a thin, pale mid-dorsal line. The legs may have blotches of dark colour arranged in irregular pattern of bands on the upper surface. Below they may be white, grey or cream and the lower surface has a granular appearance.

Members of this genus may be found under very dry conditions far from water, but still return to water to breed. Unlike other frogs, they cannot make long jumps, but progress by hopping or running. The parotid glands exude a secretion (this is usually white) when a toad is disturbed and this is irritating to mucous membranes of a potential predator, or if it gets into a cut on a hand. Some predators, however, such as some snakes and the African Civet, appear to feed on toads without experiencing these problems.

Dead-leaf Toad
Bufo brauni

Identification: A large toad, females reaching up to 110mm, males considerably smaller at 65mm. The back of this attractive toad is greyish brown with dark blotches; warts are present on the back and sides. Some individuals have a thin, pale mid-dorsal line on a dark background and this line resembles the axis of a dead leaf when the animal remains motionless amidst dead leaves on the forest floor, hence its common name. The parotid glands are large, flattened and elongate. A more or less continuous ridge of skin runs from just above the eye, includes the parotid glands and continues to

near the point of insertion of the hind limb. The underside is grey or greyish white to cream-coloured. Unlikely to be confused with any other species of *Bufo*.

Habitat and Distribution: This species is endemic to the Usambara, Uluguru and Udzungwa mountains of Tanzania. Although essentially a forest species, it may continue to survive in cleared farmland at the edge of forest.

Natural History: Males call while sitting in a stream or on rocks in a stream in the forest.

Garman's Toad
Bufo garmani

Identification: Large females to 115mm, males to 106mm. A chunky toad, usually brown or tan, with series of paired, dark-edged blotches down back. Back is warty; each wart is black-tipped. Parotid glands are large and obvious.

Usually no dark markings on top of the head. Bars behind eyes do not meet in centre. Red patches on back of thighs.

Habitat and Distribution: A savannah species, widely distributed in eastern Kenya and north-central Tanzania.

Natural History: Live in the savannah and breed at temporary pools, but will utilise permanent man-made water sources. Males usually call from edges of water bodies. Females lay double strings of over 10,000+ eggs. The call is a loud harsh *gwaaack*, lasting from a fifth to nearly a second.

Guttural Toad
Bufo gutturalis

Identification: Females to 120mm, males to 90mm, breeding individuals usually 70-83mm. Parotid glands large and obvious. Dorsal markings usually a mix of dark coloured blotches, and a pale mid-dorsal line. Some breeding individuals have bright red wash on rear thighs and underside around cloaca. White or cream below.

Habitat and Distribution: Widespread / common throughout Tanzania and southern Kenya, except moist forest habitats.

Natural History: Will feed on insects attracted to electric lights around dwellings. If molested releases a thick sticky white irritant secretion, lethal to predators that eat it (though Civet Cats and some snakes eat it with impunity). Males call from edge of breeding pools, a low hollow continuous rattling (a well-known African night sound), and mate with females as they move into water. Many eggs are deposited, in long strings of jelly. Tadpole small and black.

Taxonomic Note: This species is not clearly taxonomically defined; limits in connection with closely related species are not yet determined in East Africa.

Kerinyaga Toad
Bufo kerinyagae

Identification: Small toad, both sexes reach about 85mm. Perhaps the most beautifully coloured of the larger 'Bufo' toads. Parotid glands visible, distinct from the eye and parallel to each other. Warts on the skin are sharp-tipped and so the skin has a distinctive, rough feel. Overall colour is cinnamon to medium brown upon which are rich, dark-brown to maroon blotches. There is usually a lime-green mid-dorsal stripe and frequently two lateral areas of lime-green. In some specimens parts of the snout are also green.

Habitat and Distribution: Lives in high, flat grassland and moist savannah, usually above 1,800m. Occurs around the Ngorongoro Crater, and high central Kenya.

Natural History: Breeds in seasonal pools and flooded fields. The name refers to Kerinyaga (sometimes spelled Kirinyaga), Mount Kenya, the resting place of Mogai, God, in the Kikuyu creation story.

Kisolo Toad
Bufo kisoloensis

Identification: Females to 87mm; males smaller, up to 71mm. Its rather pointed snout is a good field character, as are the extensively webbed, relatively slender fingers. Parotid glands present and obvious. Males and females differ. The male has a smooth back without an obvious colour pattern, females have a typical toad's warty back. The back is usually uniform dull dark green to olive or rufous. Breeding males undergo a startling colour change, they turn bright lemon yellow for a short while, before returning to the normal colour.

Habitat and Distribution: Widespread in high savannah and grassland, to high altitude, occurs on the moorlands of the Aberdare Mountains at over 3,000m. Found in high central and western Kenya and southern Uganda, also from the Mahale peninsula in western Tanzania.

Natural History: Little known; Aberdare specimens were active by day around moorland pools.

Lugh Toad
Bufo lughensis

Identification: Very small, females to 33mm, males smaller, to 22mm. This is common micro-toad of arid northern zones of East Africa. Usually brown with a suggestion of patterning, and pale rectangular marks on either side of its mid-dorsal line. Tympanum is present

but hard to see. There are paired tubercles under the fingers. Usually a dark spot on the upper jaw below the eye. Extent of webbing varies. Unlike similar small toads, the underside is lightly marked with haphazard small black spots or dashes.

Habitat and Distribution: Widespread in dry savannah and semi-desert of northern Kenya and also the Tsavo area; the two populations are probably connected.

Natural History: Most specimens collected under ground debris, often near temporary huts of nomads; also under logs and rocks. Nothing known of its breeding biology but presumably lives the usual life of amphibians in dry country, i.e. emerging in rainy season to feed and breed around temporary pools and burying itself deep in the mud when the dry season comes.

Steindachner's Toad
Bufo steindachneri

Identification: A small toad, up to 55mm length. The colour pattern is typical of the genus, with dark brown blotches on a slightly paler background, with a V-shape behind the eyes. Breeding males have bright-red patches on the rear of the thighs, parts of the foot and

sometimes on the rear upper arms. Unlike many toads, the palms and soles are dusky dark brown. The toes are slightly webbed and the parotid glands are not conspicuous. The back has many warts and feels rough to the touch.

Habitat and Distribution: Occurs in woodland and savanna, known from most of the Kenya coast, Tsavo National Park, also north-east Tanzania and Kampala.

Natural History: Males call from a concealed site at the edge of the water.

Desert Toad
Bufo xeros

Identification: Fairly large, up to 100mm. Variable in colour, brown or brownish-grey, sometimes with usual subrectangular back markings, but markings often faint or invisible.

Habitat and Distribution: Widely distributed across the semi-desert and dry savannah of northern and eastern Kenya, at low altitude, with a couple of records from south-east Tanzania.

Natural History: Lives the usual life of amphibians in dry country, emerging in the rainy season to feed and breed around temporary pools; buries itself deep in the mud when the dry season comes.

Bunty's Dwarf Toad
Mertensophryne micranotis

Identification: Females to 24mm, males 19mm. A small toad of the forest floor leaf litter. Back dark brown to very dark grey or black; no definite pattern, there is usually a contrasting white area above the vent. A fine mid-dorsal line may be present. Below, white to cream with fine black dots; some areas of ventral surface translucent. The parotid glands are not conspicuous and toes have no webbing.

Habitat and Distribution: Endemic to coastal forests and woodlands of Kenya and Tanzania, inland on the Rufiji River and on the offshore islands of Tanzania.

Natural History: Easily overlooked when motionless among leaf litter. Most often seen in the early morning, and after rainfall, when it feeds on small invertebrates in the leaf litter. Breeding is unusual, with internal fertilisation. The male grabs the female under her arms, and the two remain in amplexus for several hours, while the male deposits sperm into the cloaca of the female. The female deposits eggs in small water-filled snail shells or tree cavities. The tadpoles have an unusual shape and structure, with a 'crown' (raised ring of tissue) above the eyes and nostrils.

Genus *Nectophrynoides*: Eastern Arc Toads

A genus of seven or eight small forest-dwelling toads with a unique method of reproduction; fertilisation is internal and the female retains the fertilised eggs in her oviducts, where they go through the tadpole stage in relative safety. These little toads are confined to the forests of the Eastern Arc Mountains in Tanzania, and all are on Appendix 1 of CITES, meaning no trade in these species is permitted.

Kihansi Spray Toad
Nectophrynoides asperginis

Identification: A small toad, females up to 29mm, males to 19mm. Adult males are yellow, with a dark brown lateral band, this band is less distinct in females. Fingers and toes are webbed but not extensively.

Habitat and Distribution: Known only from a few hectares of the formerly spray-drenched Kihansi River Gorge, below the Kihansi Falls, Udzungwa Mountains, Tanzania.

Natural History: As with other members of the genus, fertilisation is internal and the female retains the fertilised eggs in her oviducts, where they go through the tadpole stage in relative safety. The female then 'gives birth' to tiny toadlets. This species is fast-moving over the slippery, water-soaked rocks as well as through herbaceous vegetation of the spray zone.

Conservation Note: This species was discovered in 1996 and formally described in 1998. Once the Lower Kihansi hydropower project became operational, its required habitat, spray-dependent wetlands, were destroyed. The population crashed. As an emergency measure, 500 were taken to special amphibian breeding centres at zoos in the United States. Even the installation of an artificial sprinkler system to generate spray in the gorge has not maintained the habitat nor the populations of toads, which have been further decimated by chytrid fungus. This is one of the few African amphibians which meets the Critically Endangered criteria established by the World Conservation Union, IUCN. At the time of writing (autumn 2005) only a few Kihansi Spray Toads have been seen in the gorge over the past three years.

Tornier's Forest Toad
Nectophrynoides tornieri

Identification: A small toad, 21 to 30mm long. Quite variable in colour, usually reddish-brown above, with a dark bar behind the eye.

Habitat and Distribution: Endemic to Tanzania, occurs only in the woodland and forest of the Usambara and Uluguru Mountains.

Natural History: Lives on the forest floor among leaf litter. As with other members of the genus, fertilisation is internal and the female retains the fertilised eggs in her oviducts, where they go through the tadpole stage in relative safety.

Robust Forest Toad
Nectophrynoides viviparous

Identification: Females up to 60mm, but most males and females between 40 and 50mm, males usually smaller than females. Unmistakable; it has large parotid glands and huge, pale-coloured, strongly-contrasting glands on its limbs. The skin is smooth, without warts. Very variable in colour, the back may be black, grey, brown, tan, green, yellowish or even reddish. The underside may be black or white, sometimes mottled. The toes are webbed.

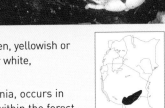

Habitat and Distribution: Endemic to Tanzania, occurs in woodland, forest, bamboo and grasslands within the forest, in the Uluguru, Udzungwa and Ukinga Mountains.

Natural History: Males may call from hidden positions, such as under leaves, but may also climb a metre or more in search of calling perches. As with other members of the genus, fertilisation is internal and the female retains the fertilised eggs in her oviducts, where they go through the tadpole stage in relative safety.

Genus *Schismaderma*: Red-backed Toad

This genus is represented by a single species; it does not have parotid glands and has a unique coloration, with a reddish, brick-red to brown back and two dark, rounded marks on the lower back. A lateral glandular fold extends along each side of the body.

Red-backed Toad
Schismaderma carens

Identification: A medium to large toad, big females reach 90mm, males slightly smaller. Unmistakable. The colour is unique: the back is brick to rusty red, with two small dark brown marks on the lower back. Creamy or light grey below. The parotid glands are not visible. A fold or ridge of skin extends along each side. The tympanum is large and obvious.

Habitat and Distribution: Widespread almost throughout Tanzania, in a range of habitats including savannah and Miombo Woodland, just enters Kenya in the southern Rift Valley at Olorgesaille.

Natural History: Breeds in seasonal pools, even those fouled by cattle. The call of the male sounds similar to the moo of a cow, and is loud and travels long distances. The black tadpoles form large swarms in the water.

Other notable species of toad found in East Africa

Cameroon Toad *Bufo camerunensis* A big warty toad, reaches a length of 90mm, resembles a square-marked toad with dark, paired blotches down the back, sometimes yellow on the flanks. Known from western Uganda.

Sooty Toad *Bufo fuliginatus* Reaches a length of 65mm, back uniform brown, there is a dark eye-stripe from the eye onto the snout. Recorded from south-western Tanzania.

Sombre Toad *Bufo funereus* A toad that grows to 60mm, with a brown back, indistinct darker markings and a light band between the eyes. Sometimes has a pale vertebral stripe. Known from western Uganda.

Lindner's Toad *Bufo lindneri* A very small toad: females reach 34mm. Grey or brown above, with orange or red tubercles, and a vertebral stripe. Recorded from Dar es Salaam to southern Tanzania.

Lonnberg's Toad *Bufo lonnbergi* A small toad, yellow-brown in colour. Reaches a length of 70 to 80mm. Known from the Thika-Ruiru area of Kenya.

Flat-backed Toad *Bufo maculatus* A fairly large toad, up to 80mm. Looks like a Guttural Toad but has not the red thigh markings. Occurs in the Lake Turkana area.

Parker's Toad *Bufo parkeri* A small toad, about 70mm in length, colour yellow-brown, with a fine vertebral line, known from sparsely wooded grassland in the Lake Natron area of northern Tanzania.

Rees's Toad *Bufo reesi* A medium-sized toad, up to 70mm length, uniform brown in colour, known from the Kihansi-Kilombero floodplain, southern Tanzania.

Square-marked Toad *Bufo regularis* A fairly large toad, up to 130mm in length. Has big parotid glands, a very warty back. Has the usual distinctive pattern, darker blotches on a brown background. Sporadically recorded from western East Africa.

Taita Toad *Bufo taitanus* A little toad, up to 31mm, with thin limbs and no visible tympanum. May be grey, tan or rufous brown. Occurs from southeastern Kenya through eastern Tanzania. The tadpoles were recently described; they have the same bizarre crown-like structure on the head as the tadpoles of Bunty's Dwarf Toad.

Lake Turkana Toad *Bufo turkanae* A large toad, up to 90mm in length; resembles a Guttural Toad. Known from the shores of Lake Turkana.

Urungu Toad *Bufo urunguensis* A small species, up to 30mm. Brownish above, with pale areas on the snout, neck and lower back; irregular black marks below. Recorded from southern Tanzania.

Lake Victoria Toad *Bufo vittatus* A small toad, up to 60mm in length, with typical 'Bufo' markings, i.e. a row of paired darker blotches on a brown background. Known from the western shores of Lake Victoria.

Beautiful Tree Toad *Churamiti maridadi* A bizarrely beautiful toad, without parotid glands or a tympanum. Only described in 2002, from the Ukaguru Mountains in eastern Tanzania. It is a deep metallic yellow with pink limbs, or deep metallic green with blue-green limbs. It reaches just under 60mm.

Loveridge's Forest Toad *Stephopaedes loveridgei* A small brown toad, up to 38mm, with white underside. The skin is covered with dark-tipped spines. Known from coastal woodland and forest in southern Tanzania.

Shovel-snouted Frogs: Family Hemisotidae

The members of this family are easily recognised by their small triangular heads, shovel-like snouts, short powerful limbs and rather round plump bodies. A small thin groove runs laterally across the head between the eyes. As the common name suggests, the head is used as a shovel when the animal digs into soft soil. The front legs are short and muscular, to assist in pushing the animal forward as it digs; the front limb muscles are three times larger than those in frogs that do not burrow forward. No other frog family in East Africa can be mistaken for this one and its members are in a single genus *Hemisus*. Three species occur in East Africa: the Guinea Snout-burrower *Hemisus guineensis,* the Short-fingered Snout-burrower *Hemisus brachydactylus* and the Marbled Snout-burrower *Hemisus marmoratus.*

They are found in a wide variety of habitats but not thick forest. Shovel-snouted frogs usually deposit eggs in burrows under the ground but near the edge of seasonal pools. When rainwater floods the pools and eventually the burrows, the tadpoles swim to the water.

Guinea Snout-burrower
Hemisus guineensis

Identification: This is a medium-sized species; females reach about 45mm, males are smaller at 32mm. Members of the genus are unmistakable. The snout is flat, triangular and hard and used for digging; the body is short, squat, and somewhat globose. The inner

metatarsal tubercle is large and the skin is smooth. The colour of the back varies; it may be black, grey or dark olive; there is a pattern of yellow vermiculations on some individuals. Males have a black chin.

Habitat and Distribution: Found in woodland, savannah and grassland. Not as widespread as the Marbled Snout-burrower but in some places the two species occur together. Sporadically recorded from south-west Tanzania, the northern Lake Victoria shore and the Semliki River in western Uganda.

Natural History: May occur in large numbers in the breeding season but remains hidden for much of the year.

Marbled Snout-burrower
Hemisus marmoratus

Identification: This is a small-
to medium-sized frog, females
34mm, males 22mm in length.
Unmistakable. The snout is flat,
triangular and hard and used for
digging; the body is short, squat,
and globular. The back is grey
or brown with darker spots or
marbling. Sometimes a thin, light mid-dorsal line is present,
and some individuals lack the darker pattern, giving the
impression of a pale grey animal with little contrast.

Habitat and Distribution: This species is common in open
habitats such as savannah, grassland and woodland. In
some places, it occurs together with the Guinea Snout-
burrower. Found virtually throughout Tanzania and southern Kenya, the only
Uganda records are the Bwamba Forest and Kidepo.

Natural History: Males call from the edge of temporary pools and are
usually hidden under vegetation. The reproductive pattern is quite
remarkable. A male clasps the large female and is dragged into a burrow
dug by her. The eggs are deposited in a cavity such as a burrow, or under a
stone or other hidden site. This nest is some distance from the water. As
rains fall, the water rises and the tadpoles swim away. If the water level
does not rise to a sufficient height, the female is able to carry tadpoles on
her back and others may follow her to water as they swim over the wet mud.

Other species of snout-burrower found in East Africa

Short-fingered Snout-burrower *Hemisus brachydactylus* Grows to
43–49mm. Brown above, with light spots and a light vertebral line. Known
only from the vicinity of Masiliwa, central Tanzania.

African Tree Frogs: Family Hyperoliidae

This family comprises all but a few species of the arboreal tree frogs of Africa, Madagascar and the Seychelles Islands. In terms of species numbers it is the largest family in East Africa, with over 70 known members; there will be many more if the Common Reed Frog (*Hyperolius viridiflavis*) 'complex' is split. African Tree Frogs range in size from the tiny 17mm Dwarf Reed Frog *Hyperolius minutissimus*, of southern Tanzania, to the 110mm Principe Giant Tree Frog *Leptopelis palmatus*, endemic to a single island in the Gulf of Guinea. Most species are relatively slender, have smooth skin and greatly expanded finger and toe tips for climbing. All members of the family have a small bony or cartilaginous structure (the intercalary element) between the last and penultimate bone of the fingers and toes: this apparently allows the expanded finger and toe tips to rotate more freely in climbing. In most, the hind limbs are much longer than the fore limbs with the exception of a few of the terrestrial species. Adult males of all species except in the genus *Leptopelis* (tree frogs) have conspicuous thick chin, or gular, glands covering the vocal sac. All known species are dependent upon water for development, which includes a free-swimming tadpole stage. Most are active at night, and different groups (genera) may be distinguished by their advertisement calls. Shape of the pupil is important in identification to genus: genera of this family have pupils that are either horizontally oval, rhomboidal (diamond-shaped), or vertical.

Genus *Leptopelis*: Tree Frogs

Recent work suggests that members of this genus represent a separate family, the Leptopelidae. They are medium-sized to large, nocturnal, arboreal frogs, always with vertical cat-like pupils, long hind legs, and enlarged finger and toe tips. The tympanum is usually distinct and visible. Unlike other members of the family, the male gular glands are absent. Males of some species have flattened glands visible ventrally where the arms join the trunk (pectoral glands). In most species, females are noticeably larger than males. Where known, reproduction in these tree frogs includes a breeding pair burying large eggs in soil near water or in a depression that will become rain-filled. The eggs seem to develop rather slowly, and the thin, slender larvae then make their way overland to nearby water. Advertising calls are rather unmusical clacks, buzzes and, in some, a cat-like whine; some species have bimodal calls, the two portions of which are radically different from each other. Members of this genus are mostly forest forms and absent from the arid, semi-desert areas of East Africa. There are a few species that are terrestrial or fossorial.

Glade Tree Frog
Leptopelis argenteus
(including *Leptopelis concolor*)

Identification: Up to 34mm. Small-ish, stout brown tree frog with non-protruding eyes; male pectoral glands absent; webbing is reduced; male and female coloration similar, usually light brown with a darker bar or reverse pyramid-shaped marking between the eyes; never any green. Northern individuals have a vague Y-shaped marking on the back, southerly individuals frequently lack the interorbital bar but have two darker brown paravertebral stripes.

Habitat and Distribution: Bushes or low trees in clearings, even plantations and disturbed areas from river deltas in south coastal Somalia south through coastal Kenya and eastern Tanzania into Mozambique.

Natural History: Calls from bushes in openings outside forest proper. Male call bimodal: atonal *claack!*, followed immediately by 2 or 3 *yiiinnggg* sounds.

Taxonomic Note: Some consider the southern striped form to be a separate species, *L. concolor*; but distributions confluent and advertisement calls identical.

Bocage's Burrowing Tree Frog
Leptopelis bocagii

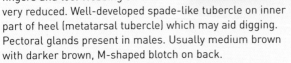

Identification: Males to 50mm, females to 58mm. Lives on ground. Large, stout frog, non-protruding eyes, lacks expanded disks on fingers and toe. Webbing on feet very reduced. Well-developed spade-like tubercle on inner part of heel (metatarsal tubercle) which may aid digging. Pectoral glands present in males. Usually medium brown with darker brown, M-shaped blotch on back.

Habitat and Distribution: Inland grassland and savannah of moderate elevation from western and central highlands of Kenya, south through western Tanzania, may occur as far south as northern Namibia and Zimbabwe (type locality Angola). Several cryptic species may be included in this distribution.

Natural History: Call long, slow *waaah* emitted from ground. Large numbers may occur but usually only encountered during major rainfall. Eggs apparently deposited in deep holes in ground, tadpoles unknown. Can form cocoon of epidermis, within which it avoids evaporative water loss during dry seasons.

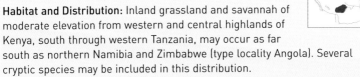

Ornate Tree Frog
Leptopelis flavomaculatus

Identification: Males to 50mm, females to 70mm. Large with bulging eyes and short snout, moderately developed webbing between toes; males have pectoral glands; male colour pattern variable but always

some green (which Glade Tree Frog lacks), males' heels and knees white-tipped; males uniform green or mix of green and brown, may have large, broad-armed dorsal inverted U-shape pattern. Females usually have high contrast, similar, light cream U-shaped pattern on rich dark brown background.

Habitat and Distribution: Dry open forest. Coastal Kenya south through most of southeastern Tanzania in various dry deciduous forests (but excluding moist evergreen forests of Eastern Arc).

Natural History: Reproduction presumably similar to other *Leptopelis* where known. In Arabuko Sokoke Forest, Kenya, where it is found close to the Glade treefrog. The call is a cat-like *weaao* or *waaao*.

Albertine Rift Tree Frog
Leptopelis kivuensis

Identification: Males to 36mm, females larger to 50mm. A high altitude forest-dependent tree frog. Both sexes have protruding eyes, conspicuous all-red irises and striking white spot on upper lip below eye. Tympanum (ear drum)

about half the diameter of eye; toe webbing rather reduced. Male pectoral glands large and conspicuous; adult males have loose darkish skin in chin area. Light to moderate brown, often with X-shaped blotch on back; frequently upper arms of 'X' are joined by an interorbital bar. Newly metamorphosed young bright green without markings.

Habitat and Distribution: Glades and swamps, riverside vegetation and forest clearings near water in montane forest up to 2800m (but three juveniles reported at around 4000m in the Virunga volcanoes).

Natural History: Has bizarre defensive behavior; when disturbed flattens its back, raises arms and legs off ground and partially opens mouth. Can hold this position for several seconds. Males call with a loud, non-musical *clack* from bushes, sedges or other vegetation between 1.5 and 2m above ground.

Notable tree frogs of the Eastern Arc Mountains

These ancient isolated mountains originate with the Taita Hills in Kenya and run south through Tanzania to Mlanje Mountain in southern Malawi. Poorly explored, their amphibian fauna appears to be highly diverse and largely endemic to these montane forests. Although unlikely to be encountered on a typical safari in East Africa, their presence nevertheless speaks to the antiquity and diversity of the East African herpetofauna.

Vermiculated Tree Frog
Leptopelis vermiculatus

Identification: Perhaps the largest Eastern Arc tree frog; females to 85mm, with rather a stout body. Female and juvenile coloration (far right) usually a vivid green with fine black vermiculations, sides are blotched black and white. Most males (above) are brown with various patterns.

Habitat and Distribution: Known from the forests of East and West Usambaras, Mt Rungwe and the Udzungwa Mountains.

Natural History: Sits quietly on branches above water. Able to change colour over time.

Parker's Tree Frog
Leptopelis parkeri

Identification: A rather slender tree frog with females up to 56mm. May be distinguished from other Eastern Arc tree frogs by its bright red iris. Colour pattern extremely variable and may be composed dorsally of wavy bands of various colours to patterns similar to tiger stripes. This is one of the most beautiful of the forest tree frogs.

Habitat and Distribution: It is known so far from the South Pare Mountains, the East and West Usambaras, the Ulugurus and the Udzungwas.

Natural History: The voice is a quiet buzzing. Fairly common in areas of dense forest.

Barbour's Tree Frog
Leptopelis barbouri

Identification: A rather small, slender, Eastern Arc tree frog (females to 43mm), identifiable by the male's bright, cobalt-blue vocal sacs. Dorsal coloration may be light to middle green with a fine lacy pattern in white; some individuals may be nearly silver in coloration. Iris of eye may be reddish on the periphery but not entirely red as in Parker's Tree Frog.

Habitat and Distribution: So far known from the East and West Usambara Mountains and the Udzungwa Mountains, but expected in the Ulugurus.

Natural History: Curiously, this species has bile pigments in the circulatory system resulting in green muscles, bone and blood. The males call from branches near streams, at a height of 2–6m. The voice is a brief buzzing.

Other notable tree frog species found in East Africa

Uluguru Tree Frog *Leptopelis uluguruensis* Another tree frog endemic to the Eastern Arc Mountains, Tanzania (East and West Usambaras, Ulugurus, and possibly Udzungwa Mountains), usually a dense green to bluish green, frequently with white blotches and/or rings in the pattern. Iris of the eye is dark; tympanum very small; voice described as a brief, unremarkable *clack*.

Christy's Tree Frog *Leptopelis christyi* Very similar to Albertine Rift Tree Frog *Leptopelis kivuensis* but lacks white spot on upper lip below the eye. Known from Budongo Forest and a disturbed area adjacent to Bwindi Impenetrable National Park, Uganda and a number of other localities in north-western Tanzania, northern Rwanda and southern Uganda.

Genus *Afrixalus*: Leaf-folding Frogs

Small to middle-sized tree frogs, similar in size and shape to reed frogs (*Hyperolius*) but distinguished from all other arboreal East African frogs by the shape of the pupil, always vertically rhomboidal or diamond-shaped (with four angles). Fingers and toes usually webbed; the tympanum is usually not visible. Male gular gland always present, round and bright yellow in many species. In a number of species the skin of the male is beset with tiny black spines on the dorsum, sides (and frequently the gular gland), giving the skin a rough appearance. Where known, all species deposit eggs along the midline of a leaf (frequently grass) above water; the outer edges of the leaf are then folded together and 'glued' over the egg mass, hence the common name. The male advertisement call is non-melodic; in smaller species it may be a prolonged, insect-like buzzing, preceded or followed by series of single, distinct *clicks*; in larger species the call is a series of low, but loud rapid *clicks* like a tiny machine-gun. *Afrixalus* species are mostly forest, moist savannah or grassland forms and absent from the arid, semi-desert areas of East Africa. About 12 species occur in East Africa.

Dwarf Leaf-folding Frog
Afrixalus brachycnemis

Identification: Sexes similar in size, up to 22mm. A very small leaf-folding frog with a narrow head, distinguished from the nearly identical Grassland Dwarf Leaf-folding Frog, *Afrixalus septentrionalis*, by absence of a mid-dorsal stripe and presence of dark asperities on the male gular gland. Dorsal skin covered with minute unpigmented spinules. When the frog is sitting, a dark brown stripe is visible on the upper surface of the hind legs. Pure white below. The male gular gland is yellow; this and the chest have many tiny, well-spaced black spinules.

Habitat and Distribution: Inhabits grassy coastal and inland riverine habitats, at low altitude, from the Juba River in Somalia south through coastal Kenya to Malawi and Mozambique, west to Singida in Tanzania.

Natural History: There are conflicting reports as to whether this species glues the edges of leaves over egg mass. Males call from emergent vegetation, sometimes close to water surface; call begins with a single *buzz*, then a prolonged, steady insect-like buzzing, which may last up to 10 seconds.

Spiny Leaf-folding Frog
Afrixalus fornasinii

Identification: The largest East African *Afrixalus*; males and females to 40mm. Both sexes have minute black spines all over the back, head, and upper surfaces of fore and hindlimbs, particularly obvious in males. The chin or gular

gland is disc-like and white, not yellow, without spinules. Two dorsal color patterns are known, not correlated with sex. In the first, the entire dorsal surface of the head, body and hind legs is uniform silver to light brownish gold with no blotches or stripes; the second pattern includes a broad, mid dorsal stripe of dark brown.

Habitat and Distribution: Breeds in ponds or flooded areas in differing habitats where grass is present including openings and glades in coastal forest. Found from Malindi southwards on the Kenya coast into Tanzania, inland in the Rufiji River area, widespread in southeast Tanzania.

Natural History: Male advertisement call is a loud, slow series of *ticks* 5–10 per second, lasting several seconds; and has been likened to the firing of a tiny machine gun. This remarkable frog has recently been shown to prey on the newly deposited eggs of other frogs during the breeding season, including foam-nesting frogs (*Chiromantis*), reed frogs (*Hyperolius spinigularis*, *H. tuberilinguis*) and perhaps those of its own species.

Striped Leaf-folding Frog
*Afrixalus quadrivittatus**

Identification: Medium-sized leaf-folding frog, females usually slightly larger than males, but in our area both sexes can reach 27mm. Unmistakable, the only evenly striped leaf-folding frog in East Africa. The back and sides are dark

brown, with three well-defined cream to light golden longitudinal stripes down the back, originating on the snout which is of the same colour. The upper limb surfaces also have a longitudinal stripe. Skin of males with light, rather inconspicuous spines; gular gland disc-like in shape and bright yellow; both sexes light and unpatterned below. No ventral spinules or asperities.

Habitat and Distribution: Inhabits pools in grassland/savannah at medium elevation, tolerant of disturbed areas, calling from man-made dams and roadside drainage ditches. Absent from higher elevation forests. In East Africa, fairly common in the Lake Victoria drainage of western Kenya, northern Tanzania and south-eastern Uganda, but distributed at lower elevations across southern Uganda, Rwanda and Burundi; known also from Kigoma Region, Tanzania, on shores of Lake Tanganyika. and recently reported from Serengeti National Park.

Natural History: Male advertisement call typical of other leaf-folding frogs, described as series of *clicks* (11–12 per second in Uganda; 6–7 in Ethiopia), somewhat intermediate between the *buzz* of smaller forms (*A. brachycnemis*, *A. septentrionalis*) and staccato call of the larger Spiny Leaf-folding Frog *A. fornasinii*. Lifestyle little known.

* We are assuming this species is distinct from a number of similar Central and West African populations distributed across the Sahel to Cameroon, currently known as *A. fulvovittatus*.

Eastern Arc Leaf-folding Frog
Afrixalus uluguruensis

Identification: Males to 25mm; females slightly larger, to 27mm. A medium-sized leaf-folding frog with narrow waist and flat head with bulging eyes. Males with very small, round, white gular gland; the males have small unpigmented spines on the dorsum; females are smooth.
A light brown canthal stripe is always present, running from tip of snout to above the fore limbs. The back varies from almost pure white with a few light brown markings, to a fine vermiculation of tiny cinnamon spots scattered evenly or irregularly over the back; this pigmentation never coalesces into stripes, spots or other recognisable shapes.

Habitat and Distribution: A forest-dependent endemic confined to the Eastern Arc Mountains, so far known from the East and West Usambaras, Uluguru and Udzungwa Mountains, Tanzania. Several endemic species of tree frogs and reed frogs occur in the Eastern Arc Mountains but *Afrixalus ulugurensis* appears to be the only endemic member of its genus found there.

Natural History: Voice described as quiet buzzing. Deposits eggs at tip of herbaceous vegetation 1–1.5m above water; does not fold edges of leaf over egg mass.

Western Rift Leaf-folding Frog
Afrixalus orophilus

Identification: A small leaf-folding frog; Ugandan males and females to about 22mm. Unmistakable, consistent dorsal pattern of two fine, non-converging, cinnamon-coloured lines on a background of light goldish-brown.

Habitat and Distribution: Apparently endemic to the eastern and western escarpment forests of the Albertine (Western) Rift above 1,500m in Uganda, Rwanda, Burundi and Democratic Republic of the Congo. Occurs with Osorio's Leaf-folding Frog *A. osorioi* at Omubuyanja Swamp, Bwindi Impenetrable National Park (1,850m).

Natural History: Reproduction, call and natural history unknown.

Osorio's Leaf-folding Frog
Afrixalus osorioi

Identification: Medium-sized leaf-folding frog (Ugandan males to 27mm; females to 29mm). A dark, dense dorsal colour pattern comprised of two mocha-coloured, broad, paravertebral stripes originating on snout and reaching

about two-thirds of the way to the hind legs. A third stripe of the same colour originates directly over the vent and passes towards the head between the two paravertebral stripes about one-third the length of the body; stripes occur against a dark brown to nearly black background; in some specimens all three stripes coalesce where they meet.

Habitat and Distribution: Occurs at Bwindi Impenetrable National Park with *Afrixalus orophilus* at above 1,800m. Also known from Rwanda and Kakamega, Kenya. There are old records of the species at Entebbe and Budongo Forest, Uganda, but it is absent in the lower elevation Kibale Forest of south-west Uganda.

Natural History: The species exhibits leaf-folding reproductive behaviour and the call is described as an initial slow *creaking* sound followed by a series of *clicks* from eight or nine per second.

Smooth Leaf-folding Frog
Afrixalus laevis

Identification: A small leaf-folding frog, the largest Uganda specimen is a 23mm male. The head is flat, the eyes bulging, and both sexes lack spines or asperities. Variable colour pattern from light golden-brown dorsally with slightly darker brown stripe through the eye, to white or gold, with a small horizontal bar between the eyes and a small, chevron mark between fore limbs and hind limbs.

Habitat and Distribution: In East Africa, found on both sides of Western Rift in forests of Uganda, Rwanda and Burundi. Occurs at Bwindi Impenetrable National Park but at lower elevations than *Afrixalus osorioi* and *A. orophilus*; fairly common at Buhoma, a popular tourist destination at 1,580m. Single record from the central Congo Basin.

Natural History: The call (described from a Cameroon specimen) is a series of single clacks; the East African specimens have not been sonogrammed. West African specimens are said to deposit eggs on leaves overhanging moving water, without folding the outer edges of the leaves over the egg mass.

Other species of leaf-folding frog found in East Africa

Snoring Leaf-folding Frog *Afrixalus crotalus* Small (up to 24mm) frog with pale yellow back, usually with faint brown vertebral line. Known from extreme south-east Tanzania. The call is a series of *clicks*, about seven per second.

De Witte's Leaf-folding Frog *Afrixalus wittei* A medium-sized frog, up to 33mm, with three dark stripes on a golden-yellow or brown dorsum. Known from south-western Tanzania near Sumbawanga. The call is a short *buzz* followed by about eight rapid *clicks*.

Shimba Hills Leaf-folding Frog *Afrixalus sylvaticus* A small frog, reaching 24mm, the back is off-white with darker speckles and a distinctive broad dark bank across the lower back. Known only from the Shimba Hills area, southeast Kenya. The voice is a series of short *clicks*.

Grassland Dwarf Leaf-folding Frog *Afrixalus septentrionalis* Reaches 23mm, a small frog, appears nearly identical to the Dwarf Leaf-folding Frog *Afrixalus brachycnemis* in all respects, but lacks a mid-dorsal stripe. Medium elevation savannah in south-east Kenya, as far west as Machakos District; probably occurs in similar habitats in northern Tanzania.

Udzungwa Leaf-folding Frog *Afrixalus morerei* Small frog (23mm), dorsum is light with pair of brown, broken dorso-lateral stripes that merge posteriorly. Endemic to Udzungwa Mountains. The voice is a long, even *buzzing*.

Genus *Hyperolius*: Reed Frogs

Delicate and beautiful, often with stunning colour patterns, the reed frogs are small to medium-sized arboreal tree frogs with horizontally oval pupils. *Hyperolius* is the most successful and speciose genus in the African tree frog family Hyperoliidae, with over 120 species. Reed frogs are found across sub-Saharan Africa from coast to coast and south to South Africa. With a few exceptions, the skin is smooth and the tympanum hidden (but present beneath the skin). Usually the skin of male vocal sac is very distensible, the gular gland is disc-like or oval and white (not yellow as in leaf-folding frogs, *Afrixalus*). Normally males are only slightly smaller in snout-vent length than females, and with a few exceptions both sexes have the same colour patterns (however, see below). Many species are brightly coloured, and populations of the poorly understood '*viridiflavus* complex' (see pages 191–193) usually occur in at least two different colour phases as adults. Where known, most species deposit eggs in vegetation overhanging water; after hatching, the tadpoles drop into the water below. Male advertisement calls are variable but are usually a single *tink, tak, creak*, or *buzz*, often repeated in series.

Argus Reed Frog
Hyperolius argus

Identification: Grows to 35mm. One of only two East African species that exhibit marked sexual dimorphism (males and females look different) for colour pattern. Males are usually fairly uniform dull green to yellowish brown with a dark thin mask (canthal line) of black or black spots extending from the tip of the snout to the eye.

Females are unmistakable; usually cinnamon to rich golden-brown on the back and sides, with large round and oblong cream to yellow blotches with even black edges.

Habitat and Distribution: Coastal habitats from southern Somalia, south through coastal Kenya and Tanzania.
Probably originally a coastal forest dweller that has adapted to the fragmentation of this environment over time.

Natural History: Males seem to prefer to call from floating vegetation like lily pads or water cabbage, eggs are laid in bunches of about 30, up to 200 per female, and probably attached to vegetation above the water surface, although there are conflicting data in the literature. Male advertisement call is usually a nearly continuous series of thin, reedy *wenk* sounds.

Ahl's Reed Frog
Hyperolius castaneus

Identification: Up to 35mm. Extremely variable in colour and pattern but the pattern always contains some elements of lime green. A dark canthal line is always present, and dorsal colouration is usually sharply delineated from the ventrum by a wavy but continuous dark line.

Habitat and Distribution: A high elevation forest dweller, particularly common in forest swamps at or above 2000m in eastern Democratic Republic of the Congo, south-western Uganda and in Rwanda.

Natural History: Nothing is known of the reproductive biology; males call from sideways positions on tall grasses and sedges. Ahl's reed frog seems to be replaced at lower elevations by *Hyperolius lateralis*, the side-blotched reed frog. Male call a fairly loud *tchick!*

Cinnamon-bellied Reed Frog
Hyperolius cinnamomeoventris

Identification: Up to 28mm. Like the Argus Reed Frog, this species is also sexually dichromatic. Males are usually light brown on the back and sides, frequently with small dark speckles and with two obvious white dorso-lateral stripes, edged in black, that run from the snout to the hind limbs. Females are always fairly uniform green without markings, although laterally may be yellowish with flecking.

Habitat and Distribution: One of the few reed frogs known to inhabit both forest clearings and savanna habitats. In East Africa, it is found from western Kenya (Kisumu and Kakamega Districts) across Uganda (where it has been found above 2,000m in Bwindi Impenetrable National Park) and extreme north-west Tanzania to Rwanda.

Natural History: Unknown, as is the reproductive biology. The male advertisement call is a series of short, distinct *clicks*.

Silver-bladdered Reed Frog
Hyperolius cystocandicans

Identification: Males to 28mm; females larger, to 36mm. Colour pattern varies from thick mustard yellow to marbled russet, translucent bluish below. Distinguished by its silvery-white bladder, visible through the semi-transparent skin of the ventral

surface, and the presence of dense pectoral glands near the armpits. The large gular gland covers the entire gular region.

Habitat and Distribution: Endemic to Kenya, in open grassland habitats in the central highlands, including the Laikipia Plateau, from 2200–2500m. It co-occurs with another Kenya highlands endemic, the Mountain Reed Frog *Hyperolius montanus* at several localities.

Natural History: Male call is a brief *chiik, chiik, chiik*, or a longer, drawn-out *criiiik–iiiik–iiiik*. Females evidently carry from 120–260 eggs; in the laboratory, development from egg to metamorphosis occurs in 80–90 days.

White-snouted Reed Frog
Hyperolius frontalis

Identification: Males to 28mm, females to 30mm. The highly-contrasting white or light golden snout on moss-green background is diagnostic. Skin rather granular; a dark canthal strip of dark spots between nostril and eye. Males have large round gular gland that covers

the throat region. The vocal sac is green when inflated.

Habitat and Distribution: Montane forest glades, up to 2000m, in Bwindi Impenetrable National Park in south-western Uganda, the Virunga region of Rwanda and the Albertine Rift forests of extreme eastern Democratic Republic of the Congo.

Natural History: Males call from leaves up to 1.5m above ground. The call has been described as a brief, hard buzzing, repeated in series of two or three. Around 24 eggs are suspended from leaves above still or slow moving water in forest clearings.

Kivu Reed Frog
Hyperolius kivuensis

Identification: Males to 34mm; females to 40mm. Snout rather long and pointed; colour varies from light or dark green to brown; usually with a continuous black lateral band extending from the nose to the pelvic region. Male gular gland is large and flat.

Habitat and Distribution: An evidently environmentally tolerant inhabitant of farmbush country and also dense wooded savannahh from western Kenya at Kakamega and Chemilil and northwestern Tanzania through the Victoria Basin of southern Uganda and northern Tanzania to Rwanda and the eastern Democratic Republic of the Congo.

Natural History: The call is a series of low coarse *creaks*. Poorly known, eggs are said to be deposited above water in the normal *Hyperolius* mode.

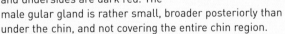

Side-blotched Reed Frog
Hyperolius lateralis

Identification: Males to 26mm; females to 29mm. Colour variable but in Uganda and western Kenya usually bright to medium dense green, with a broad irregular white or yellow, highly contrasting black-edged stripe; the hands and feet and undersides are dark red. The male gular gland is rather small, broader posteriorly than under the chin, and not covering the entire chin region.

Habitat and Distribution: Agricultural areas, savannah and medium elevation montane forest, from Kakamega, Kenya, west through Uganda in the Victoria Basin drainage to the eastern side of the Albertine Rift in Democratic Republic of the Congo, south through Rwanda to northwestern Tanzania.

Natural History: Little known. Male advertisement call is a succession of brief screams. In the higher elevations of south-western Uganda, this species appears to be replaced by Ahl's tree frog, *Hyperolius castaneus*.

Mountain Reed Frog
Hyperolius montanus

Identification: Males to 28mm; females 34mm. Often at same localities as Silver-bladdered Reed Frog *Hyperolius cystocandicans*; this species distinguishable by denser colouration, usually shades of light

and darker brown expanding on to flanks; broad brown canthal strip extends from snout to groin (absent in *H. cystocandicans*); opaque dense white to cream below, unlike the translucent ventrum of *H. cystocandicans*.

Habitat and Distribution: Restricted to the higher elevations of high central Kenya; an endemic. Occurs alongside Silver-bladdered Reed Frog at Maua in the Nyambeni Range, Limuru and Tigoni. Also extends higher (to 3350m on the Chogoria Track, eastern Mt Kenya).

Natural History: Call a succession of screams, different from the quiet call of the Silver-bladdered Reed Frog. A series of females collected at midday in tall grass at the western edge of the Aberdares National Park at around 3200m.

Sharp-nosed Reed Frog
Hyperolius nasutus

Identification: Tiny; both sexes to about 25mm snout-vent. Very sharp-nosed and elongate, usually a light translucent green overall with two narrow white dorso-lateral stripes, not usually outlined in darker

pigment. Third mid-dorsal stripe in some populations; others brownish with spots. Males have a well-developed gular gland.

Habitat and Distribution: Usually in reeds and grassy open areas in savannah. Often found with member of Common Reed Frog complex. Common in openings in *Brachystegia* woodland environments of Central Africa. In East Africa known from a few localities in coastal, central and extreme western Kenya, throughout Victoria Basin of Tanzania and Uganda to Albertine Rift (lower elevations), southward in most suitable habitats in Tanzania.

Natural History: Usually calls from grasses or sedges; a series of *ziiip*, *ziiip*, *ziiip*. Unlike most other members of genus females deposit about 200 eggs attached to submerged vegetation. Has a huge range, shows a lot of variation, and has been given several taxonomic names. Some of these may represent cryptic, undescribed species, others are probably synonyms.

Masai Reed Frog
Hyperolius orkarkarri

Identification: Largest specimen known is a 21.1mm female. Unmistakable, its extremely rough warty skin and grey colouration match the granite rocks it lives on. The hands, feet and underside of hind limbs are dark orange; the ventrum is white.

Habitat and Distribution: Endemic to Tanzania, known only from two localities, Gong Rock (Moru Kopjes) and Galen's Drift, in the Serengeti National Park.

Natural History: Call unknown; the type specimen is a female. Clearly a rock dweller, but natural history unknown.

Taxonomic Note: A study using DNA sequence determined that this species was identical to another Serengeti species, Peters' Reed Frog *Hyperolius glandicolor*. However, tissues were mixed up, and the matter is thus not resolved. Nevertheless, this frog is highly distinctive, and likely to be encountered by visitors to Moru Kopjes in the Serengeti.

Shimba Hills Reed Frog
Hyperolius rubrovermiculatus

Identification: Males to 27mm; females larger, to 32mm. A brilliantly coloured reed frog, dark brown to black on the back and sides, with bright-red spots on the head and upper surfaces. A pair of bright white canthal and dorso-lateral stripes run the length of the body onto the heels. A white lumbar band is often present; ventrum and throat yellow to orange, feet and hands orange to red. A juvenile phase is also described as generally brownish with diffuse darker spots on the back, yellow below. Males have coarse dorsal skin and a rather small gular gland; females smooth.

Habitat and Distribution: Endemic to Kenya. Known only from forest clearings in the Shimba Hills National Park and at nearby Kwale. Schiotz has suggested a close relationship between this species and Mitchell's Reed Frog of the Eastern Arc Mountains of Tanzania; the Shimba Hills are probably geologically part of this ancient mountain complex.

Natural History: The male advertisement call has been described as a scream. Little else recorded.

Spiny-throated Reed Frog
Hyperolius spinigularis

Identification: Males to 24mm; females to 30mm. Superficially similar to the white-snouted reed frog of Uganda, but white colouration may continue posteriorly as two conspicuous dorsolateral stripes or broad blotches. Breeding males with a distinctive round gular gland; this

gland, the ventrum and underside of the thighs are beset with evenly spaced black spinules (like some *Afrixalus*).

Habitat and Distribution: Usually in rather dense forest openings or in farm bush on mountain slopes. Apparently endemic to the Eastern Arc Mountain complex but distribution disjunct; known from the East and West Usambaras, the Udzungwa Mountains, and Mlanje Mountain (Malawi).

Natural History: Call unrecorded. A clutch of 150–200 eggs is deposited in flat leaves overhanging water. One of the few frogs known to attend egg masses. In 1988, at a small pool in the Kwamkoro Forest Reserve, Usambara Mountains, 31 Spiny-throated Reed Frog egg masses were discovered, 13 of which had a female on the same leaf.

Tinker Reed Frog
Hyperolius tuberilinguis

Identification: Females to 35mm; males to 33mm. Colour pattern highly variable, (green, tan, yellow, white) but adults have conspicuously pointed snouts and appear to have very large eyes (good field character): this is not a matter of size, rather the iris is

relatively small compared to the large pupil. Males have a rounded gular gland, not completely covering chin region.

Habitat and Distribution: From Malndi in coastal Kenya south through eastern Tanzania.

Habitat and Distribution: The call has been described as a series of low, coarse *creaks*, sometimes two in rapid succession. On the East African coast, the call is a loud metallic *tak!* Females deposit rather large masses of eggs in very firm jelly, suspended from stems of vegetation immediately above the water surface.

Common Reed Frogs of the *Hyperolius viridiflavus* / *Hyperolius glandicolor* complex

Taxonomic Notes: Examples of this fascinating species vary widely in colour, as illustrated in the photo spread overleaf, and in many cases it is not known whether they are just differently coloured varieties of the same species, or different species. In addition, sometimes the males, females and juveniles all have different colours. As a result, the frogs of this species are at present grouped in what is called a 'complex'; that is a group of frogs that almost certainly share a recent ancestor, and may or not be separate species. Studies taking place at present, using a mixture of the call, the molecular biochemistry, colour and distribution may shed light on the group in the future. The group is poorly understood as the colour patterns, while extremely distinctive in the female, vary from population to population. In East Africa there are at least nine identifiable populations which have been widely (but reluctantly) accepted as subspecies of the Common Reed Frog *Hyperolius viridiflavus*. Recent molecular work on a large part of the vast complex suggests that there may be several genetically distinct species within the group as a whole. Ten colour patterns occur quite commonly in East Africa which, if the recent molecular study is correct, belong to at least two species. Rather than try to describe them, we have simply included a picture of each female pattern represented in East Africa, along with brief distribution data. The different names used below reflect the confusion of the taxonomy of this group. They do not have English names either, and we have resisted the temptation to give them any until the taxonomy is further clarified.

Size: Populations variable, but the maximum size is about 33mm.

Identification: This group differs from other members of the genus in being strictly savanna dwellers, having a very short snout, and females having a transverse gular fold and depositing eggs in water, rather than over-hanging vegetation. The males have a distinctive, melodic *tink* or *ting* advertisement call.

Habitat and Distribution: Open pools and marshes of savanna habitats over most of East and Central Africa.

Natural History: see above.

continued over

Common Reed Frogs of the *Hyperolius viridiflavus / Hyperolius glandicolor* complex

Hyperolius viridiflavus viridiflavus
Eastern Rift Valley of Kenya (Nakuru), but absent from arid north. Abundant in western Kenya (Kakamega).

Hyperolius glandicolor pantherinus
Western slopes of Mount Kenya, localities such as Nanyuki and Nyeri.

Hyperolius glandicolor ferniquei
Vicinity of Nairobi and medium elevations in central Kenya, east of Rift Masai Mara Game Reserve.

Hyperolius glandicolor glandicolor
Lower elevations of south-western Kenya, Tsavo East and West National Park, Lake Jipe.

Hyperolius glandicolor ngorongoriensis
Vicinity of Ngorongoro Crater (Karatu).

Hyperolius glandicolor goetzei
Savannah of north-central and
southern Tanzania (Serengeti south
to Lake Malawi).

Hyperolius (viridiflavus) mariae
Coastal Kenya and Tanzania
(Arabuko-Sokoke Forest, Kenya;
Zaraninge Forest, Tanzania).

Hyperolius glandicolor ommatostictus
Open swamps, vicinity Mount Meru,
Tanzania (Ngare Sero, Arusha).

Hyperolius viridiflavus variabilis
Northern margins of Lake Victoria,
Uganda (Lake Nabogabo).

Hyperolius viridiflavus mwanzae
Southern margins of Lake Victoria
(Mwanza, Tanzania).

Hyperolius glandicolor pitmani
Apparently a forest form of Albertine
Rift (Omubuyanja Swamp, Bwindi
Impenetrable National Park).

Other notable reed frog species found in East Africa

Parker's Reed Frog *Hyperolius parkeri* A small green frog (to 26mm) with a pointed snout; similar to Sharp-nosed Reed Frog except larger and bulkier and two white dorso-lateral bands on green or brown background usually edged in black. Spines on limbs and undersides of legs and arms but not on gular gland as in Spiny-throated Reed Frog. Male advertisement call (a bird-like *trill*) and the fact that males are larger than females is unique within the genus. Coastal habitats in Kenya, through Tanzania to Mozambique.

Five-striped Reed Frog *Hyperolius quinquevittatus*. A small (to 25mm) reed frog reminiscent of Parker's and sharp-snouted reed frogs but with gorgeous series of longitudinal stripes; mid-dorsal stripe of bright lime-green, sharply defined in black; two paravertebral cinnamon-brownstripes on either side of mid-dorsal stripe, which in turn are sharply defined by broad, dorso-lateral black stripes; below these are two white stripes beginning on eyelids running the length to the body; these are bordered below by another pair of sharply defined black stripes; upper jaw is sharply lined in white; hind legs are also longitudinally striped dorsally in brown and white or whitish green. Male call is a single, unmelodic *creak*. In East Africa has been reported in southern Mbeya Region and Rovuma Region, near the Mozambique border in Tanzania.

Flat-headed Reed Frog *Hyperolius langi* Small forest reed frog, found Kibale forest and Bwindi Impenetrable National Park, Uganda. Males to 24mm; females to 30mm. Dull green; often dark brown triple hourglass pattern on back.

Buhoma Reed Frog *Hyperolius alticola* Large (females to 35mm), tan to gold-brown uniform reed frog, with dark canthal line from snout to eye. Males with minute spinules on dorsal surfaces; known from forests of Virunga region in Rwanda and Bwindi Impenetrable National Park, Uganda, near Buhoma.

Eastern Arc Golden Reed Frog *Hyperolius puncticulatus* Robust (males to 30mm, females to 37mm) variable, but commonly brilliant orange ground colour with a bright yellow canthal stripe outlined in black which may extend dorso-laterally 2/3 of body length; some individuals have numerous black-edged rounded spots scattered across the dorsum. Common at Amani pond in East Usambaras and all forests of the Eastern Arc Mountains of Tanzania, extends on the Nyika Plateau of Malawi and also Mlanje Mountain, Malawi.

Tiny Reed Frog *Hyperolius minutissimus* Smallest reed frog (males to 15mm), endemic to high-elevation grasslands in Iringa Region, southern Tanzania. Brownish with black-edged canthal and lateral stripe running snout to groin.

Water Lily Reed Frog *Hyperolius pusillus* Tiny, (21mm) flat, translucent green frog, pale yellow feet; like small version of Argus Reed Frog; frequently calls from lily pads or Nile cabbage leaves; eggs green, deposited between leaves of lilies / other floating plants. Common in coastal environments: southern Somalia, south through Kenya / Tanzania to KwaZulu / Natal, South Africa.

Green Reed Frog *Hyperolius viridis* Similar colour pattern to Water Lily Reed Frog but larger (to 23mm); light dorso-lateral line and yellow gular gland; reduced webbing of feet. Found in high grasslands in the Sumbawanga and Mbeya Regions of south-western Tanzania and in eastern Zambia.

Genus *Kassina*: Kassinas

A morphologically diverse genus of mostly terrestrial frogs, with some arboreal members in West Africa. Kassinas (sometimes called running frogs) are found throughout sub-Saharan Africa, with about ten currently recognised species. The pupil of the eye is always vertical like tree frogs (*Leptopelis*); the tympanum is always visible. Males and females are about the same size in most species. The hind and fore limbs are approximately equal in length in most East African terrestrial species. Male Kassinas have very thick gular glands which are strap-like and attached anteriorly and posteriorly so that the distensible part of the inflated gular sac protrudes from each side of the head when calling; frequently the tissue of the inflated vocal sac is black. With one exception (the Somali Kassina), finger and toe tips are not or only moderately expanded into digital discs. Webbing in all East African species is reduced. Usually grey to light brown with darker linear stripes or spots; these are always highlighted by lighter edges. All members of this group, the related genus of rough-skinned tree frogs, *Phlyctimantis*, and the Ethiopian snail-eater, *Paracassina*, are identifiable by a distinctive male advertisement call. The most widespread species, the Senegal Kassina, makes a beautiful, liquid, rising, *boink!* sound, much like a drop of water in a bucket. Where known, all Kassina species call with a frequency-modulated variation on this theme. Members of this group can be instantly recognised throughout sub-Saharan African by this familiar rainy season call.

Red-legged Kassina
Kassina maculata

Identification: Largest East African Kassina, males to 60mm, females to 65mm. Finger and toe tips slightly dilated. The black oval dorsal spots are highlighted by a thin light line; inner surface of groin, armpits and undersides of hind legs bright red.

Habitat and Distribution: Frequents bodies of water in forests and disturbed habitats of coastal Kenya and north-eastern coastal Tanzania, sporadic records from south-eastern Tanzania.

Natural History: Call a typical Kassina rising *quoick*, but somewhat less musical, flatter and lower-pitched than the Senegal Kassina. Males call while floating amid aquatic vegetation on surface of ponds. Extremely shy and difficult to approach. Eggs said to be deposited singly or a few together on submerged vegetation. This species is rather unlike other East African members of the genus in having much longer hind limbs relative to forelimbs.

Somali Kassina
Kassina maculifer

Identification: A medium-size Kassina; both sexes reaching 40mm. Only Kassina in East Africa with enlarged finger and toe tips. A conspicuous brown dumbbell shape from between the eyes to the level of the forelimbs is diagnostic of this species. Males have dark distensible skin on either side of the gular gland.

Habitat and Distribution: Wells and water pans at low altitude in the dry Somali Arid Zone. Originally described from Garoe, Somalia; later found in freshwater cisterns in Wajir and at Sabuli water pans near there; and in an old museum collection from Banissa, Mandera District, all in northeastern Kenya.

Natural History: Unknown, but the call has been analysed; a typical frequency modulated Kassina call, shorter in duration and more steeply rising than for other Kassinas.

Senegal Kassina
Kassina senegalensis

Identification: Both sexes to 42mm in Kenya (larger elsewhere). Rather short hind limbs; moves by running rather than leaping. Gular gland strap-like with distensible dark tissue on either side of throat. Silver-grey to gold-brown above.

Pattern may be any combination of darker stripes and/or elongate blotches, usually with fine light edging. Specimens from arid north have a reduced pattern, some authors recognize these as a separate species, *Kassina somalica*.

Habitat and Distribution: Breeds in a wide variety of aquatic habitats in most savanna-like environments save high elevation forests. Recorded almost throughout East Africa, although records lacking from north-west Kenya and north-east Uganda.

Natural History: Terrestrial. Male advertisement call is lovely, musical, liquid *boink*. Males call from under overhanging vegetation or on open ground at waters edge. Single call is hard to locate. Males recorded starting to call intermittently at a considerable distance from a breeding site. Eggs are attached to aquatic vegetation; over 200 may be laid.

Genus *Phlyctimantis*: Rough-skinned Tree Frogs

Strict forest-dwellers, very similar to Kassinas in having vertical pupil, visible tympanum, gular gland structure, tadpole morphology and even male advertisement call, which is also frequency-modulated. *Phlyctimantis* have longer hind legs, and the discs of fingers and toes are greatly expanded. They have very rounded, disc-like gular glands, which are free posteriorly. The back is dull brown or black, unmarked, but there are vivid colour patches in the armpits and groin, seen when the animals move. This coloration is similar to that of the Red-legged Kassina *Kassina maculata*. All *Phlyctimantis* also have the external downward-directed, tubular extension of the cloaca present only in *K. maculata* and *K. decorata* of West Africa, suggesting the latter two species may belong to this genus. Two of the four species of rough-skinned tree frogs are forest dwellers; two appear to breed in ponds in open grassy areas. Reproductive information is unknown.

Western Rift Rough-skinned Tree Frog
Phlyctimantis verrucosus

Identification: Sexes similar, to 53mm. A large frog with uniform dark to medium brown dorsal coloration, long arms and legs, dark irises and slightly bumpy skin. Hidden parts of the body, such as the armpits and inguinal regions are bright orange. The dorsal surfaces of the hind limbs have orange stripes, these bright areas are hidden from view when the frog is at rest. Finger and toe webbing absent; otherwise characteristics as for the genus.

Habitat and Distribution: Lives in forest at mid to higher elevation forests in Rwanda, and western Uganda.

Natural History: Egg deposition sites unknown for species of this genus; male advertisement call similar to various Kassinas but rather atonal; males may call from the ground or from as high as 3m above ground in bushes and trees.

Other rough-skinned tree frog species in East Africa

Keith's Rough-skinned Tree Frog *Phlyctimantis keithae* Known only from the Udzungwa Mountains, Tanzania. Growing to 43mm length, it is black, with minute white spots, and bright orange, yellow or pink, black barred, at the body-limb junctions.

Asian Tree Frogs: Family Rhacophoridae

Members of this family are similar to the African hyperoliid frogs but the two families differ in a number of internal characteristics. As the common name implies the Rhacophorids are mainly Asian; the three or four species of the genus *Chiromantis* are the only African representatives of the family.

Genus *Chiromantis*: African Foam-nest Frogs

A remarkable group of frogs, both physiologically and reproductively, members of this genus all have opposable 'thumbs', this chameleon-like arrangement presumably aids these heavy-bodied frogs in climbing. *Chiromantis* are large, with females usually much larger than males and usually greyish or brownish. All except the West African species *Chiromantis rufescens* are able to blanche chalk white, presumably to increase their reflectance of direct sunlight. They are unique among African frogs in their ability to excrete uric acids (like birds and reptiles), in their tolerance to heat (they can withstand temperatures of up to 40°C internally) and in properties of the skin that reduce evaporative water loss. Thus they are often found sitting exposed to the hot sun at midday, which no other African frog can do. As their name suggests, these frogs construct foam nests within which the eggs are deposited; nests are constructed on vegetation overhanging temporary water from two to twenty metres above the water. Foam is produced from a substance from the female cloaca by the churning action of the hind legs of the females and the many males accompanying her. All the males seem to participate in fertilisation. The foam nests harden overnight, eggs hatch and develop into tadpoles within the nest. Six to eight days later the nest decomposes and the tadpoles drop into the water below, where development continues. Adults are never found in water, and in arid northern Kenya adults of *Chiromantis petersi* may take refuge in the huts of nomads.

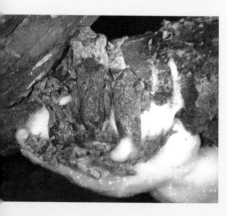

Southern Foam-nest Frog
Chiromantis xerampelina

(Female and three males
producing foam)

Southern Foam-nest Frog
Chiromantis xerampelina

Identification: Size variable, Kenya coast females to 65mm, males to 42mm. Differs from other East African species in more extensive webbing between fingers; intermediate in size between the Western and Northern Foam-nest Frogs. Coloration variable.

Habitat and Distribution: Woodland and coastal mosaic areas; tolerant of disturbed habitats. Occurs along the coast from southern Somalia, south through Kenya but spreading inland in Tanzania, south through Zambia to KwaZulu-Natal. It seems to be replaced in inland Kenya by the much larger Northern Foam-nest Frog.

Natural History: Egg masses are preyed upon by the Spiny Leaf-folding Frog (*Afrixalus fornasinii*). How the skin of these frogs resists water loss remains a fascinating mystery, despite ongoing investigations.

Other foam-nest frog species

It is often difficult to separate the species of *Chiromantis* on morphology alone. The status of some described species is under investigation.

Northern Foam-nest Frog *Chiromantis petersi* This is the largest member of the genus, with females reaching 92mm, snout to vent. It is an inhabitant of drier, more arid areas than the Southern Foam-nest Frog, and is widespread in northern and eastern Kenya, south through south-western Tanzania.

Western Foam-nest Frog *Chiromantis rufescens* This is a much more gracile, slender species, reaching 60mm; almost always brownish in coloration and reputed to have green bones. It is known from forests of western Uganda, west to the Atlantic Coast.

Keller's Foam-nest Frog *Chiromantis kelleri* This species has just been resurrected from being a subspecies of *Chiromantis petersi*; we are uncertain of the status of this species. If valid, it resembles *Chiromantis petersi*, and inhabits northern Kenya, leaving the Northern Foam-nest Frog in southern and eastern Kenya.

Ranid or 'typical' frogs: Family Ranidae

The common name does little to describe the features of its members, but many ranid frogs are easily recognised: they are the frogs of childhood storybooks, with big eyes, pointed snouts, alert postures and long legs. Many have the typical frog lifestyle of living near water or, at least, in moist conditions and returning to water to breed. Many species have considerable webbing between the toes. Other ranids have developed adaptations that allow them to survive long periods of drought and these alter their appearance to a considerable degree. These include rounded globose bodies, the possession of a large, hard digging tubercle on the foot, and the ability to aestivate, usually by burying themselves in a sealed chamber during the dry season. The family Ranidae contains the smallest and largest frogs in East Africa. In terms of species numbers it is the second largest family (the largest is the tree frogs, Hyperoliidae) with about 55 species in East Africa. Many ranids are easily recognisable. However, some of the genera (especially the puddle frogs, *Phrynobatrachus*) are complex and poorly understood, and some of the puddle frog species are very difficult to identify. This entire family is under review; there is consensus among scientists that the group is probably not a natural one and contains a number of families. We have been conservative and kept Ranidae for the time being, but have adopted some newly proposed names, for example *Amnirana* for *Hylarana*.

Genus *Rana*: African River Frogs

River Frogs as their name suggests are found in larger bodies of water, usually rivers and streams, in a variety of habitats. They are large animals. They spend a lot of time in the water, consequently their toes are webbed and they are excellent swimmers. They lack the regular, longitudinal glandular ridges of ridged frogs (*Ptychadena*) and the expanded toe tips of most species of white-lipped frogs (*Amnirana*). The taxonomy of this group is still being studied.

Angolan River Frog
Rana angolensis

Angolan River Frog
Rana angolensis

Identification: Females reach
90mm. A long-legged frog, usually
brown or green, often mono-
coloured but sometimes with darker
blotches, black specimens are
known. may have several
lengthwise, non-glandular ridges
down the back and the hind legs are
often clearly barred.

Habitat and Distribution: Widespread in savannah
and woodland, from sea level to over 2,400m altitude.
Not recorded from dry northern and eastern Kenya,
absence of records from western Tanzania probably
due to undercollecting.

Natural History: Unlike most other East African frogs it usually lives in
permanent water sources, and is apparently active throughout the year, and
by day and by night. Spends the day in the water or under waterside cover.
At night often emerges and will sit quietly on the bank, if approached it
produces a gigantic leap to get into the water. The male advertisement call
is a short series of *clicks*, followed by a short *croak*. The males call from very
shallow water or just on the banks. Eggs laid in shallow backwaters. It
seems to be tolerant of quite polluted rivers.

Other species of river frogs known from East Africa

De Witte's River Frog *Rana wittei* A medium-sized (to 70mm) robust frog,
brown or greenish, with a distinctive dark patch behind the eye.
Characteristic of high-altitude areas of high central and western Kenya,
occurs on montane moorlands on the Aberdares and Mau Escarpment.

Ruwenzori River Frog *Rana ruwenzorica* A medium-sized river frog recorded
from the Ruwenzori Mountains and western Uganda. This species is difficult
to distinguish from *Rana desaegeri* of the Albertine Rift; both species may
not be valid.

Genus *Amnirana*: White-lipped Frogs

Previously known as *Hylarana*, a genus that now includes only Asian species. *Amnirana* are attractive, fairly large frogs. They are similar to 'typical' frogs (*Rana*) but all *Amnirana* species except one are distinguished from other African members of the ranid family by the presence of expanded finger and toe tips.

Galam White-lipped Frog / Golden-backed Frog
Amnirana galamensis

Identification: Females about 85mm, males smaller, about 77mm. The general impression is of a long, muscular frog. The colour pattern is unique, with a broad, golden mid-dorsal stripe, this may be black-speckled. The lips are pale grey to white and contrast sharply with the surrounding darker side of the head. Below, whitish-grey with darker grey blotches, especially on the throat and hind limbs. This frog has a broad, dorso-lateral ridge. Fingers are relatively long and lack webbing, hind toes are webbed-finger and toe tips not expanded as in other *Amnirana*. Resembles the Angolan River Frog, but male Galam White-lipped Frogs have a dark external gular sac at each corner of the throat. Ridged Frogs look similar but have a much more pointed snout and numerous small ridges along the back, rather than a single dorso-lateral ridge along each side. The male advertisement call is a weird human-like groan followed by a strangled *yuck*, *kyuck*.

Habitat and Distribution: This species is found in woodlands as well as the coastal strip, and appears largely dependent on permanent ponds and pools, although sometimes found in moist woodland and savanna (for example Kenya coast). Occurs virtually throughout Rwanda, Burundi and Tanzania, southern Uganda and western and coastal Kenya.

Natural History: Little known.

Forest White-lipped Frog
Amnirana albolabris

Identification: Females up to 74mm, males up to 57mm. Features as for genus; in this species, the longitudinal skin folds are very distinct; the back is brown to dark olive with darker brown to black blotches. Tips of the digits expanded to form large discs: this is a useful aid to identification. The distinctive white lips contrast sharply with the other parts of the frog.

Habitat and Distribution: Moist forest in western Kenya, and in Uganda.

Natural History: Active during the night and day, feeds on invertebrates.

Genus *Arthroleptides*: East African Torrent Frogs

As the name for the genus suggests, these frogs are adapted to life in fast-flowing streams. The adult males are very large, and are easily recognised by the large, expanded tips of their fingers and toes which are extremely flat and split into two parts (bifid), a feature not found in any other East African species. Their reproduction (where it is known) is very unusual; torrent frogs lay eggs in jelly under a trickle of water, and the tadpoles live and develop within a thin film of water on rocks. This genus is endemic to East Africa and contains three species.

Martienssen's Torrent Frog
Arthroleptides martiensseni

Identification: Males reach up to 65–75mm; females are smaller. The back is dark olive green with some mottling; a dark olive to brown band runs from the nostril through the eye. Below, white to translucent.

Habitat and Distribution: Mountain streams in forest and dense woodland in the Usambara Mountains of Tanzania.

Natural History: Nocturnal, living in and around mountain streams and rivers where, with their flattened discs, they easily grip the slippery wet rocks. Juveniles have striking crossbar pattern of dark olive bands on pale background. They sit on low vegetation along forest paths and streams at night In breeding males, the forearms become greatly thickened. Eggs are deposited in a mass of jelly on rocks which receive a steady trickle of water and the tadpoles also live on such rocks.

Other species of torrent frog known from East Africa

Mt Elgon Torrent Frog *Arthroleptides dutoiti* A small frog, known from Mt Elgon on the border between Kenya and Uganda. Unobserved despite recent repeated searches on the Kenya side of Mt Elgon; this frog may be extinct.

Southern Torrent Frog *Arthroleptides yakusini* A large frog, known only from the Uluguru, Udzungwa and Nguru mountains in Tanzania.

Genus *Cacosternum*: Dainty Frogs

This genus contains small frogs with a small, narrow head, and a slender body and limbs; the toes lack webbing. The common name for the genus refers to the slight, graceful appearance of these frogs. May be confused with puddle frogs (*Phrynobatrachus*) but dainty frogs lack a tarsal tubercle; they differ from small squeakers (*Arthroleptis*) and litter frogs (*Schoutedenella*) by lack of a fine median skin fold (raphe) on the back. The dorsum is often green, but also may be brown. Most dainty frog species have undersides spotted with diffuse black or grey. Members of the genus are found at the edges of flooded grasslands and pools.

Boettger's Dainty Frog
Cacosternum boettgeri

Identification: About 25mm. See features of the genus detailed above. The combination of a small head, fairly flat body, slender limbs, and dark spots on the under surface are characteristic. Dorsal colour very variable; it is often brown or green, but may be grey or red.

Habitat and Distribution: Found in woodland, savanna and grassland in northern Tanzania and south-central Kenya.

Natural History: This species spends the dry season in hiding but emerges in large numbers in the wet season at shallow, flooded areas; often found around fields. Feeds on small invertebrates and may be active during the day. Male call a series of high-pitched *clicks*. They call during the day and at night from concealed positions at edge of water and can be very difficult to locate and observe.

Genus *Hildebrandtia*: Ornate Frogs

Frogs in this genus are large, heavy-bodied, with a large inner metatarsal tubercle for digging. They survive the dry season by digging into drying mud, forming a cocoon and aestivating until the rains come again. The beautiful colour pattern on the back, with a brown or bright green mid-dorsal stripe, is the reason for the common name for the genus, and males of most species have stark black and white patterns on the throat.

Hildebrandt's Ornate Frog
Hildebrandtia ornata

Identification: A large sized frog; females to 70mm, males slightly smaller, to 60mm. A heavily-built, compact frog; the snout is rather blunt, webbing is moderate and the inner metatarsal tubercle is large; webbing of toes is moderate. There is a complex pattern of bright

colours on the back; typically there is a broad, mid-dorsal line of bright green or golden brown or tan extending from the snout to the vent. A pair of white Y-shaped marks stand out clearly against a generally dark grey to blackish throat. Differs from similar burrowing species like the Cryptic Sand Frog (*Tomopterna*) in bright colour pattern and the Edible Bullfrog (*Pyxicephalus*) smaller size and lack of cusps on the lower jaw.

Habitat and Distribution: Found in wooded grasslands and savanna, widespread in south-east Tanzania, and in south-eastern Kenya, with an isolated recorded from Moroto in Uganda.

Natural History: Males call from the edge of seasonal pools. This species survives the dry season by burrowing into the drying mud with its large metatarsal tubercle, forming a cocoon and aestivating. The male advertisement call is a harsh bellow.

Genus *Hoplobatrachus*: Eastern Groove-crowned Bullfrog

In East Africa this genus is represented by a single species, the Eastern Groove-crowned Bullfrog *Hoplobatrachus occipitalis*, which is characterised by the presence of a distinct groove running between the eyes.

Eastern Groove-crowned Bullfrog
Hoplobatrachus occipitalis

Identification: May reach 135mm but rarely more than 120mm in East Africa. This big frog is unmistakable: it is a large, aquatic species; the eyes are on top of the head, and it always appears to be looking upwards. Toes extensively webbed, and it has long, flexible fingers. There is a characteristic groove in the skin which runs between the eyes. The colour of the back is generally grey or greenish-grey with darker markings. The groove across the top of the skull between the orbits appears as a pale line. The under-surface is white or greyish.

Habitat and Distribution: Often in permanent water bodies, but will occupy temporary pools. Essentially a west to central African animal; in East Africa it is found around the Lake Victoria basin (across to Lake Baringo in Kenya), south-west Uganda and north-west Tanzania; also Rwanda. Sporadic records elsewhere.

Natural History: Feeds on invertebrates, but also eats other frogs and tadpoles. Floats at the surface of the water (this can present a bizarre spectacle, especially at night) and, when disturbed, it skittles across the top of the water like a flat stone skipped across the water - a behaviour unique among East African frogs but observed in a related Asian species. If disturbed on the shore, it whistles as it leaps into the water. The eggs are laid in shallow water. In West Africa some people eat this frog. The male advertisement call described as a series of deep notes.

Genus *Phrynobatrachus*: Puddle Frogs

Small, often brown, warty terrestrial frogs, active by day, often common and present in large numbers. A tarsal tubercle is always present (a diagnostic feature of this genus) along with inner and outer metatarsal tubercles; there is no median skin fold. The skin is frequently covered with warts or thin, elongate glands; webbing of fingers and toes usually reduced compared with aquatic species. Most species are cryptically coloured but the colour patterns are notoriously variable; within a single population of one species, specimens can be found with or without thin, mid-dorsal stripes, with or without diamond-shaped or X-shaped markings; some may have broad bands of dorsal colour different from the rest of the body. Puddle frogs usually breed in standing water (often flooded fields or temporary pans); the eggs hatch to tadpoles. This group is in great need of study and there is confusion over names. A number of species are known from 'hotspots' such the Eastern Arc Mountains and western Uganda. At present characteristics of the male breeding call should be used together with morphological details in order to identify species. The following are some of the more easily identified, but this list should be viewed with caution: some taxa may not be valid, or may contain additional species under one name.

Coast Puddle Frog
Phrynobatrachus acridoides

Identification: Males to 28mm, females 30mm. A medium-sized, grey-brown rather slender puddle frog with a warty back; two elongate, thin, chevron-shaped glands on the back above the shoulders are always present. Toe tips slightly enlarged but no obvious toe pads as in the Arboreal Puddle Frog or Tree Frogs. Tympanum visible but not conspicuous.

Habitat and Distribution: Permanent water in moist habitats, both forested and disturbed, in savanna and woodland, from Somalia south to Mozambique, including Zanzibar, Pemba and Mafia islands; in our area widespread in southern Kenya and north, eastern and southeast Tanzania. Most common in coastal environments where it seems to replace the Natal Puddle Frog.

Natural History: Coast puddle frogs frequently call during the daylight hours. Mating call a repetitive harsh *creak*.

Arboreal Puddle Frog
Phrynobatrachus dendrobates

Identification: To about 32mm. Medium-sized puddle frog; differs from other East African species by conspicuously enlarged, tree frog-like pads on the fingers and toes. Breeding males with bright chrome-yellow gular region (similar to Usambara Puddle Frog *P. kreffti*); tympanum distinct, toes slightly webbed at base.

Habitat and Distribution: Small streams in high forest between 1000 and 2300m of the Albertine Rift in Uganda, Rwanda and Burundi.

Natural History: More arboreal than other puddle frogs, often on leaves along streams both day and night. Call a single, high-pitched, five-pulsed *chirp* of slightly less that half a second. Eggs are deposited in holes and declivities of tree branches that extend over water; adults are often found in close proximity to egg masses.

Giant Puddle Frog
Phrynobatrachus irangi

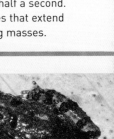

Identification: Males to 46mm, females to 51mm. Recently described, females of this species are largest puddle frogs in East Africa. Entire snout is light-orange brown, sharply demarcated from rest of the darker body by transverse line running between eyes. Small spines on soles of the feet. Webbing reduced to the base between the third and fourth toe, most of fourth toe is free of webbing.

Habitat and Distribution: Currently only known from the Irangi Forest on south-west slopes of Mt Kenya, but a population may persist at Kimande in the Aberdares; may occur throughout remaining montane forests of Mt Kenya and the Aberdares at 1000-2000m, but may have been overlooked.

Natural History: Diurnal, found along the banks of small forest streams. Males call during the day; call a loud, rough *raugh-araugh-aaaraugh*.

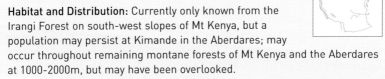

Usambara Puddle Frog
Phrynobatrachus kreffti

Identification: Second largest puddle frog in East Africa, males to 41mm as in the Giant Puddle Frog, but females smaller than the latter, averaging 46mm. Similar to Giant Puddle Frog in light-coloured snout, bordered by a sharp line between the eyes. Many have two wide, light dorso-lateral stripes. Breeding males have bright chrome-yellow gular (chin) regions similar to Arboreal Puddle Frog *P. dendrobates*.

Habitat and Distribution: Forest-dependent, found along montane streams. Endemic to the East and West Usambara Mountains, Tanzania.

Natural History: Males are evidently territorial; males observed chasing each other with bright yellow vocal sacs inflated. Unlike other puddle frogs, egg masses are attached to vegetation or rocks above stream surface. Call harsh sounds repeated rapidly, then slowing down.

Natal Puddle Frog
Phrynobatrachus natalensis

Identification: Males to 35mm; females to 40mm in our area; larger individuals reported from south of our area. Small warty frog, body squat and robust, head with rather pointed snout, foot broad, toes about one-half webbed, toe tips not expanded; males with dark gular regions with loose skin folds frequently visible along margins of lower jaw; tympanum visible but not distinct. Colour very variable; usually brown, often with a broad red, orange or green mid-dorsal stripe.

Habitat and Distribution: Widespread around Lake Victoria basin, records sporadic in Tanzania, absent from dry northern and eastern Kenya and montane forests. On the coast it appears to be replaced by the Coast Puddle Frog.

Natural History: Often abundant, breeds in any standing water, and active by day and night; call been described as a loud, rapid snoring, *errrrrrrrr, errrrrr, errrrrrr*, about three calls per two seconds; males often call in the daytime.

Dwarf Puddle Frog
Phrynobatrachus mababiensis

Identification: Males to about 18mm, females to 22mm. One of Africa's smallest frogs. Tiny puddle frog with warty skin, differing from litter frogs in possession of a tarsal tubercle, two metatarsal tubercles and lack of mid-dorsal skin fold. Differs from other puddle frogs in our area in small size as adults, tympanum not visible and webbing of the feet absent. Toe tips are not expanded.

Habitat and Distribution: Very common in marshes, ponds, waterholes, springs and flooded fields from western Kenya south through northern and eastern Tanzania, to eastern South Africa.

Natural History: Males call with a long metallic *buzz* (of about one second duration), followed by 4–6 *ticks*; calls day or night. Eggs are deposited in a single-layered mass that floats on the surface of still water.

Taxonomic Notes: We are assuming that this frog and the Ukinga Puddle Frog *Phrynobatrachus ukingensis* are the same species; the above species name has precedence.

Other notable puddle frog species known from East Africa

Golden Pond Frog *Phrynobatrachus auritus* A small puddle frog, up to 35mm length, with a golden-brown back, a fine light vertebral line, sometimes with blue-grey flanks and red upper forelimbs. Recorded from Rwanda.

Kenya Puddle Frog *Phrynobatrachus keniensis* and the **Kinangop Puddle Frog *Phrynobatrachus kinangopensis*** are small brown puddle frogs from the highlands of central Kenya. Both names may refer to the same species.

Dwarf Puddle Frog *Phrynobatrachus parvulus* A tiny frog (males 16mm, females 25mm), brown with light stripe between eye and forelimb. Known from Udzungwa Mountains and mountains around north end of Lake Malawi.

Webbed Puddle Frog *Phrynobatrachus perpalmatus* Males reach 25mm, females 29mm. Chocolate-brown above, with a light flank band and barred legs. Has well-developed webbing. Recorded from south-western Tanzania.

Rungwe Puddle Frog *Phrynobatrachus rungwensis* To 23mm. Warty frog, back grey-brown with darker markings. Known from south-western Tanzania.

Green Puddle Frog *Phrynobatrachus versicolor* Greeny-brown above, known from swamps at high altitude in western Uganda, Rwanda and Burundi.

Genus *Ptychadena*: Rocket Frogs

(sometimes called grass frogs or sharp-nosed frogs)

Easily identified by their pointed snouts, long powerful legs and six or more dorsal folds of skin ('ridges' which run longitudinally along the back; *Ptychadena* means 'wrinkled skin'). Tremendous jumpers, some can jump 3m or more; a rocket frog from Kenya, entered by Jonathan Leakey, once won the celebrated Calaveras Country Jumping Frog Competition in California. The world record, under controlled conditions, is still held by a Sharp-nosed Rocket Frog (see page 214) which covered 9.83m in three leaps. Most rocket frogs are characteristically marked with longitudinal stripes, often with darker crossbars. Males have a pair of external vocal sacs but when not expanded these are withdrawn inside (gular) slits below the jaw. Colour and patterns of species in this genus are extremely variable; within the same area one can find three or four colour 'varieties' of the same species. Thus they are hard to identify by overall appearance but can be separated by a combination of features, such as colour pattern on the dorsum, on the thighs, and the position of the openings to the male vocal sacs.

In addition to jumping away from danger, rocket frogs are experts at avoiding predators (and capture by humans) by remaining motionless then working their way quietly through tangles of grass. They often occur in large numbers. Because of their cryptic colouration and habits, they are seldom observed by the non-specialist. However, if you are walking beside a river or lake and are startled by a frog making a huge leap from almost under your feet, it will probably be a rocket frog.

Anchieta's Rocket Frog
Ptychadena anchietae

Identification: Medium-sized (50-60mm), females larger than males. No distinct colour pattern on back.

Habitat and Distribution: Typically found in grasslands near water, but can also be found some distance from water, in woodland

and open grassland. Widespread in north-western Tanzania and western Kenya, also parts of coastal strip; records sporadic elsewhere including the dry north.

Natural History: Tolerates considerable disturbance; found near human habitation and in gardens. High-pitched call described as loud, persistent *reek, reek, reek* and may be heard both day and night. One of the commonest, most abundant frogs in much of East Africa, but it has been little studied.

Golden-throated Rocket Frog
Ptychadena chrysogaster

Identification: To 53mm.
Unmistakable, the only rocket frog
species in East Africa with a bright
golden-yellow throat and belly in
both sexes. Also differs from other
species in genus in having two
dorso-lateral glandular ridges that
are interrupted, or present only on
the posterior part of back. Usually has a broad mid-dorsal
band, either light green or sometimes rusty red in colour.

Habitat and Distribution: Appear to be dwellers of forest
edges at higher elevations in western part of East Africa.
Recorded from Bwindi Impenetrable and Kibale National
Parks, Uganda. Also known from Rapogi in Kenya, Rwanda
and the Serengeti National Park, Tanzania.

Natural History: Little known, but probably similar to other rocket frogs.
Male advertisement call unknown.

Mascarene Rocket Frog
Ptychadena mascareniensis

Identification: Males 55mm,
females larger. Back is brown or
greenish-brown, usually has broad
mid-dorsal line that can be green,
yellow or brown. There are eight
dorsal folds. Below white to cream
colour. Sometimes a yellow wash on
lower abdomen. Light-coloured line
on upper surface of lower leg. On posterior surface of thigh
there are 1–2 light-coloured continuous lines that contrast
with darker mottling.

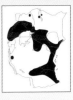

Habitat and Distribution: A widespread species along small
and large water bodies, in savanna and woodland. Widely
distributed in southern Uganda and Kenya, probably
throughout Tanzania but records lacking from the west. Sporadic records
from northern Kenya and Uganda.

Natural History: Male advertisement call a series of duck-like *clucking*
sounds, made from the edge of water, sometimes from vegetation. Recent
molecular work indicates this taxon is likely composed of many very similar
(cryptic) species.

Sharp-nosed Rocket Frog
Ptychadena oxyrhynchus

Identification: Males to 62mm, females to 85mm. Very sharp snout is distinctive; back is usually a more or less uniform light brown with scattered darker spots. In some individuals there may be an obvious brick red wash. Six or more dorsal folds. Distinct pale triangle on top of

the snout. A dark line passes from snout, through the eye, to the tympanum, then along the side of the body. No light line on upper surface of lower leg. Back of the thigh is mottled, without distinct longitudinal lines.

Habitat and Distribution: Woodlands and savanna species but able to tolerate disturbance and found in man-made habitats such as flooded fields and ditches. Known from the coast and eastern Kenya, sporadic records elsewhere, most in forest or woodland areas.

Natural History: Male call is a loud, explosive *trill*. This species holds the record for length of jump as noted in the Guinness Book of World Records.

Other species of rocket frog known from East Africa

Christy's Rocket Frog *Ptychadena christyi* Up to 55mm length. Grey, greenish or brown above, with dark spotting. Known from extreme western Uganda.

Mahnert's Rocket Frog *Ptychadena mahnerti* Up to 55mm length, recorded from the high country north of Nairobi, and around Mt Elgon.

Mozambique Rocket Frog *Ptychadena mossambica* Reaching 40 to 50mm. Usually grey, greenish or brown above, sometimes a broad tan vertebral line. Widespread in southern Tanzania.

Grassland Rocket Frog *Ptychadena porosissima* Grows to 49mm, usually distinctly striped, with a light vertebral line and dark bars. Known from north-west Tanzania, western Kenya and central Uganda.

Short-headed Rocket Frog *Ptychadena stenocephala* Up to 48mm. Grey or brown above. Recorded from western Uganda.

Small Rocket Frog *Ptychadena taenioscelis* Small, to 40mm. Usually brown above with dark blotches on back. From Kenya to southern Tanzania.

Upemba Rocket Frog *Ptychadena upembae* Up to 51mm. Usually brown with black markings and a green vertebral line. South-west Tanzania.

Udzungwa Rocket Frog *Ptychadena uzungwensis* Up to 48mm. Usually brown or grey, with dark spots along the skin ridges. Throat and groin of males deep yellow. High altitude grassland, Rwanda to southern Tanzania.

Genus *Pyxicephalus*: African Bullfrogs

These are the largest frogs in East Africa. Their calls are supposed to sound like a bull bellowing, hence the common name. Bullfrogs are large, strong frogs that spend the months of the dry season buried in the soil, aestivating; they have a strong, large metatarsal tubercle with which they burrow into the soil. They are distinguished from the similar but much smaller sand frogs (*Tomopterna*) by the possession of three bony cusps on the lower jaw. Two species occur in our area. In the past only a single species was recognised, leading to confusion over records; even now the distribution is not clear (see page 217).

Edible Bullfrog
Pyxicephalus edulis

Identification: Males reach 105mm; females slightly larger to 120mm. Unmistakeable; large, heavily-built, broad-headed frog with wide mouth and big prominent eyes. Juveniles may be confused with adult sand frogs (*Tomopterna*), but can be distinguished by presence of a thin, bright green line down back. Adults usually olive to dark green (rarely brown); males (especially breeding males) more brightly-coloured than females. Back has short folds and bumps, but not long folds or ridges. Three large tooth-like structures (odontoids) in lower jaw. Have large, strong metatarsal tubercle.

Habitat and Distribution: Mostly in low-altitude woodland, grassland and savanna, and in habitats modified by humans along the coast. Found in south-east Kenya and coastal Tanzania, inland on the Rufiji River.

Natural History: These large frogs undergo long periods of inactivity, followed by short periods of frantic activity when conditions are right. They are excellent burrowers and bury themselves at the end of the dry season using the large metatarsal tubercle as a digging tool. Male call is a short, low-pitched *yap*, like a small dog barking. Eaten in parts of Africa, hence the specific name *edulis*, i.e. edible.

Genus *Tomopterna*: Sand Frogs

A genus of small, squat, robust frogs with blunt snouts. They are proficient burrowers, and can survive hot, dry conditions; they dig themselves in using their large inner metatarsal tubercle. They resemble *Bufo* toads, but are smaller, and lack paratoid glands behind the eyes. They are generally found in woodland and grassland, often in seasonally dry areas. The skin on the back is cryptically patterned, with darker brown blotches or marbling.

Members of this genus are very difficult to tell apart and the taxonomy is in a state of flux; major changes may be expected. Recent work indicates that there are more species than at first recognised on the basis of morphology. Thus it is not possible to be certain of distributions. However, we describe below what is assumed to be the most widespread species, with notes on three other forms (see page 217).

Cryptic Sand Frog
Tomopterna cryptotis

Identification: Females to 60mm, males smaller, to 45mm. A medium-sized frog of a fairly heavy build with a rough and warty back. Colour pattern is variable but always cryptic with a complex pattern of darker and lighter browns. Below white, with greyish throat. The well developed spade-like inner metatarsal tubercle is used for burrowing.

Habitat and Distribution: Grassland, savanna or woodland. Widespread in eastern Tanzania and in much of arid northern Kenya.

Natural History: Call is a repetitive, high-pitched *warbling* sound made up of individual notes. Males call from edge of seasonal pools. May be abundant, but are so cryptically coloured they are difficult to detect, unless calling. In arid northern Kenya, males frequently call in concert with males of Anchieta's Rocket Frog *Ptychadena anchietae*. Spend much time underground in dry season; however, they can tolerate quite arid conditions, and in some areas may be active on relatively dry nights when few other frogs are active.

Other species of bullfrog known from East Africa

African Bullfrog *Pyxicephalus adspersus* Much larger than Edible Bullfrog, snout–vent length reaching 207mm and mass over 1kg; the largest frog in East Africa. Usually dark green with lighter patches, often bright yellow low on flanks. Obvious longitudinal skins folds on back. Unusually African Bullfrog males are larger than females and may enter into battles over a territory to which females are attracted. Unlike Edible Bullfrog, males of this species are active during the day, and amplexus and egg deposition also takes place during daylight hours. Distribution problematic due to confusion with the previous species, but apparently occurs in low-altitude, inland savanna areas of Kenya and Tanzania. Aestivating bullfrogs are able to secrete a cocoon around themselves to avoid desiccation. They emerge after rainstorms and begin calling, and breed frantically in temporary pools. Specimens have been reputed to emerge after seven years of underground aestivation.

Other species of sand frog known from East Africa

Tandy's Sand Frog *Tomopterna tandyi* This is a bizarre species, a result of hybridisation between two well known species, with a double chromosome set (tetraploid). At present this species cannot be distinguished from the Cryptic Sand Frog using morphology.

Rough Sand Frog *Tomopterna tuberculosa* To 45mm. Colour varies from vividly blotched, a mixture of blacks, browns, grey and whites, to uniform brown. Occurs in southern Tanzania.

Red Sand Frog *Tomopterna luganga* To just over 50mm. Rusty brown or orange above, with faint darker markings, lower flanks marbled white and black. Known from the central Tanzanian plateau.

Genus *Strongylopus*: Steam Frogs

The stream frogs (*Strongylopus*) are long-legged frogs. They look like rocket frogs (*Ptychadena*) but lack long, dorsal glandular skin ridges (short ridges may be present, however). They all have a broad, dark bar extending backwards from the eye. They have very long toes with reduced webbing. Three species are known from Tanzania, but there is debate on their status.

Fülleborn's Stream Frog *Strongylopus fuelleborni* Reaches 53mm. Has dark longitudinal stripes on a grey background, sometimes a broad mid-dorsal stripe. Widespread in the high hills of central Tanzania.

Kitumbeine Stream Frog *Strongylopus kitumbeine* Grows to about 50mm. Brown above, with darker mottling. Known from the Kitumbeine Forest, a volcano north-west of Mt Meru, Tanzania.

Mt Meru Stream Frog *Strongylopus merumontanus* To 45mm. Usually a rich red-brown above, with the usual broad dark bar behind the eye. Appears to occur only at high altitudes on Mt Meru, northern Tanzania.

Microhylid Frogs: Family Microhylidae

East African genera in this family are easily recognised: most are rotund little frogs with a small head; many have a rather flat face. Although they are usually excellent burrowers and are secretive, found under logs, stones and in leaf litter, some are also good climbers. In general, this family is poorly represented in Africa. There are but two widespread genera, *Breviceps* and *Phrynomantis*. Of the remaining six genera, *Balebreviceps* is endemic to Ethiopia. The rest (*Callulina, Hoplophryne, Parhoplophryne, Probreviceps and Spelaeophryne*) are all associated with the ancient Eastern Arc Mountains of Eastern Africa. Most species are found in forest but the common and best known to most East African residents, the Rubber Frog *Phrynomantis bifasciatus* is found in woodland, grassland and even urban areas, and breeds in temporary pools.

Genus *Breviceps*: Rain Frogs

Rain frogs are small, with rounded bodies, flat faces (*Breviceps* means 'short head') and strong, muscular limbs; they have been unflatteringly described as resembling badly made meatballs to which the chef has added a face and four legs. The males are much smaller than the females. As the common name suggests, they are usually active only during rainy periods and remain hidden for the drier portions of the year. In some South African species, during amplexus, the adjacent skin of the male and the female actually fuses together, which probably aids them in maintaining the embrace. They rapidly dig in backwards using their muscular legs and their flattened metatarsal tubercle; they can literally disappear in front of your eyes in soft soil. The eggs are deposited in an underground cavity and develop directly into tiny froglets; there is no free-living tadpole stage in the life cycle.

For a long time only a single, relatively well-known species in this genus was known from East Africa, but a second species was recently described (see page 224). However, the genus has radiated widely in southern Africa, with 15 species known there; local tradition is that these frogs can bring or withhold rain and they are consequently respected. There are almost certainly undescribed species of rain frog in East Africa.

Mozambique Rain Frog
Breviceps mossambicus

Identification: Female to 55mm, males to 22mm. Body round, limbs short and powerful. It has a large metatarsal tubercle, used as a spade to dig backwards in the soil. Dorsal colour variable; dark brown or almost black and mottled. A dark band runs down and backwards from the eye. The lips and area around nostrils are contrastingly white to ivory; sometimes the darkened area of the throat may be continuous with a dark stripe from eye to forearm, often an orange or yellow patch is present above the forelimb.

Habitat and Distribution: This species is found mostly in woodland and savanna but is also found in some coastal forests. Widespread in south-eastern Tanzania.

Natural History: Active for only a short period after the short rainy season begins. Males call – a short *chirp* (very difficult to locate) – from concealed positions. The male is much smaller than the female, and thus cannot wrap his arms around the female in amplexus. Consequently, special glands on his chest produce a 'glue' that keeps him attached to the female during mating and even while she digs the burrow and nest in which the eggs are deposited. The eggs develop directly into tiny froglets.

Genus *Callulina*: Warty Frogs

A genus with two species, endemic to hill forests of eastern East Africa (see also page 224). Both species are small, dark, globular, warty frogs with oddly long limbs, with the toes opposed to assist climbing. Similar to forest frogs of the genus *Probreviceps*, warty frogs can be distinguished by the presence of squarish, expanded finger and toe tips.

Krefft's Warty Frog
Callulina kreffti

Identification: Largest female 47mm, males are smaller. A frog with a rounded body and a very sticky, glandular skin. The limbs are relatively thin and the tips of the digits are expanded into large discs. Usually dark brown or grey, with some areas of the skin mottled grey-white. Unusually, the toes are arranged in two opposing groups, making it an excellent climber.

Habitat and Distribution: Often found under rotten logs or stones but also in banana plants into which it climbs and hides in the moist axils. Endemic to Kenya and Tanzania, known from the Taita hills and other coastal forests in Kenya, and from forests of the East Usambaras, Ulugurus, Ngurus and Udzungwa mountains in Tanzania.

Natural History: Although it is often found under logs and ground cover in the forest, this frog climbs well and males may call from 3m above ground level. No reproductive details known. It produces copious quantities of sticky secretions from the skin.

Usambara Warty Frog
Callulina kisiwamsitu
(see page 224)

Genus *Hoplophryne*: Banana Frogs

This is a little known genus of small microhylids endemic to Tanzania. *Hoplophryne* means 'weapon frog', as the males of the Uluguru Banana Frog have sharp spines on their chests and limbs. Banana frogs live in forest leaf litter and lay eggs in small amounts of water found in tree stumps or in the axils of plants. In the members of this genus, the thumb is reduced either to a group of spines (*Hoplophryne uluguruensis*, endemic to the Uluguru Mountains, see page 224) or a small stub of bone (*Hoplophryne rogersi*, endemic to the East Usambara and Nguru Mountains).

Rogers' Blue-bellied Frog
Hoplophryne rogersi

Identification: This is a small frog, females about 32mm, males about 26mm. Unmistakable, the only East African frog that is usually dark blue above. The body is very flat. There is a black band which runs from the tip of the snout to the eye and continues along the side of the body. Dark crossbars are found on the legs but these do not always contrast strongly from the base colour of the body. The undersurface and undersides of the legs are blue-black with conspicuous white vermiculations and markings. Another unique feature is the remnant thumb with a tiny bone protruding from it.

Habitat and Distribution: A Tanzanian endemic, known only from the forest leaf litter of the East Usambara and Nguru mountains

Natural History: Although regarded as a species of the forest floor, it can climb, and the female deposits eggs in water in holes in tree stumps, bamboo and other plants and the tadpoles must survive and metamorphose there.

Genus *Phrynomantis*: Rubber Frogs

In East Africa this genus is represented by a single species, *Phrynomantis bifasciatus*, the Red-banded Rubber Frog. The name refers to the appearance of the skin of the frog, which seems to be made of shiny, black rubber. It has starkly contrasting black and red markings, which warn of its irritating skin secretions.

Red-banded Rubber Frog
Phrynomantis bifasciatus

Identification: In our area females reach 54mm, males 26mm. This blunt-headed frog is unmistakable: no other East African frog has the combination of rubbery skin and black and red/orange colour pattern. Grey below with fine white spots, the throat is a dusky grey. The toes and fingers have small discs at their tips.

Habitat and Distribution: Widespread in woodland and other open habitats, frequent in suburban areas but not found in dense forest. Found almost throughout eastern Tanzania and south-eastern Kenya, with an isolated record from Lake Baringo.

Natural History: Often enters buildings in the dry season and hides in toilet cisterns and in showers. Away from habitation it burrows in moist soil, often at the base of banana plants. They climb well, aided by the discs on their toes. The melodic, electronic-sounding trilling call of males is a characteristic sound of the night, once rains have been sufficient to fill up temporary pools in which it breeds. The distinctive colour pattern probably serves to warn potential predators: the skin secretions are irritating if they get into a cut or come into contact with mucous membranes. If placed in the same bag with the Rubber Frog, other species of frog can be killed by its skin secretions.

Genus *Spelaeophryne*: Scarlet-snouted Frog

A genus of microhylid frogs that contains a single species, *Spelaeophryne methneri*, the Scarlet-snouted Frog. It is endemic to Kenya and Tanzania. It can be distinguished by its unique colour pattern.

Scarlet-snouted Frog
Spelaeophryne methneri

Identification: Up to 53mm but usually smaller, around 40mm. A squat, short-headed, round-snouted frog, with short legs. The colour pattern renders it unmistakable: a dark, black (sometimes very dark brown) microhylid frog, most specimens have a red (this may vary somewhat from brick-red to almost orange) V-shaped mark on the head, with the vertex on top of the head.

Habitat and Distribution: Inhabits forest. Endemic to East Africa; known from the Taita Hills in Kenya, the Uluguru Mountains and localities in south-east Tanzania.

Natural History: Nowhere common and often difficult to find. Little is known about the biology of this species; its skin easily comes off when handled, presumably a defence mechanism. The skin produces copious, sticky mucous. Although its coloration might seem to make it easy to detect, it is expert at simply disappearing by moving rapidly through leaf litter of the forest floor.

Genus *Probreviceps*: Forest Frog

A genus of small frogs, rather similar to the rain frogs, with fat, rounded bodies, and a short face. Four species are known from Tanzania.

Long-fingered Forest Frog
Probreviceps macrodactylus

Identification: Females to 52mm, male to 40mm. Typical microhylid frogs with a shortened face and plump, rounded body. Identified by an elongate fourth toe, dark 'mask' through the eye, and golden brown back. Flanks with a greenish-yellow wash. Usually grey below, with fine tiny white spots.

Habitat and Distribution: Forests of the North Pare and Usambara Mountains, Tanzania.

Natural History: Hides under logs and in leaf litter. Males call from concealed positions, difficult to detect. If threatened or handled, glands on the back may emit a copious thick sticky secretion.

Other species of microhylid frogs known from East Africa

Highland Rain Frog *Breviceps fichus* Recently described, females to 43mm, males 35mm, resembles Mozambique Rain Frog. Grassland above 1500m in Iringa Region, Tanzania where the Mozambique Rain Frog unrecorded.

Usambara Warty Frog *Callulina kisiwamsitu* To 30mm. Brown and warty above, with darker markings and a thin cream mid-dorsal line. Western Usambaras. The specific Swahili name means 'forest islands', where it lives.

Uluguru Banana Frog *Hoplophryne uluguruensis* To 28mm, black with silvery-white speckling and dark leg bars. The males have spines on the limb and chest. Uluguru Mountains only.

Uluguru Forest Frog *Probreviceps uluguruensis* Females to 45mm. Cream to terracotta above (sometimes black or yellow), may have purplish wash. Flanks and below purplish-brown with indistinct lighter blotches. High in Uluguru Mts.

Loveridge's Forest Frog *Probreviceps loveridgei* Females to 45mm, males to 33mm. Uniform purplish-brown above, brown below with faint dark reticulations. Mid-altitude forests of Uluguru Mountains.

Mt Rungwe Forest Frog *Probreviceps rungwensis* Females to 60mm, males to 48mm. Snout pointed, back has conical warts. Dark spots on purple-brown above, marbled below. Southern Highlands and Mt Rungwe.

Usambara Black-banded Frog *Parhoplophryne usambarica* To 23mm. Dark blue above, a black band from the snout to the flanks, dark crossbars on legs. Marbled blue-white on black below. Usambara Mountains.

African Clawed Frogs: Family Pipidae

Pipids occur in Africa and South America. They are adapted for a highly aquatic existence and have no tongue. In East Africa a single pipid genus, *Xenopus*, occurs. They are unmistakable. They spend virtually their whole lives in water (they occasionally make forays out onto wet grass or mud), and the males call under water. They have a flattened head, a streamlined body and indications of a lateral line for sensory purposes. The name *Xenopus* means 'strange foot', on account of the dark-coloured, horny claws these frogs have on some of their highly webbed toes. Their tiny eyes (relatively smaller than any other frog) are on top of their heads, allowing them to see potential prey as well as predators above them. They are bred commercially; many thousands are used in medical and other scientific research. There are six species in East Africa.

De Witte's Clawed Frog
Xenopus wittei

Identification: A medium-sized clawed frog; females average 46mm; males about 20% less. Adults can be distinguished from all other East African *Xenopus* by their totally uniform, dark-brown to chocolate back and head; no spots, markings or patterns are

present on the dorsal surfaces. The undersides are yellowish white with a few small spots (especially on legs) to heavily spotted including the throat. There is a sharp lateral delineation between ventral and dorsal colouring. The head is rounded with relatively large eyes.

Habitat and Distribution: This frog is a high-altitude species inhabiting all kinds of still water in the forested areas of south-western Uganda (Kibale Forest, Bwindi Impenetrable National Park), the Virunga Volcano region and Rwanda.

Natural History: This species co-occurs with the Jacketed Clawed Frog *Xenopus vestitus*, but advertisement calls and colour pattern are consistently different. Male advertisement call (given under water) is described as long tinkling and ringing trills, *trrrirrrirrri*.

Müller's Clawed Frog
Xenopus muelleri

Identification: Adults are large frogs, females often reach 65mm in length, males are generally smaller, about 50mm. Larger individuals are known to occur. A big clawed frog, dark to light olive above, often with considerable bright yellow colouring on the underside. The tentacle

found below the eye is at least half the diameter of the eye. Numerous lateral line sensory organs are present, giving the impression of stitch markings.

Habitat and Distribution: It is found in permanent water bodies, including highly polluted water and cattle watering ponds and pools, also occurs in slightly brackish water where freshwater streams and seepages flow into the sea. Widespread virtually throughout Tanzania and occurs on the Kenya coast.

Natural History: The skin produces copious mucous, making the animal slippery and difficult to hold in the hand. Reproduction takes place in the water; the tadpoles are filter feeders on algae. Adults are aggressive predators, and feed on eggs of fish, small fish fry, other amphibians (including tadpoles of their own species), and insects. This species is able to survive high water temperatures, and may burrow deep into the mud of drying water bodies, thus surviving conditions that are intolerable to other aquatic species. The male call is of two types: either a ticking sound, frequency 4–8 per second; or a series of 5–12 pulses of *trra, trra*.

Lake Victoria Clawed Frog
Xenopus victorianus
(see page 227)

Lake Victoria Clawed Frog
Xenopus victorianus

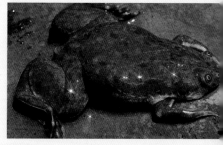

Identification: A large clawed frog, females reach 78mm, males 60mm. The back is variable in colour, often olive-green but some individuals appear more yellowish than dark green. Many small, dark spots are present on the back, as are darker larger blotches and less regular markings. The tentacle near the eye is only about a third of the diameter of the eye.

Habitat and Distribution: This species is found in dry woodland but also in forests. Occurs around the eastern side of the Lake Victoria basin, sporadic records elsewhere from the Albertine Rift Valley and Lokichoggio in north-west Kenya.

Natural History: Can survive in very dry conditions by burrowing into the mud, and may be found in dirty water such as drying cattle watering holes. Male call is a series of very short trills, *drick-drick-drick*.

Taxonomic Note: This species was once included in *Xenopus laevis* (Common Clawed Frog) but has been recognised as separate from it.

Other species of clawed frog known from East Africa

Northern Clawed Frog *Xenopus borealis* Grows to 95mm. Usually dark brown to steel-blue, with 30–40 irregular black spots, denser on the lower back and hind limbs. The call is a series of loud *flicks*, like a table tennis ball bouncing, accelerating from 2–12 per second. Known from savannah in northern Tanzania, central and northern Kenya (Mt Marsabit).

Ruwenzori Clawed Frog *Xenopus ruwenzoriensis* Females reach 57mm, males 20% less. Brownish above, with big dark spots, legs spotted ventrally. Below, yellow with black spotting, although often the throat and chest are uniform brown. The call is a series of short, high-pitched trills, *cri, cri, cri*, about two per second. Recorded only from the rain forest in the Semliki Valley, Uganda.

Jacketed Clawed Frog *Xenopus vestitus* Females to 55mm, males 20% smaller. The back is dark brown, marbled with light silver-golden to bronze chromatophores. The head is lighter coloured, with a dark collar. Throat and belly heavily spotted, except for a light median band. The call is a trill, *triing, triing*. Recorded from high country in south-western Uganda and Rwanda.

Caecilians
Order Gymnophiona

Caecilians are limbless amphibians, resembling earth-worms or small snakes. Known from tropical America, Africa and Asia, this indicates an ancient distribution on Gondwana with a subsequent fragmentation and dispersal. Poorly known and rarely encountered, they largely live below ground. East African species occur mostly in the Eastern Arc Mountains and on the coastal plain; one occurs further west in Rwanda. Sampling is incomplete, however, so new species are likely to be discovered. When caecilians do emerge, they are usually encountered in forest soils and leaf litter, but may be on the surface at night and/or after heavy rain. One genus is not found in forest but on floodplains of large rivers.

Caecilians have small eyes (sometimes covered with skin or bone) and a mouth with teeth. The number of external conspicuous rings, or annuli, is used to distinguish species. Caecilians can move rapidly through leaf litter or soil, in a serpentine fashion rather than the concertina movement of an earth-worm. If held they feel slippery, squirm vigorously, and may produce mucous from glands under the skin. Caecilians feed mostly on soil invertebrates. About 170 species are known. Two families occur in East Africa. One, the Caeciliidae, has seven species in two genera: *Boulengerula* and *Schistometopum*. *Schistometopum* species are larger, fairly thick-bodied with closely spaced posterior annuli. *Boulengerula* species are smaller and more slender, with short tentacles and a reduced eye, not visible externally. The second family, the Scolecomorphidae, has three East African species, all in the genus *Scolecomorphus*. They have eyes that may be visible when they protrude their long tentacles.

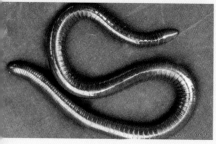

Mud-dwelling Caecilian
Schistometopum gregorii

Identification: Grows to 36cm. A large caecilian, the only one of its genus in East Africa, shiny brown/black in colour with a paler head.

Habitat and Distribution: Restricted to floodplains of some of the larger rivers; recorded from the Tana Delta

in Kenya and between Bagamoyo and the mouth of the Rufiji River.

Natural History: Found in moist soil on floodplains. Thought to be viviparous.

Taita Hills Caecilian
Boulengerula taitanus

Identification: Up to 35cm. Dark blue/grey dorsally, and slightly lighter ventrally, with the annuli marked in a pale white/blue; the head is sometimes pinkish.

Habitat and Distribution: Known only from the Taita Hills, south-east Kenya.

Natural History: Found in moist soil, and appears to be most common in old agricultural plots, but also found in forest. Oviparous with direct development. They eat a wide range of invertebrates such as termites, earthworms and fly pupae.

Ribbon Caecilian
Scolecomorphus vittatus

Identification: Grows to over 40cm.
A glossy purplish-black stripe along
the back flanked by red or pink on
the sides and belly.

Habitat and Distribution: Known
from the North Pare, Usambara,
Ukaguru and Uluguru Mountains.

Natural History: Appears to be more common above ground
than *Boulengerula*. They feed mainly on earthworms.

Other caecilians found in East Africa

Uluguru Pink Caecilian *Boulengerula uluguruensis* An unpigmented, pale
pink caecilian, head lighter in colour. Up to 20cm. Recorded from the
Uluguru and Nguru Mountains, eastern Tanzania.

Nyungwe Forest Caecilian *Boulengerula fischeri* One specimen 19cm.
A long thin caecilian, pink in colour. Distinguished by its number of annuli
(186). Known only from the Nyungwe Forest in southern Rwanda.

Usambara Bluish-grey Caecilian *Boulengerula boulengeri* Grows to 28cm.
Overall colour pinkish or bluish grey, but this darkens dorsally along the
back. The throat may be pinkish. Recorded from the Usambara Mountains.

Changamwe Caecilian *Boulengerula changamwensis* Grows to about 23cm.
Bright pink above and below. Originally recorded from Changamwe, on
mainland opposite Mombasa Island, also known from Shimba Hills and Malawi.

Tana Delta Caecilian *Boulengerula denhardti* One specimen 21cm. A long, thin
caecilian, colour pale in preservative, unknown coloration in life. Distinguished
by its number of annuli (161). Known only from the Tana River Delta.

Nieden's Caecilian *Boulengerula niedeni* A thin caecilian reaching 27cm.
Brownish dorsally, and slightly lighter ventrally in colour, with the annular
grooves slightly paler; the head is lighter in colour. Known only from the
Sagalla Hill, in the Taita Hills, south-east Kenya. Found in agricultural plots.
This species was described in 2005.

Kirk's Caecilian *Scolecomorphus kirkii* A large caecilian, reaching 45cm,
purple, purplish-pink or black above, flanks brown, below pink shading to
white. Recorded from highlands of Malawi, and Tanzania (records from the
forests of Mahenge, Udzungwa, Rubeho, Uluguru and Nguru).

Uluguru Olive Caecilian *Scolecomorphus uluguruensis* A large caecilian (to
33cm), olive or green-grey both dorsally and ventrally, occasionally with
small pale patches on underside. Known only from Uluguru Mountains.

Glossary

Albertine Rift Valley: The western branch of the East African Rift Valley, between Lake Albert and Lake Tanganyika.

Amplexus: The breeding position in frogs, wherein the male grasps the female behind her forelimbs from above and fertilises eggs as they are laid. In primitive species, males grasp females around the waist.

Annulus (plural annuli): A ring on the scale of a chelonian shell or a body segment of a worm lizard.

Anterior: The front.

Aposematic: Vivid warning coloration, indicating the possessor is dangerous or unpalatable.

Aquatic: Living in water.

Arboreal: Living in trees or bushes.

Arthropod: Animals with jointed legs, usually meaning insects, arachnids, millipedes and similar animals.

Asperity: A tiny spine on the skin, often darkly pigmented; asperities account for the rough appearance of the skin in some frogs.

Bifid: Split into two.

Canthus: the angle between the top of the eyes and tip of snout in reptiles and amphibians. Hence canthal: to do with this area.

Caudal: To do with the tail.

Cloaca: A common chamber that the digestive, urinary and reproductive systems all discharge into.

Crepuscular: Active at dusk.

Discs: Flattened adhesive structures on the tips of the fingers and toes of frogs (and the tails of some lizards).

Diurnal: Active by day.

Dorsal: To do with the back.

Dorso-lateral stripe: A stripe between the back and the sides of an animal.

Dorsum: The back.

Frequency: The number of cycles or oscillations per second. Calls of high frequency are described as high-pitched.

Gular: Pertaining to the area below and between the lower jaws; location of vocal sac in frogs and also large glands in most male tree frogs.

Hemipenes: The sex organs of male lizards and snakes, stored in the tail base.

Hinge: A flexible joint on the shell in hinged tortoises and terrapins.

Interorbital: Between the eyes.

Keel: A prominent ridge on a scale.

Montane: Living in mountainous country.

Parotid gland: A big skin gland found behind the eye in frogs in the family Bufonidae.

Raphe: A thin, continuous and permanent, non-glandular fold of skin. Located mid-dorsally in *Arthroleptis* and *Schoutedenella*.

Rupicolous: Living on or among rocks.

Spinule: small spine on the skin.

Subcaudal: The region below the tail.

Supraorbital: Above the eyes.

Tarsal: To do with the heels.

Terrestrial: Living on the ground.

Tubercle: A raised hardened skin projection, often shaped like a squat cone or a ridge, usually on the feet in frogs.

Tympanum: Essentially the external ear of frogs; a circular supported membrane located behind the eye; usually located within a recess in lizards.

Ukambani: The country of the Kamba people in Kenya, in the east between Machakos and Tsavo National Park.

Ventral: To do with the belly or underside.

Webbing: Thin skin joining the toes or fingers of frogs.

Institutions involved with East African herpetology

Department of Herpetology
The National Museum
P.O. Box 40658
Nairobi
Kenya
Tel: 00 254 20 3742131
Fax: 00 254 20 3741424
email: nmk@africaonline.co.ke
(mark for attention of herpetology)

The department houses Kenya's national preserved reptile collection. It has regional branches (e.g. Kitale, Kisumu), some of which have herpetologists on the staff.

Nairobi Snake Park
c/o National Museum
P.O. Box 40658
Nairobi
Kenya

Nairobi Snake Park has a large display of living reptiles, and knowledgeable experts on the staff who can identify Kenyan reptiles.

Kenya Wildlife Service
P.O. Box 40241
Nairobi
Kenya
Tel: 00 254 20 600800
Fax: 00 254 20 603792

Kenya Wildlife Service manages national parks in Kenya and has a staff herpetologist.

Nature Kenya (formerly the East African Natural History Society)
P.O. Box 44486
Nairobi
Kenya
Tel: Nairobi 00 254 20 3749957
email: office@naturekenya.org

Nature Kenya produces a bulletin and journal suitable for publishing local herpetological discoveries and research.

Department of Zoology and Wildlife Conservation
The University of Dar es Salaam
P.O. Box 35064
Dar es Salaam
Tanzania
Tel: 00 255 022 2410462
Fax: 00 255 022 2410480

The department houses Tanzania's major preserved reptile and amphibians collection, manages a biodiversity database, and has several expert local zoologists.

Tanzania National Parks
P.O. Box 3134
Arusha
Tanzania
Tel: 00 255 027 2503471
Fax: 00 255 027 2508216
email: tanapa@habari.co.tz

Tanzania National Parks manages national parks in Tanzania.

Department of Forestry and Nature Conservation
Makerere University
P.O. Box 7062
Kampala
Uganda
Tel: 00 256 41 543647
email: deanffnc@forest.mak.ac.ug

The department has a preserved reptile collection and expert local zoologists.

continued over

Uganda Wildlife Authority
P.O. Box 3530
Kampala
Uganda
Tel: 00 256 41 346291
Fax: 00 256 41 346287

Uganda Wildlife Authority controls Ugandan national parks, and has some expert local zoologists.

There are also snake parks in a few places in East Africa, which are often run by enthusiastic experts who will identify and assist. These include **Meserani Snake Park**, just west of Arusha on the Makunyuni road, **MBT's Snake Park**, between Arusha and Moshi, on the road up to Arusha National Park, and **Bio-Ken**, at Watamu on the Kenya Coast; there are several small snake parks on the Kenya coast, in fact, between Mombasa and Malindi.

The only association solely involved with African herpetology is the **Herpetological Association of Africa**, based in South Africa. It produces a journal and newsletter, which are suitable outlets for both scholarly and informal publications on African reptiles. For details of membership, society officers and for other enquiries please visit the HAA website at www.wits.ac.za/haa

The authors are also interested in receiving information on East African amphibians and reptiles. They can be contacted as follows:

Stephen Spawls
stevespawls@hotmail.com

Kim Howell
kmhowell@udsm.ac.tz

Robert Drewes
rdrewes@calacademy.org

Photo credits

The publishers and authors would like to thank the following for providing photographs. While every effort has been made to trace and acknowledge all copyright holders, we apologise for any errors and omissions, and invite readers to inform us so that corrections can be made in any future editions of the book.

Amphibian pictures were supplied by R.C. Drewes, and reptile pictures were supplied by Stephen Spawls, with the following exceptions:

James Ashe 91(b), 118(b), 134 (b); Ron Auerbach 141(t), Sabine Baer 189(b); Don Broadley/J.P. Coates Palgrave 52(b), 80(b), Don Broadley/F.P.D. Cotterill 149(t); Tim Davenport 19(b); R.C. Drewes 32(t), 35(t), 74(b), 101(b), 117(b), 150(br); Gerald Dunger 105(b), 143(b); Brian Finch 64; Paul Freed 57(b), 136(b); David Gower 228, 229(l), 230(t), 231(r); Wulf Haacke 95, 139(l and r); Harald Hinkel 20, 22(b), 58(t), 67(t) 90(t), 106(t), 109(b), 110(t), 119(t), 130, 133(b); Michael Klemens 74; Alex Kupfer 229(c and r), 230(b); Dong Lin 19(m), 88, 193(mr); Jill Lovett 223; Michael McLaren 100(t), 133(t), 172; Michele Menegon 168, 169(t), 169(b); Jean-Luc Perret 209(b); Laura Spawls 19(t); Stephen Spawls 164(t and b), 167(t), 170, 180 (b), 205(l and r), 206, 210(b), 212, 216, 227; Sam Stewart/Bonterra Consulting 21(l), 24(b); John Tashjian 76, 85(b) 112(b), 120(b), 151(bl and br), 153(tl and tr), 153(b); Colin Tilbury 25(b), 29(br),45(b), 58, 65(b), 70(b), 75(t), 76(b), 112(t); Miguel Vences 214, 226; Lorenzo Vinciguerra 42, 70(t), 72, 108(t), 120(t), 134(t), 135(t), 140(br); Jens Vindum 115(t), Chris Wild 103, 116(t), 138

Index of sciencific names

Index of English names

Large orders, such as frogs and snakes, are indexed to species level under family or generic groupings such as 'Reed Frog' or 'Blind Snake'.